BACK IN 1968, it seemed a corporate marriage made in heaven. General Mills, the Betty Crocker company, had wooed and won Parker Brothers, makers of *MONOPOLY*, the world's best-selling board game. The two venerable companies vowed to grow together and learn from each other—blending cake mixes with playthings, Midwesterners with Yankees, and marketing regimen with creative flair. For more than a decade Parker Brothers thrived under General Mills's generous, hands-off management.

Then inevitably, cyclical ups and downs in the toys and games marketplace shattered the connubial bliss. Parker Brothers careened from boom to bust twice during the 1977-1984 heyday of electronic and video games, putting huge spikes in the company's previously predictable pattern of growth. General Mills clamped down, changing long-established policies and counter-manding the company's retrenchment strategy. Parker Brothers—its workforce and revenues halved—was divested in 1985, a victim of one of the most massive restructurings in Wall Street history. The games company reemerged as twenty percent of a new company called Kenner Parker Toys, Inc.—which itself faced a hostile takeover as this book went to press.

Playing by Different Rules reaches deep into the histories and personalities that shaped these two companies and so fatefully brought them together. Drawing on over one hundred hours of interviews and extensive documentation, author Ellen Wojahn explores the fast-paced hustle of the toys and games industry, contrasting it with the methodical world of foods, where it can take a year to decide whether to add butterfat to Bisquick. The result is a cautionary tale, dramatically depicting the clash of culture that spelled doom not only for the General Mills/Parker Brothers merger, but for other "perfect pairings" before and since. She writes:

> In the category of failed mergers there may be shorter stories to tell, ones replete with the scandal and sleaze that are nowhere to be found

in the gentlemanly General Mills/Parker Brothers saga. But it is in well-intentioned mergers such as this one that the basic truth... comes through most clearly: Business is not business wherever it is practiced. Companies are not *MONOPOLY* properties, worth face value plus that of their houses and hotels. Companies are cultural and creative entities unto themselves— with business personalities of their own, and a social and economic worth that ought to extend beyond the current popularity of their products. Even under the most liberal of parents, they are probably better off on their own.

ELLEN WOJAHN was born and raised in Minnesota, where General Mills is headquartered. After a six-year stint in radio news, she reported on management topics and public policy issues for a Minneapolis-based business publication. Later, as senior writer for *INC.* magazine in Boston, her articles chronicling growth and change in small companies were among the magazine's most quoted and debated features. Now living and working in Brookline, Massachusetts, Wojahn writes and speaks nationally on entrepreneurial innovation and how it is changing the ways America works.

PLAYING
BY
DIFFERENT
RULES

PLAYING BY DIFFERENT RULES

Ellen Wojahn

amacom

American Management Association

This book is available at a special
discount when ordered in bulk quantities.
For information, contact Special Sales Department,
AMACOM, a division of American Management Association,
135 West 50th Street, New York, NY 10020.

LIBRARY OF CONGRESS
Library of Congress Cataloging-in-Publication Data

Wojahn, Ellen.
    Playing by different rules / Ellen Wojahn.
        p.   cm.
    Bibliography: p.
    Includes index.
    ISBN 0-8144-5861-0
    1. Consolidation and merger of corporations--United States--Case
studies. 2. Corporate divestiture--United States--Case studies.
3. General Mills, inc. 4. Parker Brothers, inc.   I. Title.
HD2746.5.W65 1988
338.8'3'0973--dc19   88-11684
                                                                    CIP

Printing number

10 9 8 7 6 5 4 3 2 1

AUTHOR'S NOTE

This book is a work of journalism. Every name, place, and circumstance described within is real. Not all of the characters named in the book participated in its research; dozens of others participated but were not named. Please consult the research notes at the back of the book for a detailed explanation of research methodology. This section also contains definitions, explanations, and elaborations of fact that might ordinarily be footnoted.

ACKNOWLEDGMENTS

Hearty and heartfelt thanks go out to all who offered time, talent, and support to this project, including: my attentive and supportive agent, Helen Rees; colleague and advisor Donna Carpenter; conceptualizer extraordinaire Larry Rothstein, and everyone in AMACOM, led by my patient and perceptive editor, Ron Mallis.

Thanks go as well to the people who lived this tale and agreed to share it with me. Many were busy executives who spent days, or their equivalent, with me—teaching me about toys and games, helping me to piece together chronologies and personalities, and entrusting me with their weaknesses and defeats as willingly as they shared their strengths and triumphs.

On a more personal level, I wish to acknowledge: my never-distant companion, Ken Doxsee; my dear friends in Boston, including the rented ones; my former colleagues at *INC.*, who sent me off to this project with good wishes; my parents, who are still hoping for the day this nurturing stuff can stop; and my great-aunt Martha, who never knew her role as literary benefactor (and no doubt would have had something peppery to say about it).

CONTENTS

THE CAST
OF CHARACTERS

Andrus, Brent. The executive vice president of toys and games for Parker Brothers, 1983–1984. Brought in from the Toy Group's international operations when Jim Fifield divided Parker Brothers's operations in half.

Anspach, Ralph. The University of San Francisco professor who invented *Anti-Monopoly* and ultimately won a trademark suit filed by General Mills on behalf of Parker Brothers.

Atwater, H. Brewster "Bruce," Jr. Former General Mills product manager and food group executive who rose to the presidency in 1977, and the chairmanship in 1981.

Bacall, Channing "Bill." A cousin of Parker Brothers presidents Edward P. "Eddie" Parker and Randolph P. "Ranny" Barton, the company's manufacturing man in post-merger days.

Barton, Randolph P. "Ranny." Grandson of Parker Brothers founder George S. Parker. Joined the family company in 1958 and rose to the presidency in 1974. He retired in 1984.

Barton, Richard "Dick." Younger brother of Ranny Barton; son of Robert B. M. Barton. An employee of Parker Brothers in the early 1970s.

Barton, Robert B. M. Son-in-law of Parker Brothers founder George S. Parker. He was the company's president from the late 1930s to 1968, when he sold the company to General Mills. He then retired to the chairmanship.

Bell, James Ford. Son of James Stroud Bell and architect of the multiple mergers and consolidations that formed General Mills in 1928.

Bell, James Stroud. Cadwallader Washburn's Pennsylvania-born successor at the Washburn Crosby Company.

Blodgett, F. Caleb "Cal." Vice chairman of General Mills in charge of the food groups and various support groups.

Boosales, James. Vice president of marketing during the establishment of Parker Brothers's product-management structure. Left Parker Brothers in 1977 to become president of another Toy Group company, Fundimensions.

Bracy, Bill. Video-era marketing executive. Prior to joining Parker Brothers in the *Merlin* era, he had worked for the Toy Group's international operations.

Dalessio, Dick. Vice president of marketing at Parker Brothers during the post-*Merlin*, pre-video period.

Darrow, Charles. The man who brought the game that became *MONOPOLY* to Parker Brothers and is credited by the company as the game's inventor, or "author."

Ditomassi, George. President of Parker Brothers's game rival, Milton Bradley of Springfield, Massachusetts.

Dohrmann, William F. "Bill." His first job stint at Parker Brothers was as marketing vice president, but he quickly shifted to similar duties in research and development. Left Parker Brothers in 1983.

Doyle, Bob and Holly. Inventors of hand-held electronic games *Code Name: Sector* and *Merlin*, among others.

Fifield, James G. "Jim." The former General Mills product manager, food-group executive, and head of New Business Development prior to becoming the vice president in charge of the Toy Group.

Gabrel, Gary. Inventor of the board game *Pente*.

Greenberg, Arnold. President of Coleco, a video-era rival of Parker Brothers.

Handler, Elliot and Ruth. Mattel executives who invented the *Barbie* doll.

Hassenfeld, Steven. President of toymaker Hasbro and member of its founding family.

Jackson, Ronald J. Parker Brothers controller and, during the hand-held electronics era, its marketing vice president. Left Parker Brothers in 1981 to join The Talbots, a women's-wear chain affiliated with the General Mills Specialty Retailing Group. In 1985 he would return to preside over the newly spun off Kenner Parker Toys Inc.

Jacobson, Jeff S. Group vice president in charge of the Toy Group from late 1984 until the spinoff of Kenner Parker in late 1985. Succeeded Jim Fifield in that post.

Jones, Bruce R. Joined Parker Brothers initially as a market researcher, but then became the marketing vice president in charge of traditional toys and games.

Kassar, Raymond E. Former chairman of Atari.

Kinney, E. Robert. Former Gorton's frozen fish company president who rose to become one of Jim McFarland's two top lieutenants at General Mills, and in 1977, the company's chairman. He retired in 1981.

Knutzen, Donald L. Parker Brothers's first post-merger marketing vice president.

Loomis, Bernard L. "Bernie." The toy marketing brains behind *Star Wars* action figures, and the *Strawberry Shortcake* and *Care Bears* lines of licensed toys. First joined the Toy Group as president of Kenner, then served as group vice president from 1978 to 1981.

McFarland, James P. "Jim." The diversification moderate who succeeded General Edwin Rawlings as president, CEO, and chairman of General Mills, and built a decentralized operation to facilitate growth of the company's varied lines of business. Was succeeded by Bruce Atwater in 1977.

Mendelsohn, Joseph. President of Kenner during the video era. Succeeded Bernie Loomis.

Morris, "Mike." Parker Brothers's vice president of sales at the time General Mills acquired the company.

Nalen, Craig. The point man on the team that orchestrated General Mills's acquisition of Parker Brothers in 1968 and built the Toy Group. Left General Mills in 1972.

Orbanes, Phil. Product-development executive during the video era at Parker Brothers.

Parker, Edward P. Grandnephew of Parker Brothers founder George S. Parker. President of the company at the time of the merger with General Mills. Died in 1974.

Parker, George S. Founder of Parker Brothers in 1883. Died in 1953.

Peisner, Art. President of Fundimensions during the video era.

Polk, Louis B. "Bo." General Mills's vice president in charge of New Ventures in the late 1960s, the man that spearheaded the conglomerate's first steps toward diversification. Lost a bid for the presidency to James P. McFarland in 1976 and left the company.

Rado, Vic. Architect of T-GOD, the Toy Group Operations Division.

Rawlings, General Edwin W. Air Force four-star general who rose to the presidency of General Mills in 1960. His sweeping reorganization of the company took General Mills out of flour and into a variety of consumer-oriented lines of business. Retired in 1968, touching off an internal power struggle between pro- and anti-diversification factions within the company.

Simmons, Henry "Hank." Parker Brothers's research and development man at the time the company was acquired by General Mills.

Stearns, Richard S. "Rich." Parker Brothers's first— and last—non-family president. Rose from assistant product manager in 1977 to president in 1984, succeeding Ranny Barton and becoming the youngest divisional president in General Mills's history.

Swanson, David F. Former General Mills salesman and food-group executive whose duties included managing the Toy Group until 1978. Then became vice chairman in charge of non-food operations. Retired in 1984.

Venditti, Arthur. Member of Parker Brothers's product design staff from *Nerf* days to the end of the hand-held electronics era.

Washburn, Cadwallader. Founder of the original Minneapolis gristmill that became first the Washburn Crosby Company and later General Mills.

PROLOGUE:

BID

*I*t was a cold, blustery morning and, typically, the jaded New Yorkers on the sidewalks paid no attention to the antique Rolls Royce or its morning-suited occupants as they passed, smiling and waving, on Park Avenue. To heck with the pomp and circumstance—Richard S. "Rich" Stearns, the 33-year-old president of Parker Brothers, rolled up the window and slouched deep into the leather seat of the white 1935 touring sedan, determined to conserve heat and enjoy the ride.

It was a special day in the life of the 102-year-old Massachusetts-based games company, or so said the news releases. Today, February 7, 1985, marked the beginning of a year-long observance of the fiftieth anniversary of *MONOPOLY,* the world's best-selling board game. As part of the commemoration, Stearns was helping transport two editions of *MONOPOLY*—one of the originals from 1935, and another hot off the presses—to the City Museum of New York. There, amid trumpet fanfares and flutes of champagne, the games would be welcomed into the museum's renowned Toy Collection.

At Stearns's side sat 52-year-old Randolph P. "Ranny" Barton, his recently retired predecessor. Barton, the grandson of the company's founder, George S. Parker, beamed contentedly—as if parading through Manhattan with a motorcycle escort was just another day's work for the Yankee aristocracy. Not for the fidgeting Stearns it wasn't—he didn't know which irked him more, the formality of the day's event (he'd always figured that anything requiring cufflinks wasn't worth attending) or its timing.

1

It had been less than two dizzying weeks since it was announced that Betty Crocker was retreating to the kitchen. General Mills, the food-based conglomerate that had been among American business's most aggressive diversifiers since the late 1960s, had put Parker Brothers up for sale along with the two other companies that made up its Toy Group, and several more that constituted its Fashion Group. The Toy Group bidding was to begin this week, amid the *MONOPOLY* anniversary kickoff and the back-pounding, lapel-grabbing camaraderie of the industry's annual ten-day sales extravaganza, known as Toy Fair.

Blasted grain-grinders, Stearns fumed silently, using the pejorative for General Mills that was popular around the office. Parker Brothers and the rest of the General Mills Toy Group had generated enviable growth and earnings for the Minneapolis food giant—by toys industry standards, anyway. Year-to-year revenue increases of 35 to 50 percent weren't uncommon for Parker Brothers alone, and the Toy Group, which came to be the largest toys entity in the nation, consistently outperformed its competitors. At peak in 1979, the Toy Group accounted for 15.59 percent of General Mills's revenues, and 19.3 percent of its profits. The group's relative return on sales met or exceeded that of the company's flagship consumer-foods business.

Granted, things had gotten considerably worse with the 1983-84 collapse of the $10 billion market for home video games. Parker Brothers's annual revenues of more than $200 million were lopped in half and the company sunk more than $10 million into the red. Toy Group sibling Kenner Products had also seen signs of declines in its licensed lines of toys, including *Strawberry Shortcake* and *The Care Bears.* Now, just when the Toy Group most needed the financial backing and managerial parenting that had led Parker Brothers to seek acquisition back in 1968, General Mills was not only refusing to reinvest but hanging out the "for sale" sign.

Two bad years out of seventeen—it didn't seem fair to Stearns. Food companies such as General Mills could plan their work and work their plan, cranking out predictably pleasing growth and earnings each year, but boom/bust cycles were a way of life for toys and games companies. Besides, as Stearns saw it, it had been General Mills that had encouraged Parker Brothers to deal itself into the high-stakes game of video, General Mills that had rewritten the rules for playing it, and General Mills—or its managers, anyway—that had prevented the inherently conservative Parker Brothers from cashing out while the company was still in the winnings. Now General Mills blamed its toys and fashion businesses for ruining its vaunted record for unbroken earnings increases. Divesting both groups would save management time and free up financial resources for its basic food business, its spokespeople said.

The "restructuring" decision had sent General Mills's share prices soaring 32 percent as investors and their analysts applauded the divestitures as "bold" and "sensible." Ironically, Stearns might have chosen the same adjectives, were he working on the other side of the fence. But he was not, and the same decision that was making General Mills seem heroic to its managers and shareholders was victimizing a company that had been called the Tiffany of the games industry. Layoffs had slashed Parker Brothers's workforce from 1,300 to 800, costing it precious talent in key departments. Budgets had undergone draconian reductions. Nowhere among the reams of *MONOPOLY* anniversary newsprint had there been any mention of that.

The abrupt halt of the motorcade several blocks from the museum roused Stearns from his ruminations. "Early," was the driver's one-word explanation for the unscheduled stop. Runners carrying walkie-talkies rushed up to find Stearns and Barton sitting on the "wrong" sides of the car. The men switched places. Minutes later, the runners returned and breathlessly switched them back. Both men rolled their eyes, and Stearns laughed out loud. A little confusion couldn't faze either man, not after the mixed signals and unexplained policy changes they'd put up with as General Mills made its now-apparent decision to divest.

Then, as now, the real annoyance was the waiting. To beat the monotony, Stearns and Barton got out of the car to practice popping out their folded top hats in unison, as they had been told to do on arrival at the museum. Between the twenty-degree temperatures and the recognized futility of either man trying to become Astaire or Kelly before the ceremony, things got a little slapstick.

"So how's it going?" Barton asked Stearns as he slid back into the car, in the hale and hearty tone of voice he used when not really expecting a thoughtful answer. Stearns responded in kind. "We're making progress," he said breezily—on nervous breakdowns, if Barton really wanted to know. But Barton didn't want to know and Stearns didn't want to tell him, so they chatted aimlessly for only a few moments before lapsing back into their own thoughts.

Flipping idly through today's press packet, Stearns had noted that a *MONOPOLY* float would be featured in the annual Macy's Thanksgiving Day Parade. Thinking of it now, as the Rolls continued on its way, he wondered who would be the float's sponsor—Parker Brothers, or some other company that might not even be in the toys business? Unfortunately, with little or no profit on its horizon and burdensome expense on the ledgers, Parker Brothers was probably worth more liquidated for its very lucrative assets, chief among which was *MONOPOLY,* than as an operating company. Parker Brothers might very well die. A lot would die with the name, as Stearns was acutely aware—the creative potential of a uniquely talented group of people, first and foremost. But not all would be lost, as some had tried to reassure him: Parker Brothers's products would live on in the marketplace so long as somebody could make money on them. To that extent, maybe today's *MONOPOLY* hoopla made sense after all, Stearns ruefully concluded.

A crowd of perhaps one hundred waited on the curb and up the stairs to the museum when Stearns and Barton alighted from the limousine. A twenty-man honor guard stood at attention, and fifty golden balloons filled with $50 bills in negotiable *MONOPOLY* money strained for release. The 140-piece band struck up a tune that no doubt seemed fitting to the General Mills employees who had planned the event: "We're in the Money." Stearns smirked and popped out his top hat on cue.

American business has become a game of *MONOPOLY.* For more than two decades companies have circled the marketplace, buying up properties as they pass GO. Sometimes these purchasers truly need and can make use of the property; more often they get caught up in the game and buy up whatever is available, hoping to keep it out of an opponent's hands. Then, when yesterday's Boardwalk or Park Place becomes merely tomorrow's

Baltic or Mediterranean Avenue, the properties are put up for
sale and the dice is rolled anew.

Much has been written about the effect of this era of mergers,
acquisitions, consolidations, and restructurings—at first from the
shareholder's perspective, then, more recently, from that of the
parent company. Experts who once lauded these portfolio-builders
and self-styled industry-reformers for their contributions to managerial efficiency and shareholder returns are now reviewing the
trend more critically. Many are gradually concluding that, as
Harvard Business School professor and corporate strategy specialist
Michael E. Porter put it in a paper published in 1987, the record
on diversification is "dismal" and that "much of the money lavished
on the corporate consolidation movement of the last two decades
may have been squandered."

Playing by Different Rules tells a story from the side of the
issue that remains largely unexamined: what happened to the
acquired stepchildren of these consumer colossi. Hundreds of American companies have found themselves in the predicament that
Parker Brothers faced in 1985, and perhaps thousands of managers
and loyal employees have been left feeling as disillusioned as Rich
Stearns did on a certain cold February day. Reasonable and well-
intentioned as the original acquisitions may have seemed on paper
years before, the resulting mergers eventually failed in the day-
to-day execution—with often disastrous results for the acquired
company.

In this book you will meet two of America's oldest and most
respected companies—one big and managerially sophisticated, one
small and highly creative. Both had products that were decades
old and enduringly popular. The big company, General Mills,
sought growth and product-line expansion. The little one, Parker
Brothers, sought growth, too—along with the management lessons
that a *Fortune* 500 corporation could teach. For nearly a decade
theirs was a textbook example of what post-merger relations should
be. Parker Brothers flourished, and General Mills reaped the
benefits.

But the late 1970s brought a series of sharp spikes to growth
and earnings charts that had arched steadily higher for so many
years. It became progressively and painfully apparent that, for
all their shared goals and similarities in style, General Mills and

Parker Brothers—like the other companies that made up the Toy Group—had deep historical and cultural differences that made them approach business very differently. One company was methodical, one was instinctive. One organization had a natural tendency to move quickly on a single person's go-ahead; the other preached the value of research and concensus.

It was the slower and more regimented General Mills that held sway. Parker Brothers's needs for flexible and nimble responsiveness to its market were subordinated to the planning and performance needs of its higher-ups—and, possibly, to the achievement goals of the managers that General Mills had placed between itself and its divisions. Parker Brothers was made to approach the hot, new video market with skills and strategies more geared to selling cold cereal. And, as will become clear by the time the reader reaches the epilogue, the repercussions lasted years beyond the day the company broke corporate ties with General Mills.

In the category of failed mergers there may be shorter stories to tell, ones replete with the scandal and sleaze that are nowhere to be found in the gentlemanly General Mills/Parker Brothers saga. But it is in well-intentioned mergers such as this one that the basic truth behind the failure of this vicious circle of merger, acquisition, consolidation, and divestiture comes through most clearly: Business is not business wherever it is practiced. Companies are not *MONOPOLY* properties, worth face value plus that of their houses and hotels. Companies are cultural and creative entities unto themselves—with business personalities of their own, and a social and economic worth that ought to extend beyond the current popularity of their products. Even under the most liberal of parents, they are probably better off on their own.

1

CHOOSE A PARTNER

*T*he long, tentative courtship was consummated in a rush, on Wednesday, the 14th of February, 1968—an unusually clear, bright, and crisp St. Valentine's Day for dreary Boston. After nearly two years of on-again, off-again approaches and casual dating, General Mills, the $870 million food giant, and Parker Brothers, one of the oldest and most respected games companies in the nation, had at last struck a deal. General Mills would buy Parker Brothers.

Randolph P. "Ranny" Barton, son of the president of Parker Brothers and grandson of its founder, was as relieved as he was elated. The closing ended what had been, for him, a long lobbying campaign. For almost a year, he had been quietly persuading the family to do something—to sell, go public, or bring in some private investors—anything that would give the venerable company more of a cash cushion and help the family to diversify its financial portfolio before his father, Robert Brown Morrison Barton, "retired" to the chairmanship.

Since an agreement had been reached with General Mills the previous October, Barton had felt as if his town had been wired for electricity, or his fastball had been called up from the minors. This merger would usher Parker Brothers into the world of managerial sophistication he had glimpsed during a short course for budding executives at Harvard Business School, Barton thought. Good company that it was, Parker Brothers could use an injection of business know-how, a dose of sophistication—as could most of the inbred stodgy toys and games industry.

7

Had the press known what was taking place on that winter morning, the business pages likely would have portrayed these corporate nuptials as the wedding of the season. Parker Brothers and General Mills were, after all, veritable pillars of corporate America. The very mention of their names conjured up happy scenes of traditional homelife: a Betty Crocker cake rising in the oven; boxes of Cheerios and Wheaties lining the cupboard; a game of *MONOPOLY*—or *Risk,* or *Sorry!* or *Clue*—sparking good-natured competition in the family room.

As it was, there was no popping of champagne corks, no gallant toasting or speechifying, and not a single mention of the irony of it being Valentine's Day—just half-a-dozen tight-lipped men signing an endless procession of documents in an unused cubbyhole of a law office deep in Boston's financial district. The headlines that day would focus on the Winter Olympics, where American figure skater Peggy Fleming had just won a gold medal, and, as usual, on the growing carnage in Vietnam. A new book, *Quotations of Chairman LBJ,* was eagerly awaited from Simon & Schuster, according to the morning's *New York Times.* The stock market continued bullish in a rapidly expanding economy. And "Laugh-In" was the hit of the TV airwaves.

When time came to pass the check, 38-year-old Craig S. "Skip" Nalen, the point man on General Mills' hot-footed venture team, gazed wistfully at the many zeros on the draft. "Geez," he remarked, he'd "never expected to be handing over a check like this." This was his third acquisition since joining General Mills in 1965, and it was by far the most costly of the bunch. The $47.5 million figure represented payment in full, double or triple the book value of the company. In his most severe, my-dear-young-man tone of voice, 68-year-old Robert Barton replied that he'd never expected to be accepting such a check, either—not for Parker Brothers, the company his wife's father had founded back in 1883.

Nobody lingered to chat when at last the midwestern millers and the Yankee gamesmen stood and closed their briefcases. Nalen grabbed a taxi to Logan Airport in hopes of catching the next flight to Paris, where he had people to see, and, if all went well, a company to buy. Robert Barton made the 30-mile drive back to company headquarters in Salem, Massachusetts, alone. There the old clapboard factory was running full tilt to keep up with the

Steve Largent
Olive Garden

demand for *Instant Insanity,* a four-cube brain-teasing puzzle hailed as the industry's runaway hit of the year. And Parker Brothers's executive vice president of sales, Ranny Barton, was bound for New York City to spell his cousin, Eddie. Edward P. Parker, soon to be named president, had been holding down the company fort for the first three days of the annual Toy Fair.

But first the younger Barton had an errand to run for his father. Tucking the check into his breast pocket, he strode to the bank to, as his frugal father had instructed, "get the money working for the family" as soon as possible.

It was a shared desire for growth that had brought Parker Brothers and General Mills together. General Mills was in the middle of a diversification drive unprecedented in the food industry, the ultimate goal of which was to become the preeminent consumer-products conglomerate in the country. Its food business was built on proud but languishing staples such as Gold Medal flour, Betty Crocker mixes, and Cheerios and Wheaties cereals. With that as a foundation, plus a variety of acquisitions in packaged foods, fashions, and specialty retailing in the talking stages, the 39-year-old milling company seemed well on its way toward the primacy it sought.

Now General Mills had turned its acquisitive eye to another potential profit center—the $2.5 billion market for toys and games. General Mills had zeroed in on the world of children's playthings for the lure of the industry's comparatively high profit margins. Both toys and games ran circles around food in margin performance, and, of the two, games were the more lucrative. A company like Parker Brothers pocketed as much as 70 percent on some individual board games, and regularly produced overall pre-tax margins of 20 percent.

But General Mills's interest was not entirely selfish, or even financial. The Minneapolis millers saw themselves uniquely suited to bring much-needed operational and marketing expertise to the toys and games industry, much of which was notorious for its staid and largely unschooled ownership. With good reason: General Mills had been lauded for its prowess in scientific management skills almost since the day the company was formed. What's more, its corporate personality was the very soul of constancy—a virtue seldom ascribed to most of the erratic and irrascible family-owned companies in toys and games.

These attributes scored big points in Salem. Parker Brothers was well aware that it needed to broaden its horizons. The 85-year-old company, founded by a 16-year-old games fanatic named George S. Parker, had long depended on the sales of American parlor perennials such as *MONOPOLY,* which dated back to the Depression, and foreign-designed or unprotectable winners that dated back far longer.

But since the advent of television in the 1950s, board game sales had begun to trail off, and much of the company's new sales growth had come as the result of so-called action games that, being made of plastic, were more aptly termed playthings than games. With George Parker dead since 1953, and his son-in-law successor, Robert Barton, aging, the third generation—composed of cousins Eddie Parker, Channing "Bill" Bacall, and Ranny Barton—now dared wonder aloud how long the company could stick to games alone. How many new products, of any kind, could be developed solely with the capital generated from the profits of the old ones?

It wasn't that Parker Brothers was in trouble: In fact, the company had maintained an almost unbroken history of year-to-year growth in revenues and earnings, almost without lifting a finger. The previous five years had been particularly successful, with volume growing at 20 percent per year. But it seemed unwise to Eddie, Bill, and Ranny to continue betting the company's future on its past—especially in a world where sales were made less frequently through the word-of-mouth endorsements and free publicity Parker Brothers had used so successfully during its history and more often through the combined clout of savvy marketing plans and healthy advertising budgets.

Much as the thought made him shudder, president Robert Barton had gradually conceded that the company might have to expand into toys to grow, if not to survive. And like the *MONOPOLY* character of the same name, it might need a Rich Uncle Pennybags to be its backer and banker.

The elder Barton's decision to consider new internal development and seek outside investment marked the first real strategic change in eight decades and two generations of management. In many ways, the Parker Brothers of 1968 was a carbon copy of the business it had been at the turn of the century. It remained the product of George Parker's imagination, shaped and molded by the times and the town where he lived and built his company.

Since its establishment in 1626 as the first town in the Massachusetts Bay Colony, Salem was known as a community of contrasts and contradictions. The same straitlaced Puritan town that ushered in the witch trials in 1692 also welcomed a high-living class of merchants and sea captains who made the Revolutionary port a new world Venice in the eighteenth century. When shipping died out during the War of 1812, due at first to a trade embargo and then to the introduction of clipper ships too big for Salem's shallow harbor, the city attracted an increasingly blue-collar and immigrant population. Tanneries and cotton mills provided the city's livelihood during the industrial revolution, springing up beside the gabled homes and shops of old world craftsmen.

Young George Parker grew up the very embodiment of Salem's shifting fortunes and philosophies. As the third and youngest son of a well-to-do merchant, the tall and gangly youth dreamed aloud of world travel and a newspaper career while spending afternoons playing parlor games with school pals—usually chess (an import from China) or, more frequently, games of his own invention. American-made board games of the day were too preachy for young Parker's taste.

Strange as it may sound to twentieth century ears, games were not always considered amusements, and games-making was far from playful—particularly in Puritan America. Puritanism (once defined by pundit H. L. Mencken as "the haunting fear that someone, somewhere, may be happy") instructed against the pursuit of idle pastimes, including "unlawful, crafty and deceitful gaming." Cards and dice were considered tools of the devil in colonial times, and an attitude somewhere between distrust and disdain followed all such diversions into the nineteenth century. Not until 1843 were board games designed for family entertainment, and, even then, morality was the predominant theme.

The Mansion of Happiness was the first published American board game, invented by Anne Abbott, a minister's daughter who simply signed her work "By A Lady." The object of the game was to move through virtuous spaces such as "Honesty" and

"Temperance," marking spiritual advancement, while avoiding the trials and temptations of "Poverty" and "Perjury." Other Abbott games followed, with names such as *Pope and Pagan,* and *Reward of Virtue.*

With the arrival of the industrial revolution, however, games became more acceptable as a means of enjoying new-found leisure time. Game companies sprung up along the eastern seaboard, but their mission remained largely instructional. For example, Milton Bradley of Springfield, Mass., which was founded earlier, in 1860, and in time became Parker Brothers' friendly rival, focused its early games on educational themes such as spelling and geography.

George S. Parker was undoubtedly not the first young man to be more interested in financial rewards than those of the educational or spiritual variety, but he created a sensation when he carried the attitude to games-making. In 1883, at the age of 16, Parker invented *The Game of Banking.* The object of the game, consisting of 160 cards and a "bank," was to see who could become richest with borrowed money. Parker's game-playing pals encouraged him to put it on the market.

Two Boston publishing companies rejected the game and sent its inventor packing. But the second suggested that if George was such a believer in his invention, and so hell-bent on getting the game on the market, why didn't he put his money where his mouth was and publish it himself? If the suggestion was a bluff, young Parker called it. He persuaded his high school principal to grant him a leave of absence, cashed out his $40 savings account, and with 500 games hot off the presses, launched a three-week sales swing through Boston and Worcester, Massachusetts, on south to Providence, Rhode Island.

That first sales push brought a profit of almost $100. With it, Parker established the George S. Parker Company. Several years and several games later, he invited his brothers, Charles and Edward H. Parker, to join him in the business. The company became Parker Brothers, and the awkward youth at the helm grew to be a big, regal man whose white hair matched his moustache and goatee, not to mention his heavily starched shirts. No one in his family could recall seeing George wearing anything but a coat and tie—not even while taking one of his exploratory tramps through the woods, or picking blueberries, or teaching his young grandson, Ranny Barton, to wield a hatchet.

Still, Parker never lost his childlike delight in hunkering down over a challenging board game. A talented and exacting inventor, Parker demanded excellence in the quality of play for all his games. "There are many games on the market which, though bright and interesting in external appearance, are found dull and unentertaining when played," commented the young entrepreneur. He insisted on play-testing games that were still on the drawing board for hours with friends, family, or employees until he had ferreted out the errors and refined the rules to their simplest form. Parker Brothers pledged itself to publish only those games that "look well, play well, and sell well."

George Parker grew bolder with his success. Not long after *Banking* was introduced, he published *The Strange Game of Forbidden Fruit*, brazenly advertised as offering "no instruction, but quantities of fun." He also ventured into the previously taboo area of the occult, with games such as *The Black Cat Fortune Telling Game* (1897) and *The Hand of Fate* (1910).

Ironically, it was profits from older, more moralistic games that helped finance Parker's new forays. By the turn of the century, Parker had bought up the rights to the games made by the oldest and most straitlaced gamesmaker of all, the W. and S. B. Ives Company. The two Ives brothers, also from Salem, had been dead more than three years in 1887, when the purchase gained Parker Brothers control of *The Mansion of Happiness* and other Abbott-designed games. Parker may have considered them fuddy-duddies, but without the Ives assets, his company's "fun" would have been sorely limited, for lack of cash.

There were, however, times when young Parker's definition of entertainment failed to jibe with that of the marketplace. For example, *Ye Witchcraft Game* was pulled off the shelves at the turn of the century when occult-sensitive Salemites proved it would take more than 200 years before they would find enjoyment in a topic so associated with the witch trials and executions that divided their community. Parker was undaunted. With a flexibility that would teach his company how to deal with many booms, busts, and outright flops in years to come, young Parker resisted any urge to buck or wait out the resistance. Instead, he chalked up the flop to experience and replaced the game with a new entry. His sense of timing, of paramount importance in both games and toys, was one of the greater legacies he left the company.

Over the decades, George Parker charmed America with games honoring individual feats and historic events. In honor of the westward expansion of the Gay Nineties, he put out a game called *The Gold Hunters* (depicting both the Alaskan and Yukon gold rushes) and a puzzle called *Pikes Peak or Bust.* He memorialized the bravery of popular heroes such as Charles A. Lindbergh, Admiral Byrd, and, in the gangster days of the 1930s, *America's G-men.* Reflecting his formative years in Salem, he also focused heavily on travel, with games such as *The Amusing Game of Innocence Abroad, Crossing the Ocean,* and *Game of Ports and Commerce.*

Parker took to the road with his products, proving himself to be a cagey salesman—the kind who could sell a crate of games for $20 to one retailer and pull $30 for the same lot across town. But he was always a sorry sight when it came to day-to-day management. To cope with the company's persistent financial and operational disarray, he recruited son-in-law Robert Brown Morrison Barton, the Baltimore lawyer who had married his daughter, Sally. Barton arrived as heir apparent in 1932, just as the company had seen its revenues halved, from $900,000 to $450,000, by the Depression.

Lanky, bespectacled, and serious to a fault, Robert Barton quickly earned a reputation within his industry as "the judge"— and not just because of his legal background. Barton went to great pains to preserve his aura of decorum, and with it, his competitive edge. Though partial to a good glass of red wine at home, Barton wouldn't drink at industry events—not even during the boozy get-togethers accompanying the annual Toy Fair. (He said he feared blurting a company secret, though most assumed he was making sure he wouldn't miss anyone else's slip of the tongue.) Nor did Barton routinely offer the many varieties of sweetheart deals that were common in the business. In an industry where a retailer could argue to postpone payment for eight or nine months after shipment—i.e., after Christmas sales were posted—Parker Brothers' iron-clad policy was payment in ninety days. Barton never underestimated the clout of his father-in-law's company or its increasingly indispensable products. He kept his prices higher,

his discounts lower, and simply dared balkers in the retail trade
to do without Parker Brothers' popular catalog of games.

The undisputed king of that catalog was *MONOPOLY,* which
came along in the hard times of the Depression. Thousands, maybe
millions, of Americans can recite the well-publicized saga of the
unemployed heating engineer and laborer from Germantown, Pennsylvania, Charles Darrow, who dreamed up the real estate speculation theme as capitalist escapism from the economic woes of
the time. According to the legend, he chose names to attach to
his mythical properties by recalling the streets and byways of his
favorite vacation spot, Atlantic City, New Jersey—now-historic
names such as Boardwalk, Park Place, and Marvin Gardens.

Darrow drew the first versions of *MONOPOLY* onto round
sheets of linoleum and sold 17,000 of them at $4 apiece—nearly
a 100 percent markup. Then he took the game to Parker Brothers,
the world's premiere game company at the time, and asked George
Parker and Robert Barton to buy him out of the business. "Taking
the precepts of *MONOPOLY* to heart," he quipped later, "I did not
care to speculate."

But, to Darrow's surprise, George Parker summarily rejected
MONOPOLY. Ever dedicated to the "play value" of his products,
Parker cited the game for fifty-two fundamental playing errors,
led by the fact that the game couldn't be completed within the
forty-five minutes that Parker considered to be the limit of a
family's attention span. However, when Darrow subsequently peddled 200 games to FAO Schwarz in New York, and a Parker
family friend reported that *MONOPOLY* customers had cleared the
shelves at Wanamakers in Philadelphia, George Parker changed
his mind and bought up what remained of Darrow's 5,000-game
inventory on consignment.

Within months the whole lot was gone, according to company
lore, and Parker Brothers, assuming another popular fad had run
its course, prepared to move on to different products. Robert Barton
memoed a halt to production in December of 1936. But orders
soon started piling up so fast in Salem that they had to be stored
in laundry bags. By February, Parker Brothers was selling 20,000
copies of *MONOPOLY* per week. Within a year, *MONOPOLY* had
singlehandedly restored Parker Brothers' revenue to the $1 million

mark it would have achieved by 1930, were it not for the Depression.

Darrow's eagerly awaited sequel, *Bulls and Bears,* was an unmitigated flop, however. "Lightning never seems to strike twice in this business," shrugged Robert Barton. Darrow retired at forty-six to raise orchids and cattle in rural Pennsylvania—and to collect royalties, of course, on the best-selling board game in history.

George Parker died in 1953, at the age of 86. Witnessing his passing, concurrent with the twin arrivals of plastic and television, some predicted the end of a game-playing era. But Robert Barton—joined in management by his garrulous nephew, Eddie Parker, a poker-faced cousin, Channing "Bill" Bacall, and in 1957, his rather diffident son, Ranny—carried on the Parker family tradition with a succession of perennially popular games: *Risk. Careers. Mille Bornes. Clue.*

Times had changed. So had faces, trends, and, with *MONOPOLY*'s hotels now made of plastic, even material had received tweaks of transformation. But in an era that became known for its worship of corporate growth, expansion, and sophistication, Parker Brothers stayed stubbornly small and self-consciously focused on the power that came of people, products, and profits—not portfolios. Robert Barton saw to that.

If Parker Brothers was immune to strategic and managerial change, General Mills took regular doses of it, like castor oil.

While competitors traditionally rode out rough spots in their food businesses, General Mills had a history of putting itself through large and painful restructuring efforts every twenty years or so, always patting itself on the back for its "adaptability, responsiveness, and responsibility." A spate of acquisitions would be followed with divestitures, and inevitably, another round of acquisitions. Regimes of centralized management would suddenly shift to decentralization, only to drift back once again to the tight-reined control of headquarters.

By the late 1960s, by its own reckoning, General Mills had gone through four distinct strategic phases: an emphasis on flour milling (1928–1945); a maturing milling business expanding into packaged foods (1945–1959); a shift from commodities to a consumer goods (1960–1966); and the full-fledged foray into consumer products that began in 1966 and led to the acquisition of Parker Brothers, among others. What lines of business General Mills chose to grab, and how long and tightly it held them, all depended on the climate of the times and the curve of General Mills's most important performance measure, its earnings-per-share trend. It is, and always has been, an investor's company.

General Mills was born in a raging bull stock market, the kind that continues to spur mergers, acquisitions, and large-scale industrial consolidations today. The milling conglomerate was created of the combined resources of a handful of ailing flour mills in the Midwest—the oldest of which was the Washburn Crosby Company, a mill founded on the Mississippi River more than sixty years earlier by Cadwallader Washburn.

Washburn, a middle-aged Mainer, had entered milling following a career of Jeffersonian diversity including stints in law, farming, education, politics, real estate, and the military. With a partner, another Mainer named John Crosby, he expanded the mill a decade later into a spanking-new, six-story monolith that dominated the frontier and cost an outrageous, at the time, $100,000 to build. The locals called the behemoth "Washburn's Folly." When most of it was blown sky high in a May 2, 1878, grain dust explosion, the ensuing fire leveled half of the Minneapolis riverside milling district and killed eighteen men. The structure had hardly been rebuilt when Washburn went to the grave in 1882. Crosby followed in 1887.

The company nonetheless survived and became one of the region's principal flour mills, guided by successor James Stroud Bell, a Quaker who had migrated west from Pennsylvania to manage the company. But it was his son and post–World War I successor, James Ford Bell, who would bring the company to world prominence.

Like other milling companies of the 1920s, Washburn Crosby was getting muscled around in the market by bigtime bakers who had begun doing their own buying and milling of grain. While declaring the merger craze of his day "heartless, soulless and depressing," and predicting that "such maneuvering could not come to good," the younger Bell figured if he couldn't beat them, he'd join them. Conglomeration, he conceded, was probably the best solution to his growing competition problem. He began enlisting the support of some of the richest and most prominent financiers in the country in preparation for just such a move.

Within months, in mid-June of 1928, Bell had managed to closet these moguls, along with representatives of some twenty milling interests, at the Ritz-Carlton in New York City. Round-the-clock talks ensued, and the pajama-clad Bell signed the papers to form the new company in the wee hours of June 22. The stock, issued at $65 a share, sold out unsolicited in Chicago at $86.

Five months later, General Mills had grown to include twenty-seven associated companies in sixteen states. With a total daily capacity of 81,700 barrels of flour, 5,950 tons of commercial feeds, 72,000 pounds of cereal products, and storage space for 36 million bushels of grain, General Mills had become the largest grain miller in the world.

From its earliest days, the company that became General Mills was tireless when it came to finding new ways to exploit new products or extend the product cycle of older brands. When changing ideas on what constituted beauty in the feminine form resulted in would-be flappers eating less cakes and breads, Washburn Crosby propped up sales with an "Eat More Wheat" campaign. When a new type of flour was developed, General Mills executives—often apron-clad for the photographs—would take to the bakery and prove to homemakers that their brand produced the best-textured and highest-rising breads and cakes.

But it was never the company's intention to remain merely a flour miller. The elder Bell challenged his managers to diversify far and wide, well beyond mere milling concerns. "Our biggest assets rest in our Good Will, our merchandising ability, and our efficiency in the use of publicity. These must be carried into new fields of profit opportunity. Our line of thinking and experience fits us to exploit projects that have their roots in the soil that grows wheat. We may follow the trunk of the tree to its utmost tip, but we also should not be averse to grafting new branches upon it."

In the mid-1920s, the company introduced Wheaties, the world's first ready-to-eat cereal, with the world's first commercial jingle—played on the company's own radio station in Minneapolis, named WCCO for the initials of the Washburn Crosby Co. The jingle premiered on Christmas Eve of 1926, sung to the tune of a popular song of the day, "She's a Jazz Baby":

"Have you tried Wheaties?
They're whole wheat with all of the bran.
Won't you try Wheaties?
For wheat is the best food of man."

But the best example of the marketing and promotional genius for which General Mills remains known today is Betty Crocker. The fictional spokeswoman was the brainchild of in-house advertising wizard Samuel Chester Gale, who felt General Mills needed a signature over which to send recipes and helpful tips to consumers—someone with whom the average homemaker could identify. Her face came to grace the label of a line of prepackaged foods, she was the sponsor of the call-in shows for homemakers on WCCO Radio, and, by the mid-1930s, the mythologized Betty Crocker was voted the second best-known woman in America, behind Eleanor Roosevelt. Soon her face was emblazoned aside the company's Big G logo on an increasing variety of prepackaged foods and mixes.

The onset of the Depression intervened to slow the company's development, however. The elder Bell's last act as chairman was to launch a two-stage centralization plan designed to help the company weather the economic storms to come. By 1935 General Mills had organized its twenty-six federated companies into four product groups. By 1937, the company had liquidated and dissolved all existing subsidiary companies and folded their operations into what became only two divisions of the parent company: Flour and Feed, and Grocery Products.

This trimming and streamlining, combined with conservative fiscal management, increased the company's consolidated net income and tripled its average earnings goals. General Mills managed to pay a dividend straight through the Depression, one of only eighteen national companies that could boast such a record. After World War II—during which General Mills did its patriotic part by producing ordnance and medicinal alcohol—there were but eight companies that had maintained perfect dividend records.

Wall Street called them "The Golden Eight," and General Mills
was high on the list.

With peace came change. Founder James S. Bell had once
said General Mills should be free to make locomotives if it wanted
to, and while the company didn't fancy itself on the rails, the
company aggressively pursued a strategy of decentralized diversification after 1950. Two divisions became five, and, in the hope
of utilizing electronic and metal-bending capacities left over from
the war, General Mills expanded far beyond its basic food business.

The new configuration was the brainchild of Charles H. Bell,
another descendant of James S. Bell, who took over the presidency
in 1952. Though twenty years of centralization had seen the
company through social and economic turmoil, it had left a very
top-heavy organization to compete in these go-go years. As the
baby boom stimulated demand for convenience foods, Bell deployed
his excess manpower in the development of new packaged foods.
But he didn't stop there. Reaffirming his grandfather's assertion
that General Mills had the management expertise to go into any
markets that might suit its fancy, he pointed the company toward
any and all products that "travel the avenue to the home." There
were forays into appliances, electronics, and chemicals, none of
which paid off. Losses mounted as General Mills discovered that
manufacturing capacity and management capability didn't necessarily go hand in hand. For all its vaunted caution and expertise,
the company had blundered into markets it knew nothing about.
Corporate earnings hit the skids.

A period of retrenchment and soul-searching followed in 1959
with Charles Bell's decision to hire an outsider, General Edwin
W. "Big Ed" Rawlings. The burly and gruff man, who parted
his hair severely down the middle, was at one time the youngest
man ever appointed a four-star general in the Air Force. He began
his General Mills career as a financial vice president. Within two
years he had risen to president and chief executive officer, and
was launching one of the most sweeping corporate overhauls
American business had yet seen.

Rawlings' first step was to sell or close all of the ailing
mechanical and electronic operations. The executive marched Betty
Crocker back to the kitchen, where she could spend her time on
more lucrative lines of consumer business: ready-mix foods, cereals,

and a new category, snack foods. Pre-war levels of profitability were restored.

Rawlings then developed a revised corporate philosophy built upon three basic tenets: management capability, commitment to growth, and economic realism.

In seeking "management capability," General Mills set out to build itself a younger, better educated, and more competitive workforce. Rawlings committed the conglomerate to hiring twenty MBAs a year—and not just any number-crunching MBAs would do. He wanted the ones with a flair for risk and entrepreneurship, the ones who sought merit promotions, rather than the safety of the seniority ladder that so many of General Mills' executives had climbed.

Vowing his "commitment to growth," Rawlings pledged the company to continued expansion, both through acquisitions of existing companies and internal product development.

Most important, in the name of "economic realism," Rawlings questioned the company's historical emphasis on commodities and forced every division and profit center to justify its existence on paper. There would be no sentimental favorites anymore; every product, commodity, and category was deemed expendable. Those operations that couldn't pass the earnings test would be closed down or cast aside, whether they were newcomers or old standbys like Wheaties or Cheerios.

Taking his philosophy to surprising lengths, Rawlings liquidated the company's feed divisions and closed nine of its seventeen mainstay mills between 1962 and 1966. The moves cost the company over $200 million in annual sales. True to Rawlings's predictions, these actions freed up resources and talents that could be channeled into areas of higher profit and growth potential. But they also slowed the rate of earnings growth he had worked so hard to boost, and worse yet, cost the company some of its market supremacy.

Unfortunately, while General Mills was still talking about new products, the competition was testing them. For decades General Mills had been the number-one company in flour milling and cake mixes, but the company lost its cake-mix crown when rival Proctor & Gamble introduced the Duncan Hines brand, catching Betty Crocker with her apron off. The conglomerate took the setback the midwestern way: with frozen grace, soul-rending humiliation, and steely determination.

Recognizing that the company's belt had been cinched too tightly to promote volume growth—and the earnings growth that is its byproduct—Rawlings decided to go on a buying binge. Cajoling the board of directors into putting the acquisition failures of the 1950s behind them wasn't easy, but Rawlings managed. He sent Betty Crocker on her largest and widest shopping spree ever, with virtually the whole consumer-products world her market. Her only instruction was to come home with solid, respected companies whose growth was mostly ahead of them. The matron, no longer housebound, would become a career wife.

Rawlings told an ambitious lieutenant, Louis B. "Bo" Polk, to appoint some young hotshots to a new-ventures team and fan them out in all directions. Toys and games was one of the first industries to shape up as a *bona fide* target, thanks to a serendipitous discovery made by the man who would eventually negotiate the Parker Brothers acquisition, Craig Nalen.

In late 1965, soon after Nalen had been hired away from Proctor & Gamble (where, ironically, he had worked on the Duncan Hines team), the young recruit happened through one of General Mills's research laboratories. He noticed an array of marble-sized balls that reminded him of Kix cereal, only bigger. He learned that when moistened, the blobs would grow and could be sculpted like clay. Kids would have a field day with this stuff, he thought. And, being made wholly of natural protein, the youngsters could munch on it all day without having to get their stomachs pumped.

Nalen was perhaps overly enthusiastic. The resulting product, named *Lickety Stick,* was pulled off the shelves after its first few months of lackluster test marketing. But the product planted the seed of an idea in Nalen's head.

It was the first time, to Nalen's knowledge, that General Mills had seen any real connection between its stodgy food business and the ephemeral world of toys and games. The closest they'd gotten to this point was putting trinkets in Wheaties boxes. The more he thought of it, the more the pairing seemed to make sense.

This, as much as anything Nalen had seen on a business-school blackboard in his days at Stanford University, seemed to exemplify the business understanding of the concept of synergy—

in which the pairing of two different organizations produces results of which neither would be individually capable. Toys would add another figurative leg to General Mills's stool. At the same time, General Mills could offer that toy company the benefits of management expertise, working capital, and access to huge blocks of commercial time on children's TV programs. It generally took more than a year of negotiations, and more money than a small, family-owned toy company could spend, to win the plum positions that General Mills controlled. Nalen figured it'd be a snap to convert some of General Mills' minutes to toy ads.

Polk heartily approved of Nalen's idea, but admonished him to confine his interest to companies that were demonstrably more than just a flash in the pan. To win the support of General Mills's skeptical board of directors, Polk would need Nalen to come up with proven track records and established brand franchises.

Nalen's first target was Rainbow Crafts of Cincinnati. There was nothing scientific about the selection; it was simply a company for sale, and Nalen knew it had popular products—he'd been picking its leading entry, Play-Doh, out of his living room rug for years. Besides, Play-Doh's formula was 80 percent high-grade flour, and General Mills's laboratories had found that Rainbow could reduce its production costs with a lower-grade flour. Now, *that* was what the board of directors called synergy. After General Mills's acquisition, the $3 million enterprise tripled in revenue within as many years.

But one company does not a diversification strategy make. The budding toy group needed to gain size and prestige, and fast, if it weren't to get lost in the everyday shuffle of this major food company. Polk and Nalen needed to find a more substantial business to buy—preferably one with real name recognition to capture the board's attention.

Parker Brothers came immediately to mind. The company was an anomaly in the toys and games business, in that it had both a history of stability and the reputation for quality that is necessary for lasting growth. Most of all, it had the brand franchises that General Mills was so keen on—*MONOPOLY* being just one of a half-dozen examples. Nalen called and asked for a visit. He jetted to Salem within the week.

Talk about a solid, no-nonsense business: If the good guys back in Minneapolis didn't go for this, thought Nalen on arriving at Parker Brothers, they wouldn't go for anything.

Walking into the stark, clapboarded headquarters building was like walking back decades in time, to the 1940s—no, the thirties at the latest. Nalen announced himself and turned to take in the dark and cramped anteroom of this rambling wooden structure. It couldn't have been more than 20 feet square. There was an old gateleg table in the entryway with a lamp on it, and two leather armchairs on either side. The walls were bare but for their dark paneling. A few scattered magazines were the only non-functional items in the room. Stereotypical New England sparcity, if ever he'd seen it.

A graying woman peered out from behind the arched cashier's window where she served as receptionist, telephone operator, and order clerk, wondering which "Mr. Pahka" he wanted to see. Then she nodded not toward the elevator, which would soon be torn out for lack of use, but toward the plant itself. "Up the stairs," she instructed him.

Nalen strode into the hum and clatter of the plant, stepping around the woodworking shop where playing pieces were being lathed, and past a press spitting out canary-colored *MONOPOLY* money in $500 denominations. Nalen gawked right and left as he walked, noticing the wide, planked floors of the factory and the warm light of incandescent lamps on old mahogany office doors and credenzas. He ascended the back stairs to the offices on the second floor.

This was a far cry from the steel desks and fluorescent glare of headquarters in Minneapolis. General Mills's home office was a dark-glassed cluster of rectangles on a landscaped suburban knoll, where Betty Crocker's big red spoon was used like an arrow to direct the hordes of salesmen and touring schoolchildren that overran the building each day. The corridors of the complex were tastefully decorated with selections from the company art collection. The top executives' offices were arrayed around an atrium filled with greenery.

Parker Brothers had no such accoutrements. Reaching the top of the stairs, Nalen found himself in an L-shaped hallway featuring several recessed display cases, each bearing an assortment of past and present Parker Brothers games. From a corner office there emerged a ramrod-straight man with white hair and round, steel-rimmed glasses. Escorting Nalen into his office, Robert Barton offered the briefest of pleasantries. Then he sat down and shot his cuffs, signalling his intention to get down to business. He understood, he said, that Nalen's company wanted to buy his.

Nalen nodded. The 36-year-old former marketing trainee, like Polk and much of his team, was known as a smooth talker and a natty dresser. Nalen was reminiscent at a glance for a young Jack Kennedy, though more for his winning smile and affable gait than any physical resemblance. Others might have been fazed, meeting the spit-polished countenance of the man who sat before him, the man who had written the rules—all seven sets—to *MONOPOLY*. But Nalen wasn't even breaking a sweat. He was too young, too brash, and far too much in a hurry to waste time on deference. Nalen took a deep breath and launched into his pitch.

Yes, he told Barton, General Mills was in the process of expanding its base in the world of consumer-products, and particular attention was being paid to opportunities in toys and games. After all, if the conglomerate could sell Cheerios and Wheaties to kids and their moms, why not toys? In return, what General Mills offered a fine company like Parker Brothers was the working capital and management expertise it needed to achieve yet more of its already impressive growth.

Barton nodded as he listened, and soon he asked Eddie and Ranny to join him. But when the old man stood to end the meeting, Nalen found scant encouragement to be gleaned from his handshake. "It's really the younger generation's decision," he said.

After his initial visit in 1966, Nalen continued to touch base with Parker Brothers every other month or so, each time asking if there was any interest in further discussion of an acquisition. He had dinners with Ranny, and went sailing with Eddie. After a few months, Nalen knew he'd won the confidence of the two heirs. Still, he was put off every time he raised the possibility of a sale. "The time isn't right," said Ranny Barton. "Not yet," agreed nephew Eddie Parker, the man next in line to Robert Barton's throne.

Clearly, it was the elder Barton for whom the time was still "not right." Nalen, growing impatient, moved on. He went to Milton Bradley, where his pitch was rebuffed. Chalking up his difficulties to independent-minded New Englanders, Nalen thought he might have better luck on midwestern turf, where Kenner Products was on the block.

Nalen approached Kenner reluctantly. Compared to Parker Brothers or Milton Bradley—well, there was no comparison. Kenner was bigger than Parker Brothers, but it didn't have the profits or the product stability General Mills was looking for. With the possible exception of Kenner's Betty Crocker E-Z Bake Oven, the company didn't have a single brand franchise to interest the board of directors.

Kenner was originally a soap manufacturer that introduced an in-box premium, a suds-shooting gun called the Bubbl/Matic, to compete with Proctor & Gamble's giveaways. The profits from the soap went down the drain, but the gun was a hit. It changed the company's destiny, in fact. Since then it had been one trendy toy after another, each as forgettable as the last.

But Kenner was for sale, and that was criterion enough. Nalen and Polk agreed that it would be better for General Mills to buy it than somebody else. Already other food giants were following General Mills into non-food businesses like sheep, hiking prices and slimming the pickings. Using similar get-while-the-getting's-good rationale, Nalen and Polk bought Craft Master Corp., makers of crafts and paint-by-number sets, and a variety of games companies in Europe. Then Nalen made one last pass at Parker Brothers.

The elder Barton greeted General Mills's renewed interest as cordially as ever. But this time he was more specific in saying that the sale decision wasn't his to make. It was up to his son, Ranny, he said.

Nalen found the suggestion laughable. He'd enjoyed getting to know Ranny, and considered him thoroughly charming, but the son had yet to show more than a fraction of his father's style or savvy. Robert Barton, whom Nalen characterized as "one tough hombre" in reports back to headquarters, had a knack for drawing forth every unstated motive and disguised consequence, while his son seemed to maintain a firm grasp of only the obvious. Where

Robert Barton was quick and precise, Ranny Barton's considered speech pattern was broken up with long pauses that tended to knock a conversation out of sync. Instead of saying "uh" to cue listeners to thought in progress, a blank look crossed Ranny's face as he fell silent, creating a gap that Nalen and others invariably tried to fill just as Ranny began to speak again. Nor had the amiable Ranny been blessed with Eddie's personal magnetism. Eddie Parker attracted adoring throngs as he walked through the plant; Ranny's visits prompted only pleasant nods of recognition.

Nalen had to assume that Robert Barton was stalling, or at the very least, trying to use the negotiations to propel his son into a more responsible role in the family company. The latter made more sense: After all, Ranny's mother owned more than 50 percent of the company's stock. Her son would have to take a more visible role sooner or later.

But Nalen, like many others before and since, had miscalculated Ranny Barton's influence with his father, if not his skills. Since returning from his few months at Harvard Business School in 1964, Ranny had kept up a steady drumbeat for the hiring of more MBAs and the establishment of a marketing squad. Young Barton had learned in the ivy-clad halls how much could be done to sophisticate a company's operational methods, and accordingly, how little was being done in the toys and games industry. In discussions with his father, Ranny went so far as to declare that Parker Brothers would probably never achieve anything of significance if it remained just another stagnant and inbred family company, never taking the risk required to move ahead. It was like playing *MONOPOLY:* Any player who chose to sit back and play it safe deserved to lose, and probably would.

The elder Barton acknowledged that he had been slow to gauge the growing impact of discount stores, restricting his games to high-margin but low-volume department and specialty stores. And, instead of heavily promoting new products each year, Parker Brothers mostly relied on the sales of its staples. Yes, under Robert Barton, the man himself conceded, Parker Brothers's main managerial goals had been to protect the company's good name, and build its bottom line.

With typical forthrightness, Robert Barton then took his *mea culpas* public, and in so doing, laid out the germ of a plan for change. As he disclosed in a *Business Week* article, "We want to make our business grow faster." The story revealed that Parker Brothers was in the market for some working capital, perhaps that which could be derived from an over-the-counter stock offering. The preliminary plan was to sell about 20 percent of the company to investors. Then, after the offering, the elder Barton would move up to the chairmanship and let Eddie and Ranny take the reins more firmly in hand.

Up until then, Robert Barton thought he preferred almost any option to selling. For years he had retained the services of Lehman Brothers, the New York City investment banking firm, expressly to rebuff acquisition offers. But gradually he had realized that selling was, in fact, the only option that seemed truly palatable. Borrowing was out of the question. There was scarcely a dime of debt on Parker Brothers's balance sheet, and Barton hated even the suggestion of going begging. Going public, too, had lost its intrigue as Barton realized that he would have to open his books to scrutiny.

Still, it seemed a shame not to be able to tap into the perceived shareholder value in toys and games. Wall Street's markets were booming with a rally that dated back to 1964 and President Kennedy's growth-spurring tax cut. The stock tables of the *Wall Street Journal* made it clear that there were probably plenty of people out there willing to bet on a healthy business like Parker Brothers's.

One day Robert Barton folded his newspaper on the stock pages, and called his son, Ranny, into his office. Had Ranny noticed that toy stocks were selling at twenty times earnings?

Ranny said he had.

Might it not be time to reconsider selling?

Ranny said he thought it was.

The elder Barton asked Eddie Parker and Bill Bacall to join them. Going public remained an option, he told them, explaining his change of heart, but he couldn't help but think a stock offering was merely putting off the inevitable. "Twenty percent this year, another twenty the next—why not do something and be done with it?" Besides, there was the matter of the public scrutiny of Parker Brothers and its financial statements. Few had known exactly how profitable the company was, and the flinty Robert Barton preferred to keep it that way. Selling out seemed a compromise that would achieve Parker Brothers's goals without costing the company its privacy or dignity.

Another consideration argued for an outright sale: The family had "too many eggs in one basket," added Ranny Barton, and a sale would allow the family to cash out and diversify its interests. Right now most of the family wealth was tied up in the company.

No one would dispute that the Parkers lived well. The weathered photos in the family album typified leisure-class life of past decades—midi-clad women brandishing croquet mallets, capped and ascotted men playing games of *Camelot* with grandfather George, or *Sorry!* on the family sailboat. The genteel sport of sailing was a big part of family life—Ranny was hardly out of knickers before he took a hand at the helm.

But there was less cash than met the eye. Though the family had servants and the children attended private schools, there were few extravagances. Young Ranny's childhood allowance was 25 cents per week, which gave him about enough for two comic books and an ice cream.

Be that as it may, what the family really needed from its riches was not a ritzier lifestyle, but security. If Robert Barton died tomorrow, how would his heirs scrape together the money to pay the inheritance taxes? Selling all or a portion of the company would make the family's finances more liquid.

As the options had clearly narrowed down to but one, a sale, there had lingered a single question in Robert Barton's mind: Was General Mills the kind of corporate parent that Parker Brothers would want? The rest of the family thought so, pointing to the conglomerate's age, its upstanding reputation, and its recognized management skill.

"They do seem to be our kind of people," mused Robert Barton of the millers. Unbeknownst to his underlings, he had jetted off to Minneapolis for a closer look some months earlier. He arrived at General Mills headquarters with the flu and an even bigger dose of the doubts, but he came away a believer. Obviously, the grain business was not the toys business, and cereal wasn't *MONOPOLY,* but Barton found comfort in noting that the Minnesotans favored the same Brooks Brothers suits as he. There was a lawyerly quality that General Mills brought to the bargaining table that felt, well, familiar. And, despite being a midwestern company, many of General Mills's top managers had a decidedly eastern, prep-school orientation that was also soothing to Barton. He sat silent for only a moment.

"Fine. Call Mr. Nalen."

Nalen took the call from Ranny with more curiosity than excitement, not expecting any big news.

Parker Brothers had reconsidered, the young Barton told him, and the family now wished to entertain the idea of acquisition. Could Nalen be in Salem the next morning?

Indeed he could, Nalen replied, brightening considerably. To prove his willingness to talk turkey, he'd have his boss, Bo Polk, in tow.

Nalen and Polk flew in on the corporate jet. The six men—the four Parker heirs, plus Nalen and Polk—gathered in Robert Barton's Spartan office, the walls of which were unadorned but for pictures of his sailboats, past and present. Robert Barton named the figure that the stock tables suggested was right: $47.5 million. Polk muttered that the price was high. High or not, Barton affirmed, it was *his* price. He walked to the door. "Would you gentlemen like to caucus?" It was not a question.

After an hour, and a flurry of telephone calls to the highest echelons in Minneapolis, Polk and Nalen emerged from their consultations. "We have a deal," Polk announced, extending his arm. Barton's eyes narrowed behind the rims of his glasses. He was a cynical, cautious, often superstitious man—the kind who would leave a room before he'd be the thirteenth person to sit at a table.

"How firm is this?" he asked.

As firm as any agreement could be without a formal vote of the board of directors, Polk replied.

Barton wordlessly accepted a hearty handshake. He had Polk and Nalen back on the jet by noon.

In the weeks that followed, General Mills's due-diligence team bustled about the business of counting inventory, examining royalty contracts, and verifying the company's many trademarks and copyrights. A good deal of energy went into checking the ten-year sales trend on the prize of their purchase: *MONOPOLY,* which was a $20 million asset in its own right and accounted for about half of Parker Brothers' annual sales.

When lawyers for the two companies came up with a list of 150 items in dispute (disagreements over conveyances and the like), it was Ranny Barton who took it upon himself to remove any obstacles to the acquisition. He sat down with the attorneys and, within two days, hammered out amicable solutions on each and every point of contention. Ranny, like others on both sides of the deal, spared no effort in assuring that the acquisition moved forward. To him, as to most others, it was taken as an article of faith: These companies were meant to be together. Both had the intangible assets of gentlemanly management, quality products, and consumer respect. And each shared a strong desire for increased growth and position in the marketplace. If that wasn't a corporate marriage made in heaven, what was?

When at last all was in readiness the elder Barton broke the news of the acquisition to his workforce. He climbed stiffly onto a table in the third-floor collating room of the Parker Brothers factory, the only location in the rambling, barn-like facility that was large enough for general announcements. Upon hearing that Parker Brothers had been sold, an uncertain hush settled over the room, which Barton rushed to fill. Nothing was going to change, he said. Games would still be made in Salem. Not only would everyone keep his or her job, he reassured the crowd, there would be more and better opportunities available through the growth that General Mills would help spur. Already he knew that the company pension plan was going to be improved. With that, at last there was warm applause and scattered cheering from the factory workers assembled.

Word of the merger quickly spread to the rest of the toys industry, where it was greeted with great interest, but little surprise. There certainly was no question of why the Parker family had chosen to sell out; General Mills's diversification copy-cats had been unabashedly prowling the toys industry with check-books in hand—among them Walter Kidde, CBS, and Quaker Oats. No, the big question was how much General Mills paid: How would anybody else know how much to ask for their own family dynasty if they weren't privy to the going rates?

There was, however, speculation in the business press as to how much General Mills would seek to recreate Parker Brothers in its own image. Wasn't a business like Parker Brothers's a little too inbred and idiosyncratic for a food company to run? The answer, from both sides of the deal, was yes.

"The most precious thing General Mills has gained from its acquisitions," said Craig Nalen, "is the entrepreneurial identity of each company." He said Parker Brothers, like many of its other newly acquired divisions in toys, fashion, and specialty retailing, would "stand on its own two feet."

Robert Barton chimed in to say his heirs would be accepting technical guidance from General Mills management, nothing more. "This is the kind of business that people . . . must grow up in," the retiring executive declared. Intentionally or not, Barton went on to take a poke at the ambitious MBAs of General Mills, adding, "You couldn't remove an A-student from a business school and put him in a company like ours." After all, what on earth did a diploma have to do with picking good toys or games from among the bad?

2

SHUFFLE AND CUT

*E*very time they turned around, it seemed, Eddie Parker and Ranny Barton found themselves up to their armpits in General Mills brass—cereal marketers, administrative staffers, public relations men, and members of the board of directors.

Just days after the final papers on the acquisition were passed, Parker Brothers was inundated at Toy Fair with Minneapolis-based visitors. A dozen or more General Mills executives—anybody who could find an excuse, it seemed—had journeyed to New York to catch a glimpse of this hot new acquisition and its hit brain-teaser, *Instant Insanity.*

They crowded Parker Brothers's sixth-floor showroom, leaned against the Windsor chairs that were part of the drawing-room-inspired decor, and fiddled with the products displayed on the library-like shelves. They watched, fascinated by the first-name familiarity of manufacturers and major retailers in the toys industry, and listened in wonder as friendships and past favors openly dictated sales and distribution terms. By comparison with the highly regulated and standardized food industry, this was the smoke-filled room of a political convention. Looking awkward in their curiosity, the visitors observed and occasionally took notes.

Invariably, after an hour or a day of shadowing Eddie Parker, Ranny Barton, or their staff, the Minneapolis visitors would want to take their hosts to dinner. The offers were politely but firmly declined. "Gentlemen, we are here to service customers," said Barton, over and over again. "I'm sure you understand."

Barton explained that The American Toy Fair, sponsored by the Toy Manufacturers of America, Inc., was no longer the make-or-break sales forum it had been in decades past, but it was still where those who weren't ready to buy were prepped for the order-takers who would pay their visits later. This was also the place where the rumors started, where company and individual reputations were made, and where those reputations were far more quickly and gleefully broken. Barton and Parker said they had to stay where the action was. "Of course, of course," said the Minneapolis visitors, furrowing their brows with concern, "we understand completely."

But the traffic didn't ease much when Toy Fair ended; the influx of visitors followed Parker and Barton back into Salem. Sometime that spring, Nalen—now formally the head of a $91 million division consisting of toys (Kenner and Rainbow), games (Parker Brothers), and crafts (Craft Master)—telephoned Barton from Minneapolis to ask how things were going. "I have just one request," sighed Barton. "Please stop all these daggoned"—he always said daggoned when he meant doggoned—"*hangers-on* from coming out here. They're becoming a pain in the neck."

Bells went off in Nalen's head. Though he hadn't been around to see it with his own eyes, he had been told that General Mills had run its appliance and electronic businesses into the ground in the 1950s as the result of just this kind of over-eager attention. Nalen agreed to try to cool some of the ardor at headquarters. He didn't want General Mills looking over Parker Brothers's shoulder, or even seeming to do so. Not only was the company eminently qualified to take care of itself, it had a quirky individuality that Nalen didn't want to see interfered with.

Nalen had come to view Parker Brothers and its parent as different in ways that stretched beyond obvious factors of size, industry, or geographic location. For all its outward reserve, Parker Brothers was a warm, cohesive place, where people were free to create—and did so mostly for the joy of doing so. General Mills, on the other hand, was somewhat the opposite: loose and friendly on the outside, but bruisingly regimented on the inside. Few moves were made there without taking the measure of their motive and impact, and anybody who didn't achieve was "attrited."

General Mills glided through its markets like the biggest duck on a northern Minnesota lake—serene on the surface, all churning feet underneath. The company had a reputation as a modern marketing machine that made heavy demands on the time and energy of its executives, most of whom hailed from the nation's most prestigious business schools. Outsiders used words like well-oiled, methodical, and bureaucratic when talking about the millers. The company was the Marines, they said, minus the crewcuts. It seemed to be forever charging up some hill, led by a platoon of young go-getters vying for the opportunity to plant the flag.

Since the days of James Stroud Bell and the Washburn Crosby Company, the organization that became General Mills was staffed by young men in a hurry to get somewhere. Some of them were Minnesota Swedes, Norwegians, and Germans, but just as many were well-educated Yankee transplants. Bell referred to these young managers as his "kindergarten." "Bring your own desk," the new recruits were told, and they quickly learned to pack not only lunch but dinner. Sixteen-hour days were expected on all days but Sunday, when workers were let out "early"—that is, after the office closed at 6 P.M. More contemporary stories told of how flights of newly promoted executives competed to be the first to arrive in their new digs, believing that even an hour's edge might yield a slight edge in seniority. The most determined of these hopefuls started moving their boxes into the executive wing at the crack of dawn on the appointed day.

At Parker Brothers, on the other hand, work was play. Even the company history, self-published in 1973, was entitled *Ninety Years of Fun.*

Days at Parker Brothers were filled with the laughter of games being played and tested by employees. At lunch, there were boisterous card contests, the most popular of which was a game called "Oh Shit." At management functions, the entertainment often included blue limericks recited by a well-lubricated salesman who invariably ended his performance by raising his glass and intoning, "More oil, more oil." Executives had been seen on the roof of the building flying Black Hawk kites (a product that Parker Brothers sold briefly). Their intramural pranks, such as hiding one another's cars or shorting each other's paychecks, were legend. And on many summer afternoons, you could have rolled a bowling ball through the executive offices and not hit a member of the Parker clan. All three top men in the corporation—Robert Barton, Eddie Parker, and Ranny Barton—were avid sailors who never let work get in the way of a sunny day's recreation.

It would fit a romanticized scenario to say the Parkers and Bartons were a tightly knit clan, but that wasn't the case. In fact, cousins Ranny Barton and Eddie Parker hadn't met until just before Ranny joined the company, at which time he and his wife bought a house next door to Eddie. Nor did the Parkers and Bartons socialize much, and they certainly weren't the types to wax sentimental about the grand old company. But there was within the New England reserve they shared a rare and unspoken atmosphere of teamwork. While the four top family members each had their own areas of expertise, job descriptions hadn't been allowed to become weapons of turf protection. Janitor or president, they pitched in and did what was needed to be done, guided only by a faith that they extended to the entire workforce: that whoever took on the task could be trusted to do it right. If there was between them any of the rancor or infighting so common to family-owned businesses, the world was none the wiser.

In contrast, General Mills laid out its job descriptions in minute detail and operated within a fairly rigid class structure. Management encouraged intra-organizational conflict and individual competition as a means of separating winners from also-rans. To the victors went the spoils of pay and position—but rarely public acclaim. General Mills preferred to do its business in what has been called "an atmosphere of addition, division, and silence." Seldom does it put its operating managers before the public. The conglomerate prefers to portray its accomplishments as those of a company, not of any one person. The elder Bell set the pattern: He referred to all individual mistakes, no matter how egregious, as "our error," and all triumphs as "our success."

Parker and the Bartons, on the other hand, encouraged employee participation at any and all levels, receiving a suggested manufacturing modification from an assembly worker with as much respectful interest as if it had come from family. During the last frenzied weeks before Toy Fair, nearly everybody pitched in to build prototypes and paste together promotional material. Some employees became models for box art. Herculean efforts were put forth apparently with little regard as to what the payoff might be, though management at Parker Brothers endeavored to give extraordinary contributors their time in the limelight. When a family member took to the road to promote a new product, invariably one of its designers went along, an equal partner in the promotion.

In running what he now called the General Mills Fun Group, Craig Nalen considered it his calling to preserve Parker Brothers as he would any of the other divisions: independent and unique. He sought to introduce only those ingredients necessary to accomplish the growth and managerial development goals General Mills had set for itself in acquiring the company.

Still, autonomy was not freedom. Nalen fully expected to supervise key aspects of staffing and operations. Both Kenner and Parker Brothers were told to adopt General Mills's accounting conventions, for example. Part of that change involved switching from a calendar-year system to the General Mills June-to-May fiscal year, which matched the old crop year (and in some quarters, was still referred to by that name). It may have seemed a small alteration to Nalen and his higher-ups, but it was revolutionary in an industry whose single focus and year-end peak was Christmas. The change put Parker Brothers, and Kenner as well, completely out of sync with all industry data collection. Furthermore, because it tended to push pre-Christmas shipping more into May than the traditional August, it initially annoyed some retailers.

Nalen also made personnel changes. As much as he appreciated Eddie Parker and Ranny Barton, and as admirably as Parker Brothers had performed under their reins, Nalen didn't consider them or their underlings managerial whiz kids. In terms of managerial skill and savvy, many of them seemed the Yankee equivalent of good ol' boys.

Still, Nalen knew that Eddie Parker would never abide a thorough house-cleaning. Instead, Nalen diplomatically worked newcomers into several key positions in the company—first a controller, then a marketing man, then somebody for manufacturing. He did his level best to make Eddie think the changes were his own.

There was but one brief skirmish. The supposedly retired
Robert Barton stepped back into the picture unbidden to fire
Henry "Hank" Simmons, Parker Brothers's longtime research and
development man. Nalen, who happened to consider Simmons one
of few men in Salem worth his salt, was furious. "For better or
worse, General Mills owns this company," Nalen lectured Barton
when the older man arrived in Minneapolis in a huff. And, while
the conglomerate didn't pretend to know how to make games,
General Mills did know a thing or two about good management
and growth.

Nalen proceeded with his loose-tight management strategy
secure in the knowledge that he had historical precedent on his
side. General Mills had been built by men who believed in eyes-
on, hands-off management. Cadwallader Washburn, recognized by
historians as a business genius, was far more interested in planning,
financing, and staffing his various enterprises than in running
them. Later, James Ford Bell had created General Mills to be
only an umbrella for its operating companies, allowing each division to work for "its own individual goals, according to its own
whims and capabilities."

"We don't make a single sale of our own," the younger Bell
liked to say. The milling firms bought the wheat and milled it,
while General Mills, the parent, handled the merchandising, marketing, advertising, and financing. "Our aim is to give the maximum of help to our associates with the minimum of interference,"
he said.

This was Nalen's goal for the budding Toy Group as well.
But, whether it was recognized internally or not, General Mills
hadn't conducted its affairs on the Bell or Washburn models in
quite a while. The line that separated corporate staff from the
staffs of the various rival food groups in Minneapolis had grown
very thin, and many of those at the top echelon—Rawlings and
Polk excepted—considered the non-food companies as interlopers
that had to go along if they expected to get along. With General
Mills headquarters pushing for control and Parker Brothers pulling for autonomy, Nalen found himself acting the role of the go-
between almost from the day the merger papers were signed.

Despite pressure to more fully integrate his group into the
company, Nalen was reluctant to tamper with the images or

business relationships of his divisions. For example, there had been talk of weaving the Big G trademark into Parker Brothers's swirled logo, and although Nalen had been intrigued by the idea, he wasn't terribly disappointed to see it die. His main interest had been in using General Mills's proven clout to help sell Parker Brothers's products. In-house studies showed the change wouldn't influence consumers one way or another.

Later, Nalen outright discouraged corporate recommendations to throw out Parker Brothers's longtime advertising agency, the Boston-based Badger, Browning & Parcher firm. The suggestion was to appoint one New York or Chicago mega-agency to handle the account for the entire budding Toy Group, in the interest of efficiency and coordination.

Using a single big-city agency to represent both Parker Brothers and Kenner would be all but unworkable, as Nalen saw it. If there was one thing he had learned in his first year working with these organizations, it was how truly polar they were—not only with General Mills, but one to another.

You could tell them apart in a group meeting immediately: The Kenner staffers (the liberals) were the ones who looked less comfortable in their suits, as they generally wore open collars or polos at work. The day-in, day-out uniform of Parker Brothers (the conservatives) may have been occasionally jacketless, but never casual. Nalen found that he could walk into Parker Brothers unannounced at any time, and though he might find the Salem executives on their hands and knees moving a game piece around a board or in their stocking feet to test some new group participation concept, their ties and cufflinks stayed resolutely in place.

Kenner was the bigger, trendier company. It had spunk and guts, and Nalen marveled at how nonchalantly it tackled the risks inherent in its business. But as he saw it, its breathless pace combined with a strong-armed management style to produce a Machiavellian atmosphere that increased turnover and lowered morale.

Parker Brothers, on the other hand, was almost laissez-faire, particularly now that the strict Robert Barton had handed off the reins to Eddie Parker. Clock-watching simply wasn't part of the culture. People worked late, or came in on weekends. They also left early. Nobody got rich working there, but they had reason to stay. Turnover was nearly nil, and service records of twenty to fifty years were common. In fact, most of *MONOPOLY*'s original production team was still on the job in Nalen's day, as was the man who used to demonstrate games at Grand Central Station for the company in the 1920s and 1930s. No doubt there also still existed a salesman or two who had peddled moonshine from the false bottom of a valise during Prohibition.

Nalen had done his level best to try to build cohesion within the toys group, with only limited success. Relations between Parker Brothers and Kenner, for example, were like baked Alaska—toasty as they seemed on the outside, it was hard to coax an internal thaw.

Some of the differences between the various companies in Nalen's group were cultural. Yankees from New England (Parker Brothers), Jews from Cincinnati (Kenner), and Italians from Toledo (Craft Master) simply approached life and business with divergent attitudes.

But Parker Brothers did more than its part to separate itself from the rest of the group—not from the Italians or the Jews per se, but from the toys industry that Kenner and Craft Master represented. The games industry was another animal entirely, maintained the Salemites.

Call it arrogance or pride, Parker Brothers—for all its determination not to take business too seriously—was unremorsefully aware of its status as an American cultural icon. Its staffers considered the company a creative niche unto itself, and many observers agreed. In a business heavily populated by fast-talking, cigar-chomping entrepreneurs, the gamesmakers at Parker Brothers were known for their stiff-upper-lipped grace and easy going charm. Amid a rough-and-tumble industry, known for deals done in four-letter words and rolled sleeves, Parker Brothers kept its collective shoes shined and its elbows off the *MONOPOLY* table.

Even the jargon was different. Considering itself more a publishing house than a manufacturer, Parker Brothers termed new games not "products" but "editions." Individual games were not "units," they were "copies." And games designers were not inventors, they were "authors."

Of the two companies, Nalen frankly preferred Parker Brothers, partly because there was little or nothing he could do that could faze president Eddie Parker. With Kenner and its founding Steiner family, it had been armed war from the beginning.

The Kenner acquisition deal had been structured on an earn-out that was almost immediately disputed, and eventually litigated. Under the agreement, Kenner's owners had been paid not in stock or cash, but rather through a pre-determined percentage of the profits that Kenner would generate over the first few years following the sale. A floor on the agreement protected the Steiners, while a ceiling guarded General Mills's interests.

The trouble was, the two parties proved to have differing goals: General Mills was in it for the long haul, so the corporation wanted to see high levels of reinvestment, and correspondingly, relatively low earnings. The Steiners, on the other hand, saw it in their interest to force every cent they could to the bottom line. In the ensuing struggle, Kenner's performance began to suffer and the company slipped into the red. Nalen and the Steiners were soon pointing the finger of blame at each other.

It was this earn-out squabble that began to draw unfavorable attention to the toys group, then known as the General Mills Fun Group. The Kenner and Parker Brothers acquisitions of 1967 and 1968 had kicked off a series of copycat mergers, resulting in a major consolidation of the toys industry. General Mills, understandably, felt very much in the spotlight for being the trend's instigator, and it didn't take kindly to the public embarrassment of Kenner's declining performance and unseemly turf wars.

The scrutiny came from both inside and outside General Mills, but the debate it renewed was strictly internal: Was it or was it not right for General Mills, a food company, to have diversified into non-food businesses? At Minneapolis headquarters, patience had been thin with the diversification program almost since the day that chairman Ed Rawlings had initiated it. And the disgruntlement grew as General Mills's acquisition activity continued and expanded.

After the toys and games acquisitions, General Mills went up the road from Parker Brothers to Gloucester, Massachusetts, and acquired the 100-year-old, $72 million Gorton Corporation, the largest independent producer of packaged frozen seafood in the country. Later that year, 1968, General Mills moved into jewelry with the purchase of Monocraft, Inc., the New York-based maker of Monet costume jewelry. In 1969, General Mills acquired David Crystal, Inc., whose labels included Izod, the sportswear manufacturer, and Knothe Brothers Co., Inc., which made men's belts and sleepwear. Then General Mills entered specialty retailing with the purchase of a direct-mail, hobby and craft company called LeeWards. Finally, with an eye toward participating in the "long-term growth of away-from-home eating," General Mills entered the restaurant industry, buying several chains, but pledging to develop only "the most promising." Key among the acquisitions was the Red Lobster Inn, a three-unit chain in Florida. And these were just the initial incursions to industries such as frozen food, fashions, specialty retailing, and restaurants. By 1970, General Mills was touted as "a power to be reckoned with in non-food areas."

From 1961 to 1969, General Mills acquired thirty-seven companies in the United States and abroad, thirteen of them during the period of frenzied activity between 1966 and 1969. Six were divested in the same eight-year period. On Wall Street, the conglomerate's stock price rose from $24 to $60 within two years after the acquisition phase began.

But the acquisitions had left General Mills a factionalized place. The tensions weren't simply those between food loyalists and non-food interlopers; they were pressures of age and experience. The Rawlings plan, with its varied goals and strategies, constituted a major organizational shakeup. It brought in a new cadre of brash young men, most of them MBAs with an energy and style that was unfamiliar if not unwelcome to some of the old guard.

Among them, diversification strategist Bo Polk was by far the most ambitious. Tall, athletic, charming—Polk's hard-charging energy, his sense of humor, and above all, his taste for life in the fast lane, set him apart from the stoic company men of General Mills.

Under Polk, the diversification drive had taken on the air of a military invasion with its atmosphere of haste and secrecy. In board discussions, acquisition targets were labeled with cryptic combinations of letters and numbers, such as S–8, B–9, G–6, P–2, or C–5. Prior to a vote, directors would sometimes be heard whispering to one another: "What's K–9?" Or, swept away by the slick presentations of the MBA-trained "song and dance team," as Polk's venture team became known to some, a bemused director might turn to one of his fellows after a vote and ask, equally *sotto voce*, what company he had just voted to let General Mills buy.

Accompanying the jargon and the spit and polish was a prevailing attitude that there wasn't time for anyone to think too deeply about what General Mills was doing or why. Throughout the mid-1960s, the company had been in a "feverish haste to acquire before the other fellow got in ahead of us, or the FTC [Federal Trade Commission] shut off our water while it took a long look at the available supply," said board member Gerald S. Kennedy in his memoirs. Every time the board bought more than one company in a given industry, or amassed more than a two or three percent market share, it expected the federal trust-busters to be breathing down the company's neck—and with good reason, as it turned out. In 1969, after years of snack-food acquisitions, the agency prohibited General Mills from buying any more chip producers for ten years.

But the real reason for Polk's hurry was less the Feds than the old guard themselves. From the day Polk had taken on his diversification duties, Rawlings had advised him that General Mills would not take to change kindly. The new-venture team would have to work quickly and quietly. Polk told Nalen and the rest of his new-venture squad that if they didn't keep racking up acquisitions, and fast, the establishment—a word just coming into vogue then—would manage to drag things back to the earlier, more sedate pace that Rawlings believed had jeopardized General Mills's future.

General Mills had always been a company full of young talent, but never before had the youngsters found such power so quickly. New career ladders were established with the continued expansion of General Mills's business, and they were far shorter than those that made up the latticework of the food bastions. Soon it seemed that each of the company's new ventures were being run by an MBA who hadn't yet hit age forty. These young men had friendly but serious competition from a handful of Rawlings proteges on the other side of the company as well. For example, a near-sighted and gawky 39-year-old named H. Brewster "Bruce" Atwater oversaw about $400 million in annual sales, as a group vice president for such old-line products as Betty Crocker mixes, Gold Medal flour, and *Cheerios.*

So peach-fuzzed were the troops, in fact, that major business magazines began referring to the company's "youth kick." With its ranks and columns of blue-suiters in horn-rimmed glasses, the place sometimes seemed more like the Ford Foundation, observed *Business Week,* than a major U.S. corporation.

Older executives chafed against the attitudes of the newcomers, most of which they wearily attributed to business-school training. Board member Gerald Kennedy complained about the increasing sobriety of annual reports, even in good years such as fiscal 1968. "The letter to the stockholders reads like a homily on economics at an ecumenical service participated in by the deacons of the Yale Divinity School, the choir of the Harvard Graduate School of Business Administration, the rooting section of the Internal Revenue Service, and a few Johnny-come-latelies from the staff of the *Wall Street Journal,*" he wrote. "Frankly, it is as dry as a dustman's throat just before the five o'clock whistle blows for knock-off time."

Meanwhile, little of the growing factional tension escaped the architect of the changes. Stressed beyond his previous effectiveness, Rawlings lost much of his commanding air—and with it, the faith of his troops. It didn't take much prodding to secure his resignation as chairman on December 31, 1968.

The battle to succeed Rawlings became a referendum on General Mills' diversification program. Polk was the heir apparent, given his public visibility and recent accomplishments as spear-carrier for Rawlings's diversification strategy. That strength was also his liability. There were many within General Mills who had been less than happy with the wholesale revamping of the company, and who now jumped at the chance to vanquish Polk and regain control. It looked to be a good fight.

Polk, however, forfeited before the bell rang. Inexplicably, he missed several key management meetings and generally showed flagging gumption in the face of the very formidable pressure that the food establishment was putting on him. His subsequent disintegration as the leading candidate was to be expected, the pundits said. Polk was the kind of hotshot that General Mills tended to find and exploit to advantage every couple of decades, they said, but such gadflies always fell short of gaining real power. That had been, and always would be, reserved for the progeny of the establishment.

But the hard-liners didn't win this contest. A compromise candidate carried the day. He was the advocate of less aggressive growth, James P. McFarland—a bald and roly-poly South Dakota-born accountant with a Dartmouth MBA. Joining General Mills in 1934, he had risen through the commercial food side of the company, gaining a reputation as a decent man and a good manager as he went. Stating that General Mills had grown too big and complex for one man to manage, McFarland created a triumvirate, dividing some of his duties between the next two men in the chain of command. "This is no one-man fiefdom," he later told a reporter. "I don't think a company built on one individual's thinking is correct."

Polk subsequently left General Mills to head Metro-Goldwyn-Mayer, Inc., the Hollywood studio. Spurned in his quest for the chief executive officer's post, Polk departed with the politically correct explanation: lack of advancement. He wanted to be president of a company, he said, and he was going somewhere he could do that. Again the pundits nodded sagely: That's what all the exiting hotshots said.

Upon taking over, McFarland's stated goal was to build an "all-weather growth company." At a woodsy Wisconsin retreat held soon after his promotion—amid camp songs, chalk talks, and a passionate endorsement of non-food expansion delivered by Nalen—McFarland exhorted his skeptical executives to consider the acquisition strategy "a means of making the Big 'G' stand not for goodness, but greatness."

Still, McFarland publicly emphasized that it was not the company's goal to turn its back on its food business. "We're just broadening our base in what we know best, consumer marketing," he shrugged, noting that the new ventures catered to the same basic market that General Mills had always served: women and children. So, emphatically no, General Mills wasn't diversifying simply for the joy of putting its fingers in new pies. "We're skittish about [going into acquisitions merely with the aim of] conglomeratizing." In words that clearly echoed with the miserable experiences of the 1950s in electronics and appliances, McFarland concluded: "We don't want to enter an unfamiliar market and get killed."

But that's what some food stalwarts already saw happening in some corners of the company. With Kenner's earn-out difficulties, the firmly entrenched food forces began itching to take Nalen's hill—ostensibly to shore up flagging performance in the young toys group, but just as likely to prevent another outsider, namely Nalen, from gaining a firmer foothold in the company. Few at or near his level had forgotten his speech at the Wisconsin retreat, or the way McFarland had quickly made key phrases of Nalen's talk into corporate slogans. Food executives, led by a sales-trained up-and-comer named Donald Swanson, urged that toys and the other non-food groups be reined in and watched more closely. These non-food groups needed tough controls, he said.

McFarland, a professed fan of divisional autonomy, responded by imposing a rigorous set of goal-setting and performance-tracking requirements. He established a schedule of divisional and corporate meetings. And, to the delight of the national business press, the jolly McFarland began turning up in person for spot-checks at operating units—all in the name of keeping in touch. Then he brought Swanson in over Nalen's head, and Nalen began planning his exit. By 1971, when Nalen's operating managers had recognized the *de facto* shift in power and began reporting to him only as a courtesy, Nalen had decided to join investors in buying out a small company of his own. There he could continue playing the entrepreneurial role he had so enjoyed during his acquisition-hunting days.

Until Swanson's ascendancy was a *fait accompli,* Nalen had argued strenuously against the man's involvement in toys. Turf considerations aside, Nalen thought he knew full well where Swanson's basic beef came from: He was uncomfortable with the unruly nature of the toys and games businesses and thought they could be tamed. Kenner and Parker Brothers may have differed from one another in style, but it was becoming increasing clear that neither bore a whit of resemblance to the way General Mills did its business.

Like Swanson and others of his higher-ups in Minneapolis, Nalen had been amazed at how incorrigible the market for toys and games industries could be. For all his good intentions of teaching these companies a thing or two about management, it had grown increasingly clear that managerial ignorance or stodginess wasn't really the problem to be solved. As much as the companies may have recognized the value of scientific management technique, their markets didn't seem to respond to it.

Nalen had learned through firsthand experience with the rapid rise and fall of *Instant Insanity* that when a toys or a games company had a hot product, it virtually sold itself. If it grew cold, no amount of advertising money, or technological innovation, or smart positioning, or anything else in General Mills's bag of tricks, was going to change things. The business had the attention span of a nine-year-old, and no matter how Mom coaxed and cajoled, yesterday's toy was still only that—yesterday's toy.

Unlike the food industry, where public acceptance and good promotion sustained winning products into two or even three decades with scarcely a repackaging, the most popular toys and games—with rare exception—spent minimal time on the market. Product life cycles weren't bell curves in toys and games, they represented a single, spikey peak seldom more than three years in length. If the product didn't get "knocked off" (copied) by competitors and undercut in price—sometimes before the original even cleared the Toy Fair showroom—they usually succumbed within a year or two to consumer boredom.

The real management science in toys and games was timing: Getting into a market was never easy, Nalen had learned, but getting out without losing your shirt was far more difficult. Invariably, the falloff in sales was faster and more dramatic than anyone or anything could predict. Smart companies moved on at the first sign of hesitation in sales growth, and usually to an entirely new sort of product.

There were exceptions to the serendipitous rule, of course. A relative handful of toys and games each generation managed to outlive the cycles and become classics. *Raggedy Ann* and *Raggedy Andy* dated back to approximately 1910, as did *Tinkertoys. Slinky, Silly Putty, Mr. Potato Head, Erector Sets,* the *Yo-Yo, Scrabble,* and *MONOPOLY* were all pre-1950 phenomena. *Barbie* dolls have sold millions per year since they came on the market in 1959.

In games, Parker Brothers's roster of staples was remarkable. While most of the rest of the industry derived about 80 percent

of its revenue each year from new products, Parker Brothers
derived that much from its old warhorses—among them *MONOP-
OLY, Risk, Sorry!* and *Clue.* Still, not even with its staples could
Parker Brothers be considered a stable company—not by General
Mills's standards.

While General Mills had tailored everything in its operations
to produce steady, uninterrupted growth from quarter to quarter,
Nalen's quarterly reports from his divisions jerked up and down
with the year's natural cycle. As much as 70 percent of all toys
sold at retail were sold during the six weeks before Christmas.
By the first of the new year, the old toy year was over, orders
had yet to come in on a new one, and sales slumped so badly
that layoffs—something unheard of among the meticulous planners
at General Mills—were an annual event. Because the marketplace
was so fickle, performance also fluctuated from year to year, first
soaring then plunging with the fortunes of just one or two products.

In Minneapolis, such "erratic" behavior was a sign of bad
financial planning at best, total incompetence at worst. Many
General Mills executives, for example, wanted to know what
managerial foolishness had allowed *Instant Insanity* sales to drop
through the floor just a year after its triumphal introduction—
and what further oversights had prevented another product from
being ready to replace that volume? As much as he explained that
hits like *Instant Insanity* could never be relied upon as anything
but the icing on Parker Brothers's cake, the message fell on deaf
ears. Couldn't more research and testing make it easier for Kenner
and Parker Brothers to pick winners? headquarters asked.

At General Mills, research and development was a thoroughly
planned endeavor, involving thousands of man-hours and millions
of dollars. All available data on the marketplace and the competition
was exhaustively analyzed before the corporation so much as lifted
a finger to introduce or modify a product. The company sometimes
took more than a year to carefully test and explore whether even
a relatively simple formula change should be made—whether
butterfat should be added to Bisquick, for example.

This make-or-break attitude toward research and testing dated
back to Bell's day. He encouraged employees to "Think it big and
keep it simple," exhorting them to know no limits in formulating
their ideas, but to keep the implementation of those ideas man-

ageable—by doing the extensive research that he believed kept process predictable, and therefore, simple. To Bell's way of thinking, instinct was a dirty word. He wanted his company run on "facts, not opinions."

Toys and games, on the other hand, thrived on instinct and experienced guesswork. Because time frames in the industry were so compressed, the tendency was to avoid all but the most necessary market testing and take reasonable risks grounded in years of industry experience. Inventors went on their guts, knowing only that next year's hit would be something completely different than this year's. The manufacturer's role was generally limited to spotting the bright ideas as they came in the door.

At Parker Brothers in the late 1960s, research and development was centered on a large room where games were laid out for inspection. Some were unsolicited from amateurs, while others came from established design firms—but the total number of games submitted per year seldom dropped below three thousand. Those concepts that weren't deemed either hopelessly boring or permanently mired in the public domain (and therefore difficult to trademark) underwent what was called play-testing.

It was a process that had grown little in sophistication since George Parker's day. Turn-of-the-century sepia-toned photos showed women sitting with game boards or cards, their hair upswept and knotted in the Gibson Girl style, their dresses tucked and gathered with brooches at the neck. Styles had changed with the decades, but the practice did not. Play-testing remained a key development activity, and one that still fell mainly to the women of the company. "Nobody was ever fired at Parker Brothers for playing games on the job," went the in-house joke.

When a game had cleared the initial play-testing hurdle, each product then went on to try to earn the hard-won okay of management: Eddie, Ranny, Channing (Bill), and before his retirement, Robert. Once they got their hands on it, it was rare that a game went into the product line unaltered.

These men subjected the games to every twist and turn of fate they could imagine. Whether it was for fun or in the interest of play-testing science proved debatable, but bluffs and fakery were always part of the testing "rigor." "We connive and we cheat," Ranny Barton was fond of saying. It was a technique he learned from his grandfather. When George Parker didn't like how he was faring in a game, he'd arrange to catch one of his heavily starched cuffs on the edge of the board while lifting his hand to scratch his nose. Playing pieces flew everywhere. When play resumed, the old man was invariably in better position.

Because General Mills took its product development so seriously, and devoted so much time and attention to its every stage, all setbacks, delays, and outright abandonments of products were greeted with dejection and animosity. After all, the parties involved had invested several years of technology, test marketing, equipment, and personnel in each new venture. It became a part of their lives.

But Parker Brothers, like Kenner and many other toys and games companies, made it a practice not to look back. There wasn't time. Toys and games companies operated in a state of barely controlled panic, as a few weeks on one side or another of a development schedule could determine whether the product was this year's entry or next year's. Also, because so much of a company's fortune depended on the good ideas that came through the door unexpectedly, product lines were assumed to expand or contract, or get completely revamped, within a week of Toy Fair— just to accomodate a new idea, or eliminate one that had already been scooped. Those toys and games companies that couldn't endure a flop or move forward after a hit weren't flexible enough for the industry. They didn't last.

Parker Brothers inherited a more studious attitude toward product development and testing with the arrival of the new research and development man that Nalen hired to replace Hank Simmons, a prep-school pal of his named William F. "Bill" Dohrmann. Dohrmann began bringing in groups of children and their parents to be observed through one-way mirrors as they examined and compared various toys and games. But, despite an advertising background and a bias toward testing practices that came from a stint on the General Mills account at the Chicago-based ad agency of Needham Harper & Steers, Dohrmann—like Nalen—soon discovered that research had fatal limitations in such a volatile industry. It was enough to drive you crazy: A product that came through with flying colors in testing could flop in the marketplace. At the same time, an in-house flop could become the hit of the industry several years running. Dohrmann quickly became like every R & D man in the business—he came to believe in his own talent as a judge of product. His gut instincts were as good as anybody else's—which weren't always good enough.

When instinct failed, it typically failed big. In 1969, Dohrmann licensed the name and image of the occasional *Laugh-In* guest who was later married to Miss Vicky on the *Tonight Show,* only to watch the so-called *Tiny Tim's Game of Beautiful Things* gather dust on the shelves. Dohrmann endured another flop in 1970, with the introduction of a messenger game called *Oobi.* From the moment the outside inventor had brought it into his office, the otherwise sensible Dohrmann had been enchanted with this red, egg-shaped object with the big, friendly eyes.

"I'm *Oobi,*" it said on the side of the hollow orb. "I contain a message to another human being. Please further my journey an inch, a foot, or a mile. Add a note, if you wish. Then help me to the next nice person like yourself."

Dohrmann thought it was the passive sort of toy that flower children would buy for their children. But *Oobi* laid an egg. "The few people who did buy them invariably handed them to airline stewardesses," Dohrmann reported. "It didn't take long before all the stewardesses were groaning and saying, 'Uh-oh, here comes another creep with his goddamned *Oobi.'*" The product lost $300,000. Having picked up the industry's attitude toward such setbacks, Dohrmann shrugged off the failure. "I fell in love, what can I say?"

But these bloopers were far more the exception than the rule in the first few years after the merger. Parker Brothers was receiving from General Mills the financial and managerial backing it needed to pass GO, as it were, to become more than just the maker of board games and card games. With Dohrmann's guidance, along with the marketing and manufacturing expertise of several more General Mills imports, Parker Brothers began to move ever closer to the mainstream toys industry. The aim wasn't simply to seek new conquests, but rather, to avoid being left behind as the market shifted away from the traditional board games that were Parker Brothers's bread and butter.

Parker Brothers's 1970 introduction of the foamy *Nerf* ball created a sensation, and contributed to a doubling of Parker

Brothers's revenue to $36 million within three years of the merger. Only *Instant Insanity* sold better. The original *Nerf* ball was a four-inch polyurethane foam orb that came to Parker Brothers in the spring of 1969, as part of an indoor volleyball game. It looked like a good stocking-footed game the likes of *Twister,* and with good reason: It was made by the same Minnesota-based independent inventors.

The game was being tested by a group of employees led by Dohrmann when several executives, including Ranny Barton and Eddie Parker happened into the room. Dohrmann spotted Eddie, and hurled the foamy orb at him, both of them laughing as it bounced harmlessly off his forehead. Eddie tossed it back to somebody else, and soon the group was lobbing the blobs around the room, as if the volleyball net didn't exist. Dohrmann and Parker stared each other with wide-eyed wonder of revelation. "You know what that is, that's a ball," said Eddie, meaning just a ball, not a volleyball. "A ball that won't wreck the house," concurred Dohrmann. He could hear the voice of his mother and all others, admonishing the kids to quit throwing things around before they break something. Well, here was a ball that wouldn't turn the living room into a shambles.

As development proceeded on the foamy ball, Parker Brothers considered all sorts of outerspacey names—"Orbie," and "Moon-ball"—the latter inspired by astronaut Neil Armstrong's moonwalk on July 20, 1969, at the height of the product testing. But the product was named *Nerf.* Dragsters at racetracks were fitted with so-called nerf bars to protect the body and chassis as they were pushed out of the pits, in-house designer Arthur Venditti recalled. But the name was chosen less for its meaning than its sound: *Nerf* rolled off the tongue all round and cushiony, like the product itself. The *Nerf* ball became the first product to wear the label "A Parker Toy."

Many observers viewed Parker Brothers's entry into the toys market with the same amused interest that Harvard might attract if it started offering tool-and-die instruction: It wasn't completely unreasonable, but it did seem out of character. Some focused their skepticism on the *Nerf* ball itself. A retail buyer for a big chain on the East Coast adamantly refused to carry the toy, saying not only that it was overpriced, but that the almost ridiculous simplicity of the thing was an insult to the intelligence of his customers. He came around, though, when those presumably offended customers began pillaging the aisles in search of *Nerf.* That stampede was not an isolated incident: At Jordan Marsh, one of Boston's leading department stores, an entire shipment of *Nerf* balls sold out in a single day.

As was often the case with the biggest hits in the toys industry, *Nerf* had timing on its side. It was introduced just as the trial of the Chicago Seven was winding down, amid revelations of secret bombing runs in Cambodia and the National Guard shootings of four young protesters at Kent State. *Nerf* offered a mindless sort of diversion that was welcome in such a troubled era. Some people made beds out of the balls, others used them in lieu of wallpaper, creating a weird padded-cell effect. A disc jockey in the South created a fictitious *Nerf* League, for which he announced scores and standings each day.

Nobody connected with Parker Brothers or General Mills cared how or why the product clicked with the public; only that more than 4 million of them were sold in their debut year. To General Mills's further delight, the growth was achieved without denting profits: Parker Brothers's revenue and earnings continued a steady uptick of 15 to 20 percent per year.

Parker Brothers could have stopped right there with *Nerf*—and probably would have, had it not been for marketing man Don Knutzen, who possessed a General Mills-inbred knack for expanding a product line. He took the *Nerf* phenomenon many steps further, with other sorts of indoor sports equipment. There were *Nerf* softballs, *Nerfoop* basketballs, even a *Nerf* football. It looked like Parker Brothers had found itself a new staple—or rather, a new line of staples.

Still, it remained very much a one-product company. *MONOPOLY* was Parker Brothers's unmatched revenue producer and its revered symbol. Once, at a weekly product-review session, designer Arthur Venditti made a disparaging remark about the game as he sought to highlight the attributes of a game then in development. *MONOPOLY* wasn't balanced, he said—meaning that if a player started to lose, there was little that he or she could do to alter fate. A smiling but serious Eddie Parker leaned heavily on the forever wobbly mahogany conference table. "Don't you ever say that again," he chided Venditti in a gentle tone. "That game pays our rent."

Even as Parker Brothers widened its focus to include trendier toys and games, it devoted almost as much time, energy, and money to the upkeep of *MONOPOLY* and the rest of its ever-popular roster of board games. Year in, year out, the company indulged any event or stunt that tended to keep a name such as *MONOPOLY* before the public and strenuously discouraged anyone or anything that threatened to diminish the role of the game in American culture. When college kids played the first life-sized version of the game, or took it underwater, or vied for *MONOPOLY* endurance records, Parker Brothers was there. When someone tried to use *MONOPOLY* for their own gain, or took actions that might reflect badly on the game, Parker Brothers was also there. It was just such a defense effort that brought Ranny Barton out of the shadows of his father and cousin, and into the company's spotlight.

Parker Brothers had gotten a telephone call from its public relations office in New York City in September of 1972 advising the company of a *MONOPOLY*-related flap in Atlantic City, New Jersey. It seemed city fathers there proposed to rename Mediterranean and Baltic Avenues, two fixtures on the *MONOPOLY* board. Students, most of them from nearby Princeton University and calling themselves Students to Save Baltic and Mediterranean Avenues (SSBMA), mobilized against the effort. To Parker Brothers's delight, the matter became a cause célèbre overnight, producing a kind of publicity opportunity that couldn't be bought at any price.

Parker Brothers president Eddie Parker planted his tongue firmly in cheek and took pen in hand, warning that the repercussions of proposed the changes would cause near revolt among the legions of *MONOPOLY* maniacs. "Would you like to be the man to tell a *MONOPOLY* fanatic from California that the streets he came to see no longer exist? Would you be willing to take the responsibility for an invasion by hordes of protesting *MONOPOLY* players, all demanding that you go directly to jail, without even the dignity of passing GO?"

In January of 1973 the matter came to a hearing, and Parker Brothers was only too glad to accept an invitation to add its two cents' worth. As he was the only family member available that day, Ranny Barton was tapped for the job.

The event, in Ranny's eyes, rivaled the Watergate hearings that had begun the previous summer. There were camera trucks everywhere, their cables snaking toward a jam-packed auditorium. As Barton arrived, he heard a representative of the U.S. *MONOPOLY* Association announce that his organization intended to ask the U.S. Department of the Interior to step in and protect the "historic" names. A spokesman for the SSBMA then took the lectern and made the issue a metaphor for class struggle: "Baltic and Mediterranean Avenues have represented the last resort of the underdog to hold out against the repressive forces of Boardwalk and Park Place powermongers," he declared.

When Ranny Barton took the lectern, camera lights flicked on. Amid the clicking and whirring, this rather stiff young executive made a surprisingly impassioned speech. It would be "a disservice to both the game and the city" if the street names were changed, he said. "Millions of people look forward to passing GO, collecting $200, and landing on Mediterranean or Baltic Avenue."

When the question was called, the vote was unanimous: Even the commissioner who had originally advanced the proposal now rolled over and recommended its defeat. Barton was practically carried out on the shoulders of the cheering crowd. Outside, reporters pressed Barton for comment. Was this a victory for Parker Brothers? Ranny turned, faced the lenses, and smiled broadly. "It's a victory for the country, not the company."

The event came to represent a final exam in a leadership course that Ranny Barton had been taking most of his life. Almost exactly a year after his performance in Atlantic City, Barton found himself with unhappy reason to test his new-found capabilities. Eddie Parker, the company's revered president, died of lung cancer on January 1, 1974. At age 61, almost twenty years Barton's elder, Eddie had become like a big brother to Ranny. Ranny loved him. And, like most others associated with Parker Brothers, he couldn't imagine the place without Eddie's rollicking good humor.

But Eddie's passing was more than a personal loss to those who knew him. His death threw Parker Brothers into managerial limbo, raising for the first time the question as to whether Parker

Brothers would remain a family-managed company. Ranny was the next family member in line, but it was by no means clear to anyone, including Ranny, that he was the man for the job.

Ranny Barton was Robert and Sally Barton's first child of three, born in 1932, the same year his father joined Parker Brothers. There wasn't a time when young Ranny didn't know his family was in the games business, but it wasn't until he was age eight or nine that he set foot on the premises. He toured the *MONOPOLY* factory in the tow of grandfather, founder George Parker.

It was George Parker who was most responsible for grooming Ranny for leadership. While Robert Barton, tended to his young son's nautical skills (Ranny first took the helm of the family boat while still in knee-pants) it was his grandfather who gave him his earliest instruction in personal style and deportment. Upon noticing that his grandson's nose skewed slightly to one side, the exacting and appearance-conscious George Parker advised the boy to "sleep with it the other way." For years, young Barton never hit the pillow without making sure his nose was correctly positioned.

Barton joined Parker Brothers straight out of the University of Virginia, and quickly took on many of the social responsibilities attendant to being a Parker relation. That included a variety of noble endeavors and public appearances. Barton was warmly welcomed into the Yankee culture of the area; with his flared nostrils and shy grin, his face had the appeal of a young Joe DiMaggio. But many of the engagements called for elocution skills that Barton was painfully aware he lacked. Once, when slated to hand out awards at a local YMCA ceremony, he was stricken with stage fright more than a week in advance. That was that: He availed himself of every opportunity to speak, even putting himself on the annual pre-Christmas Parker Brothers product-introduction tour. Though he remained halting in one-on-one conversation, Barton became smooth and mellifluous onstage.

Still, Barton had always felt mixed emotions about the family company and his calling there. He aspired to the leadership role that was to be his for the asking, yet he yearned to be more to his coworkers than just "the S.O.P."—the son of the president. He wanted to be recognized by his peers for his own skills and leadership qualities, though he knew such acceptance would be hard to come by in the shadow of his ancestors. What camaraderie he found as a young adult was among his fellow sailors.

That summer following Eddie's death, Ranny took three weeks off to cruise the New England coast, and to do some deep thinking about his future. In many ways, this was an unwelcome dilemma—one he hadn't expected to face barely into his forties. If he chose to seek the presidency, he would be hitching himself semi-permanently to the yoke of the family business. Was that what he wanted? Thanks mostly to the General Mills acquisition he had helped engineer, Barton had the money to say no.

Barton remained undecided until he returned to Salem and discovered that several of his managers had been advocating themselves for the job, among them marketing man Don Knutzen and one of Barton's closer friends, the limerick-reciting salesman, Mike Morris.

The emergence of competition pulled Ranny off the fence. He called Minneapolis immediately and told Toy Group head Don Swanson, Nalen's successor, that he intended to assume the presidency of Parker Brothers.

"Wonderful," said Swanson. "Can you be here tomorrow?"

"You bet I can," said Ranny.

If General Mills welcomed Barton's candidacy, it was in part because the company admired his style—Barton had an elegant amiability that the milling company considered the essence of corporate bearing. But nobody, including Ranny himself, would have described Barton as a master strategist. On the contrary, there were those who suspected him to be a dilettante, someone who would quit the minute the going got tough. And, in early 1974, it was as tough as Parker Brothers had seen it in quite some time.

With the Arab oil embargo under way and worldwide recession looming, the plastic that had come to play an ever-greater role in the design of Parker Brothers's new action games had become scarce and dear. It was a time of caution and retrenchment, one in which the company needed to do all it could to monitor expenses and reduce exposure to further economic difficulties. Now more than ever, Parker Brothers needed strong, consistent leadership.

All Barton knew about business was what he had learned in his fifteen-year stint at Parker Brothers, during which time he had started on the production line and meandered through a variety of low-level sales and product-development positions. Beyond that experience and his short-lived executive-development training at Harvard Business School—which he often said "nearly killed" him—his only credential was as the S.O.P., the label he so much wished to outgrow.

In the Minneapolis interview, Don Swanson kept asking Barton if he understood the depth of the commitment that would be required of him as president of Parker Brothers. Swanson, an affable but determined General Mills veteran known since coming into the Toy Group on a tough-control platform as a fellow who took his business seriously, pressed on. Did Barton realize that the business was changing, and that there could lie difficult days ahead? Did he think he could stick with it? Barton nodded throughout the meeting, but left without any clear vote of confidence from Swanson. In fact, ten days passed before Swanson contacted him again. At that time he asked Barton to return to Minneapolis once more, this time with a written summary of his management goals and proposed operational strategies.

Barton arrived in Minneapolis in November of 1974 with a single sheet of paper. Swanson snapped it up with a flourish. The Toy Group executive's eyes widened with interest as he scanned the page. It was clear from what he was reading that this scion wanted very much to score points with General Mills.

Barton had hit General Mills with its own Big G, advocating growth. With revenue of $35 million, Parker Brothers was then roughly in fourth place in toys and games—behind Mattel, Louis Marx, and games rival Milton Bradley (whose $40 million revenue was heavily augmented by a school-supply business). In his opening paragraphs, Barton said he believed that Parker Brothers could join the upper ranks of the industry leadership. But first there would have to be a series of internal changes made.

The remainder of Barton's memo could have been a page from the General Mills playbook. Barton called for a thinning and a reshuffling of most of the company's top tier of management, something Eddie Parker had been notably reluctant to embark upon. Barton also foresaw a need to rethink and revamp the

company's production systems and facilities. He also hoped to
expand manufacturing capabilities by moving administrative functions off-site. Most of all, he wanted to further increase the
marketing emphasis of the company and use the new-found skills
to develop new staples in market categories previously beyond the
Parker Brothers's purview. The possibility of developing a construction toy was under discussion, he noted, and there was also
talk of investigating the game potential in the new microprocessing
units on the market.

Swanson's eyebrows arched ever higher as he read. As much
as he concurred with Barton's suggestions, there was more change
in his hands than he could approve on his own, he said, stepping
out of his office in search of higher authority. Swanson returned
with General Mills CEO E. Robert Kinney, the former president
of the newly acquired Gorton's frozen fish company. Kinney, one
of McFarland's two top lieutenants, simply pumped Ranny's hand
and wished him well.

"There's your okay," Swanson said as the door clicked closed
on Kinney's heels.

It was a moment of pride and triumph unlike any Barton
had experienced in business before. He strode out of the Golden
Valley headquarters high as a kite. He would prove his merit at
Parker Brothers—and he'd do it on General Mills's terms.

3

ROLL THE DICE

*N*o doubt about it, there had been days when Ranny Barton wished he had given up the family business for a few more weeks on the sailboat. The change he had so embraced had come harder and faster than Barton had expected, and to Barton's considerable disappointment, it had not always made him a hero. Sometimes it seemed everybody in the company was perturbed with him. For a man who had always fallen just short of being one of the guys, the animosity was hard to take.

The year 1975 was one of great upheaval at Parker Brothers. Barton was seeking to revamp facilities *and* reorganize personnel at the same time. As departments were packed up and moved from one end of the old clapboard factory to another, some of the more familiar faces at Parker Brothers disappeared. Barton showed the door to his brother, Dick, and asked cousin Bill Bacall to resign. Marketing man Don Knutzen went back to Minneapolis. Awhile later, Barton fired boyhood pal Mike Morris, who had served as both vice president of sales and vice president of finance.

The dismissals shocked the workforce into rare displays of sarcasm and dissent. "Don't bring a lunch on Monday, just in case," went the snide joke on one particularly bloody Friday. The following week, a handful of second-tier managers got together and wore yellow shirts, as their means of tying a "yellow ribbon around the old oak tree" in protest of the personnel changes. Later, Barton professed not to have noticed the gesture.

Though many employees assumed otherwise, General Mills had ordered little if any of this reshuffling. The conglomerate had let it be known that staffing was Ranny Barton's exclusive domain—with the exception of the controller's slot, which was permanently reserved for promising young General Mills-trained executives. With that proviso, he could fire at will, and he could hire from inside or outside, according to his whim.

Barton reminded the most experienced of his critics that he was not the first man to do a shuffle-and-cut at Parker Brothers. During the Depression, Robert Barton had gone so far as to fire the entire company, forcing his workforce to line up the next day for "whatever positions may be open." He then used the opportunity to realign the company and eliminate some deadwood. One trained bean-counter, for example, was informed that the only job he was qualified for was that of janitor—take it or leave it.

Ranny Barton didn't relish playing the bad guy. But, as Parker Brothers neared $40 million in revenue, it was getting too big and too complex for the old team to run it. He couldn't have a sales manager like Morris, who wore straw hats and galoshes, and a manufacturing man, like Bacall, whom Barton believed spent the better part of his day with the *Wall Street Journal* spread across his desk. It wasn't more managers Barton needed: "I need stars!" he exclaimed.

Barton put the word out: Parker Brothers, no longer the loose yet stodgy operation over which his cousin, father, and grandfather had stood so lovingly sovereign, was seeking bright, ambitious MBAs—preferably those with line experience in major consumer corporations.

Gradually but grudgingly Barton's veteran staffers came to accept that Parker Brothers had to respond to growth and progress with new ideas and talent. But Barton didn't endear himself with the workforce when it became apparent that he preferred to turn almost exclusively to General Mills for recruits. On this subject he was immovable: He knew General Mills veterans were well-trained, Barton said, so they represented the easiest, fastest, and cheapest means of staffing up. After all, there were plenty of General Mills executives dying to come to work for Parker Brothers, particularly those who thought that leaving Minneapolis might put them on a faster track. Why should Barton pay an outside firm to do his headhunting when he could simply make a phone call and let General Mills parade the candidates through?

Interestingly enough, it was the managers who had already come from Minneapolis who complained most loudly. These early General Mills emigrés had quickly grown loyal to Parker Brothers and the surrounding community. Many of them had bought themselves a colonial cottage in the woods, or a Cape-style home on the shore, and vowed never to return to the land-locked prairie of Minneapolis again. Nor did they miss the big-company atmosphere they left behind. Compared to the regimented atmosphere of General Mills, Parker Brothers was, in the jargon of the time, a funky place to work. They didn't welcome even the slightest spectre of General Mills hanging over Parker Brothers, because they knew it could only grow bigger and more ominously pervasive with time.

"You're filling the place with spies!" Barton was warned. First it would be people, then it would be policies, and maybe even products. How long might it be before General Mills started drawing the artwork on the game boxes?

Barton said he wasn't worried about "spies." First, he had nothing to hide from his corporate parent. Second, he didn't see anything wrong with General Mills exerting some influence. "I don't have any illusion as to who my boss is, or who owns us. If General Mills says something should be done, that's what we're going to do, whether I agree or not. I know when to fight, but I also know when to get off it and stop fighting. I know who's paying my bonus."

But it was not simply personnel matters that made managing such a strain for Barton in the first few years of his presidency. He was also drawing fire for a decision to build a new administrative headquarters building—not in blue-collar Salem, but in the bucolic adjoining community of Beverly. The decision to split the company into two locations had borne bitter fruit within the organization. Barton's wage force—most of which would stay in Salem, at the original Bridge Street plant—derisively referred to the $2 million, 50,000-square-foot project, located on one of the fairly large bodies of water that New Englanders call ponds, as "Camelot." Worse yet, Salem city fathers alleged that Barton had unfairly spurned the town. A scathing editorial in the local newspaper alleged that Parker Brothers had grown "insensitive, computerized, systematic, cold, [and] impersonal" since being bought by General Mills.

It never seemed to stop, Barton lamented. Just as one controversy died down, up popped another. Barton's ulcer kicked up just mulling over the varied pressures he and his company faced.

On top of everything else, Parker Brothers found itself in the midst of a nasty trademark suit against a University of San Francisco economics professor, Ralph Anspach, who was marketing a trust-busting game called *Anti-Monopoly*. Not only was Anspach asserting his right to use the word "monopoly" in his title, he was questioning the very validity of Parker Brothers's trademark on *MONOPOLY*. General Mills put attorneys on the case four deep. Parker Brothers won the showdown in 1976, the decision forcing Anspach to bury 40,000 of his games in a southern Minnesota landfill. But it wasn't to be the last that Parker Brothers heard of Ralph Anspach. The case was on appeal.

Stressful as it was to be running the company, however, Barton rarely second-guessed himself. He fervently believed that the changes he had made were for the better. Where product was concerned, Parker Brothers had thrown nothing but doubles since Barton assumed the presidency. As the company exceeded $50 million in revenues, Barton could proudly say it was no longer the erratic, idiosyncratic, family-run plantation that General Mills had originally purchased. It was now a well organized and highly successful division within an increasingly visible and impactful group of companies corporately known as the General Mills Creative Products Group, but generally referred to as the Toy Group.

In fiscal years 1975 and 1976, as the country was emerging from a recession and a crippling oil embargo, the Toy Group outperformed all competitors domestic and foreign, with sales increases of 15–20 percent per year. Better yet, earnings were up more than 35 percent each year.

On the strength of the Toy Group's performance, plus that of rebounding cereal and flour sales, General Mills's earnings per share reached $1.60, more than double those of pre-diversification days. In fact, on the strength of its acquisitions—by now nearing a total of sixty separate purchases, forty of them non-food entities—General Mills's sales had nearly quadrupled, from $668.9 million in 1968 to more than $2.6 billion in 1976. Earnings passed the

$100 million mark in fiscal 1976, and the company now provided a total return to investors of 9.7 percent per year—nearly twice that of the food-industry median.

Barton gladly accepted kudos for his company's contributions to the Toy Group, but never without turning some of the praise back on headquarters. With General Mills behind it, now as much in the role of advisor as banker, Parker Brothers continued to hold its 20–22 percent net margins as it grew. It seemed impervious to the double whammy of a sagging economy and a declining population of toy-age children that battered its competition. Though the company borrowed heavily for working capital, Parker Brothers was proving to be a consistent net cash generator to General Mills. In fact, Parker Brothers was throwing off so much money to headquarters that it quickly joined General Mills's biggest internal food divisions, such as the Big G cereal division, on the list of the five top profit contributors.

Some years Barton didn't know what to do with all the money. Chagrined, he would report that he had painted the walls, re-landscaped the grounds, set aside a reserve, and, gosh, Parker Brothers was still going to post more profit than planned. It got to be an annual event—he and his managers praying that a late snowstorm or a sudden boxcar shortage would keep a shipment or two on the rails into the next fiscal year. That way the figures wouldn't arch too high and wreak havoc with General Mills's image for flawless performance projections.

But if there was one thing Barton was proud of, it was the fact that Parker Brothers had made its strides without losing its strong sense of identity. General Mills CEO Jim McFarland and his Toy Group executive, Don Swanson, had seen to that.

While former Toy Group head Craig Nalen had worried how the General Mills hierarchy and its corporate policies might interfere with the competitive strategy of the Toy Group companies, Barton harbored no such concern. He took to both McFarland and Swanson immediately. Barton found McFarland to be integrity personified, a tough but true leader whom Ranny was "always thrilled to speak with." Swanson, too, had Ranny's respect as an advisor and sounding board. Despite his early statements that toys "needed control," Swanson—who also had supervisory responsibility for Toy Group siblings Fashion and Specialty Retailing—

proved to be the kind of manager who established a level of policy and planning rigor, then left product and personnel decisions to his underlings.

"We'll never know the toy business like you do," McFarland and Swanson often told Ranny. Maximum help, minimum interference—that was the watchword attributed to General Mills years before. Barton ran his business as he chose, and General Mills backed him with working capital and management support.

Barton unflinchingly sought advice in Minneapolis whenever he was unsure of General Mills's philosophy or needed an arbiter for the conflicting advice he sometimes received from his staff. Not all of the consultations were formal sessions over a desk. Sometimes Barton flew in for back-channel meetings with legal or financial officials, meeting them in their homes and never bothering to cross the threshold of the headquarters building in Golden Valley. Whether it was technical assistance, personal advice, or merely reassurance, there were people at General Mills who stood by to help. The door was always open.

Barton couldn't have imagined a more ideal arrangement: Management expertise from Minneapolis was his when Barton needed it, yet never hanging overhead or tripping him from underfoot when he didn't want it. The people at Parker Brothers only saw General Mills executives on the premises for two formal occasions a year—for the setting of fiscal-year revenue and earnings projections in the spring (known as "spring program"), and for long-range planning in the fall. If Swanson were so inclined, he might attend two product-review sessions in between. But up to certain levels of strategic importance or financial cost explicitly detailed by General Mills guidelines, Parker Brothers, like the other divisions, called its own shots. In fact, more than seven years after the merger, most people who happened upon the information that General Mills owned Parker Brothers were surprised. They'd never seen the company as anything but independently owned.

Restless with his success, Barton began talking reorganization again in fiscal 1976. This time it would involve not just personnel, but deep and broad-based change in how Parker Brothers designed and sold its products. In joint meetings held at headquarters, an obviously growth-hungry and change-thirsty Barton fairly drooled over General Mills's marketing expertise and research capabilities, whence came most of the milling company's innovations in product line. Surely Parker Brothers could benefit from a similarly regimented approach to the consumer, he volunteered.

In Minneapolis, executives listened with pleased interest. If General Mills was initially concerned about the young successor's willingness to dig in and get his hands dirty, the fears now proved groundless. Barton seemed completely sold on making the structural alterations necessary to build a more aggressive company, and on doing it the General Mills way.

The project that came to occupy most of Barton's waking thoughts and many of his conversations with Minneapolis executives was a further strengthening of the marketing presence he had proposed to Don Swanson in seeking the presidency. Key to the change was the establishment of a facsimile of the brand-manager system that General Mills had copied from the likes of Lipton, General Foods, and Proctor & Gamble, and installed with the help of some of their expatriates. The structure formed the chassis on which all General Mills products rode from test kitchen to supermarket.

General Mills's brand-manager system was fast becoming the stuff of business legend. When reporters journeyed west of Minneapolis to General Mills headquarters, seeking to account for the conglomerate's exemplary performance in its post-diversification years, the brand-management system invariably got a goodly chunk of the credit.

Under the brand-manager system, each young manager was godfather to a product—individually responsible for coordinating its research, development, marketing, advertising, and sales support. In effect, the brands thus became a companies within a company, each with a young MBA presiding.

The system was often cited for its ability to organize and empower the product-development process. But there was little that was speedy or streamlined about it. For every example of a young brand manager cutting red tape with a unilateral decision, there were three stories of inexplicable delay. The same system that allowed one brand manager—Nalen's old roommate, H. Brewster "Bruce" Atwater, Jr.—to make the daring decision to replace the inferior-but-popular *Betty Crocker Instant Mashed Potatoes* with the new and unproven *Potato Buds* in the early 1960s also bred caution on seemingly simpler alterations. For example, when the brand-management group for *Kix* cereal realized that the 35-year-old product's low sugar content and lack of artificial flavoring and coloring had as-yet-unexploited consumer appeal, they proposed to push those attributes in its packaging and advertising. It was an idea that was to boost *Kix* sales volume to its highest levels ever. But it took almost a year to get the new strategy up and running.

General Mills regarded the cumbersome nature of the product-manager system as one of its bigger pluses. It *ought* to be hard for new products to get to market, the thinking went. A brand manager *should* have to fight to start up the bandwagon of internal support that convinced higher-ups of a product's worthiness. Besides, having young marketing recruits run the brand-management gauntlet tended to help separate management wheat from chaff. Competition for corporate funds and executive-suite attention was so fierce at the brand-manager level, and progress so inherently slow within the structure, that only the most facile, tenacious, and gutsy of the bunch survived.

Accordingly, almost since the days of James S. Bell's "kindergarten," General Mills had purposefully overhired for every position in marketing. Each year a new "class" of MBAs moved into the cubbyholes, each member vying for opportunity and recognition. Like law students or medical residents, most of the thirty or forty brand managers in each class would end up dropping out—into a division, a subsidiary, a staff position, or if failure was truly disastrous, the street.

But rarely was anyone fired. Those who didn't overwhelm management knew it was time to start looking if they were assigned a so-called exit brand—one that was an obvious dead end. If someone from a class behind was promoted ahead of someone more senior, it was time for the one passed over to run, not walk, to the boss's office with a letter of resignation.

Only a handful, perhaps eight, of these brand managers would make it to the next rung on the executive ladder, that of marketing director. But those who made the cut—as Atwater had in being promoted to food-group responsibilities—were considered to be the company's fast-trackers. It was Atwater again who was tapped to move up to the third chair in the executive suite when Jim McFarland retired as chairman. From 1977, when McFarland stepped aside and former Gorton's executive Bob Kinney took over, thereby ushering Atwater into the chief operations officer's slot, there would be few management bigwigs who hadn't made it through the brand-management hazing.

Barton knew that installing a similar web of product-development gatekeepers was going to be complicated, and with its elite corps of business-school-trained managers, expensive. Neither fact diminished its appeal to Barton. He was a man fascinated with newness. Anyone could see that who witnessed his concurrent decision to level a 30-room, 18,000-square-foot, 1905-vintage mansion overlooking the harbor in picturesque Manchester, Massachusetts, to create a new one-story family home.

Barton knew the establishment of his *product*-manager system (so named because his company had none of General Mills's *brands* to manage) would immediately telegraph to customers and competitors alike the news that Parker Brothers was marching to a jazzier beat than any of his forebears had laid down. Once a product-driven company, in which development decisions were made on guts and sales experience, Parker Brothers intended to become market-driven. What to make and when to sell it would now depend on the results of a variety of market-sampling and sales-projecting techniques.

So, flush with the success of its *Nerf* toys, Parker Brothers welcomed a new and younger crop of MBAs, most of whom were funneled into positions as product managers, assistant product managers, or marketing researchers. What resulted was a marked upswing in creative energy—so much of an upswing, in fact, that the main trouble for Barton was harnessing it. The place seemed to be crawling with smart, ambitious people looking to make a difference.

One of the newcomers was Richard E. "Rich" Stearns, a tall man with a sweep of blond hair and a beard that hid a baby face. Stearns was a 25-year-old graduate of the University of Pennsylvania's Wharton School of Business who had grown bored with his two years of sales promotion and regional market planning at The Gillette Company in Boston. He saw an ad for an assistant marketing manager at Parker Brothers and thought it would be fun to work in toys. With an impulsiveness that would prove typical, Stearns decided to apply for the job. He dug out a newly printed sheaf of resumes and sent the top one to Salem. He never had to so much as fold another one. In February of 1977, he became the second MBA hired for Parker Brothers's budding product-management group.

Someday there would be a dozen or more product managers at Parker Brothers, Stearns was told in his first week on the job. Each of these product managers would hold wide-ranging responsibility for a narrow slice of the company's product line. For now, however, there were but three such managers on staff. Two of them came from General Mills headquarters, and the third, like Stearns, from Gillette. Each had an assistant such as Stearns in training.

But Stearns quickly discovered that he wasn't merely carrying a clipboard for his boss. Like the other assistants, Stearns had decision-making input into the development of four or five different games and puzzles. Each of them was an integral part of a team that included designers and engineers, of course, but also the vice presidents of marketing and R & D. As a group, they reported directly to president Ranny Barton himself.

Stearns hadn't known what to expect of executives in the toys and games industry, but he was pleased by those he found at Parker Brothers.

Bill Dohrmann's cultured air was particularly striking to Stearns. Dohrmann was Hotchkiss and Princeton, with a bachelor's degree in English literature. In his rep tie and blue blazer, Dohrmann was much more a preppie than the overgrown eight-year-old that Stearns might have expected to find in such a job. Yet, Dohrmann was far from the average headquarters import: The guy knew all the inventors, spoke their language, and got as flipped out over a good design as anybody else did.

Controller Ronald J. Jackson, a serious and methodical General Mills transplant in aviator glasses, was just moving into the company's marketing slot as Stearns was settling in. Jackson succeeded another General Mills import named Jim Boosales, who had been shifted over to the presidency of another Toy Group company, Fundimensions. (Based in Toledo, the company's core was Craft Master Corporation, one of Nalen's original acquisitions, plus the toy-train maker, Lionel Corporation, and other hobby companies.) Jackson's promotion was greeted with some trepidation, Stearns gathered. The Michigan State MBA had lived and breathed financial management since joining General Mills in 1966 and Parker Brothers in 1971. Most people involved with product development at Parker Brothers feared he would be a veritable wet blanket on creativity with his persistent questioning of everything's price and level of risk. Still, who could dislike a man whose entire face blossomed into a boyish grin when he laughed?

Bruce Jones was another General Mills import in Stearns's new-found milieu. Jones had come from General Mills in 1974 a marketing research man, but per Ron Jackson's promise, he was shifting into duties that would put him in charge of marketing traditional games—a shift in track that wouldn't have been possible back in Minneapolis. Auburn-haired, mustachioed, frequently furrowed of brow, Jones was a man of firmly held ideas and a lot of stubborn energy. But, like Stearns, he had an ear for a sarcastic turn of phrase, and he never lacked for an amusingly deprecating label for someone who was making his life difficult. At his laconic best, Jones's speech patterns evoked a world-weary W.C. Fields, but when excited or angry, his voice could leap a scratchy octave—and get stuck there.

And Ranny Barton? Well, he fairly reeked of an aristocracy that Stearns, a used-car salesman's kid from Syracuse, could never fully comprehend—not even after his stints at Cornell and Wharton. Stearns had to work for every inch he got; Barton's dues—relatively speaking, anyway—had been largely paid for him. By 1977, Barton was far from the diffident young man who had quaked at the thought of representing his father's company in public. With his resonant baritone and confident bearing, Barton now seemed, to Stearns, to have been born to shake hands and sign off on decisions. His cheerily calm demeanor was a source of wonder to a high-rev personality like Stearns. The younger man delighted, as well, in Barton's low-key, unself-conscious attitude toward authority. Barton's idea of a power lunch, for example, was a hamburger and a chocolate "Junior Fribble" at the local ice cream parlor.

There were plenty of oldtimers who could and did tell Stearns that the company had tightened down and stiffened up since "the good old days" before General Mills came on the scene, but Stearns wasn't complaining. As far as he was concerned, one of the best things about the company was the atmosphere of unfettered opportunity Parker Brothers fostered even for newcomers like himself. Shortly after joining the company, Stearns saw a magazine story on children's author Beatrix Potter, and brought the idea of a game based on her stories to Dohrmann. Dohrmann concurred with his interest, negotiated the license, and told Stearns to design the game. It hit the market the following season.

Amazing, thought Stearns: He and the others with product-related responsibility could be just like George Parker, each one a single-headed, doubled-handed game-development machine. Just as George had been decades before, Stearns was in the business of capturing the public's imagination. He stayed up nights playing new games and struggling to write coherent rules for them. It proved to be a humbling experience, particularly when Stearns would go to the one-way window of the play-testing room and see parents and children trying to make sense of rules that had seemed so clear to him at midnight the night before. On the other hand, there was great pride in knowing that someday he could stroll through a toy store, point out a game such as *Curious George* or *The Little Engine That Could,* and whisper to his children that "Daddy helped make that game, and that one, and that one. . . ."

But even newcomers like Stearns could see that Parker Brothers was a company in transition. No longer was turf shared in the way that company legend said family members Ranny, Robert, Eddie, and Bill had shared it years before. As departments grew and individual responsibilities shrank, managers stood guard over their territory, lest one of Ranny Barton's infamous reorganizations pull it out from under them like so many rugs.

Almost from the day Barton took over in 1974, there had been a run-and-gun rivalry between the newly enfranchised marketing department and the former powers of the company—R & D and sales. The lines that divided these departments had overlapped and become blurry with the company's growth, yet to the chagrin of many of the oldtimers, it was the wisenheimers in finance and marketing—people like Jackson, and Jones, and even young product managers like Stearns—who suddenly seemed to control a disproportionate share of decision-making influence. Hands-on experience in toys didn't carry all the weight anymore; an MBA, or line experience in Minneapolis, counted for plenty.

Not long before, the route to influence, and possibly the presidency, began in sales or R & D, but no more—to the growing irritation of people like Bill Dohrmann, who had consciously decided to carve a career out of R & D. As late as 1974, Dohrmann secretly believed he could become the company's first non-family president. But now the fast track paralleled General Mills's, running from finance or manufacturing to marketing, and from there, non-stop to the executive suite. Dohrmann kicked himself for having chosen the shorter career ladder.

Back in the post-merger days when Robert Barton fired R & D man Hank Simmons, Dohrmann had been presented by Craig Nalen with a choice: Did he want to take over research and development, or stick with marketing? Dohrmann thought that working the product side would be more fun, and besides, it was clearly the company's pole position.

It wasn't for long. The power of the marketing department grew with each successive jobholder, and by the time it had become Jim Boosales's slot, and subsequently, Ron Jackson's, all other management jobs in the company were pale by comparison.

Once out from behind his ledgers and into the marketing slot, Jackson proved to be a firm, dynamic leader—easily the power behind Ranny Barton's throne. Jackson doubled the marketing budget almost overnight, and with Barton's approval, set himself up as the gatekeeper on a variety of decisions that sales and R & D formerly made. Suddenly sales was being second-guessed on how to position and move merchandise, while the results of the product testing that Dohrmann had encouraged and increased at Parker Brothers was sometimes turned against him and used to shoot down Dohrmann's authority along with his ideas.

Jackson, like Boosales before him, made it plain that he regarded Parker Brothers as a talented but undisciplined operation that could benefit from the regimen of a detailed marketing strategy and a set of strict financial controls. The prevailing view, post-merger, was that Parker Brothers had long thrown too much product at the wall. It was a problem that Parker Brothers shared with many other companies in the toys industry—too many product introductions, too much bread cast upon the water, and therefore, too many expensive flops. The goal was to rein in the creative staff, make them justify their decisions with data, and thereby limit the number of product introductions per year. Instead of doing twenty good games per year, why not make thirteen or fourteen really great ones?

Few disagreed with the basic philosophy. It was simply the basis on which the "good" would be separated from the "great" that created bones of contention, and sometimes confrontations. Marketing and R & D were supposedly checks and balances for each other, but people in R & D had only to check the balance of power to see it had shifted decisively in marketing's favor.

One day, at one of the product-review meetings where R & D's Bill Dohrmann held court, a young assistant marketing manager—the first one hired, then no more than a week on the job—piped up and asked Dohrmann about the wisdom of the latter-stage development plans he had just heard detailed. The young product manager pointed to what he considered to be a lack of market information and registered alarm. "Are we really sure we should be doing this?" he asked. Dohrmann's jaw dropped. Who did this young marketing punk think he was?

"It used to be that if I said something got in next year's line, damn it, it got in the line!" Dohrmann later complained to Barton. Dohrmann's main beef, however, was not in any recent failures to get products into the catalog. Rather, he felt that the marketers, led by Jackson, neither understood nor respected the fickle creative force that drove the toys industry. If they did, argued Dohrmann, they would know that nothing, certainly not research, could obviate or even mitigate the risk of the toys and games business.

Good numbers didn't guarantee good products, Dohrmann said. Guts and timing accounted for that—neither of which showed up on marketing's printouts or indices. And as for finding the good ideas in the first place, as much as these young product managers might think there was a scientific method to be employed, Dohrmann had learned from hard experience that there was no substitute for instinct.

"Why do these people think they can take their marketing gurus, and their 20 percent of the budget, and thereby quantify and predict the success of a toy or a game?"

While Dohrmann steamed, the sales troops fought back with pranks. At one sales meeting in early 1977, then-marketing vice president Boosales and controller Jackson went to the garage of their hotel to collect their rented car from the attendant, and a veritable parade float rolled out instead. The vehicle had been gaudied up by the sales staff, hood ornament to tailpipe. There were streamers on the door handles, fuzzy dice on the windshield, and a woman's bra flying from the antenna like a flag.

Harmless as most of the inter-departmental sniping was, it was symptomatic of real and deep tensions within the organization. Barton began to feel that a good share of his management time was devoted to barking "in my office in ten minutes" to pairs of managerial siblings. He professed to have little patience with the constant sparring, but, knowingly or not, he encouraged it.

Ranny Barton never pretended to be an intuitive manager, the kind who focused all eyes upward with his self-assured decision making. He preferred to keep business at arm's length, relying heavily on the concensus that rose up the ranks. In the absence of concensus, he was the almost reluctant arbiter of tie votes and dogfights. Still, Barton preferred to manage on an as-needed basis, capitalizing on the ambition of his young turks to get things done.

And despite the carping and sniping—or maybe because of it—golly, could they get things done. As Barton watched, this new crop of managers redefined his company as something more than the maker of "tortured cardboard," as Stearns and the other restless product managers had come to call traditional board games. By 1977, two particularly revolutionary product ideas were on the drawing boards: a construction toy and a hand-held electronic game. Both of these products had begun to take shape at his underlings' suggestions, soon after Barton assumed the presidency.

Riviton, the construction toy, was billed as "a toy that makes toys." It featured flexible plastic shapes of various sizes and colors, including wheels, brackets, and panels. With a hand tool that placed reusable rubber rivets, children could connect these pieces to assemble a variety of toys (such as trucks, boats, planes, and buildings).

A construction-toy project was a fairly major departure for Parker Brothers, simply because it involved more metal and plastic than the usual paper-related stuff of the company's board games. And because there was no presumption that *Riviton* would foster group or game-like activity, it represented a far deeper incursion into traditional toy territory than *Nerf.*

Non-food chief Don Swanson and the others at General Mills were skeptics from the beginning. But Parker Brothers had done its homework. The construction-toy segment of the market had become one of the fastest-growing categories in the business, more than doubling the growth rate of the entire toys industry. The Danish construction set, *Lego,* was the giant of the market, with the lion's share of all construction toys sold. But its sets of interlocking blocks were targeted at children between the ages of 3 and 6. Tinkertoy- and Playskool-brand products divided up the market for ages 2 to 5, and *Erector Sets* accounted for nearly all sales in market for kids aged 12 and up. Parker Brothers hoped to fill the hole, the 6-to-12 age bracket, with *Riviton.*

The sense obvious in this strategy scored points, but it was mostly in recognition of Parker Brothers's growing reputation as the fair-haired child of the Toy Group, by virtue of its superior profit picture, that the conglomerate signed off on the *Riviton* project.

But if *Riviton* was considered a departure from the norm, the research that led Parker Brothers into electronics was a relative space shot. In considering the field electronics and computerized games, Parker Brothers hadn't had to go beyond its own four walls to find the doubters. In fact, had there not been key competitors testing the same waters and research that indicated board games might be made obsolete by semiconductor technology, the idea of introducing an electronic game would likely have been killed for lack of guts.

The working moniker of Parker Brothers's first device described its object: *Sink the Sub.* Players attempted to track down a constantly moving vessel, to gauge its depth, and then shoot to destroy. There were no wooden playing pieces, no dice. *Sink the Sub* had lights that flashed and buttons to push. The only thing that made it seem familiar and game-like to Parker Brothers was the fact that the sub movements were tracked on a map.

The inventors of the gizmo were Bob and Holly Doyle, a bespectacled pair of astronomers-turned-physicists-turned-designers from Cambridge, Massachusetts. The two Ph.D.'s had grown disillusioned with the aerospace projects they had been working on in and around Harvard University and decided to get out of the soft money of publicly funded research. They steered instead for the hard-cash business of electronic games. In early 1975, they began pitching prototypes to Parker Brothers, promising the company that just one of their ideas, properly developed, could produce revenue of anywhere from $20 million to $100 million per year. How could Parker Brothers help but sit up and take notice?

On their first rounds, the Doyles showed off three tabletop games, each for two players, and one game which was of the individual, hand-held variety. None had a name, and nobody in R & D jumped for joy. Dohrmann reminded the Doyles that Parker Brothers was in the *family* game business—as in more than two players, preferably blood relatives, sitting around the table at home at night. The game they called *Sink the Sub* had better group-play potential, the Doyles asserted upon introducing it to Parker Brothers several months later. But Parker Brothers continued to drag its feet.

The main reservation was technological. The introduction of microprocessors would open up a brand-new—i.e., scary and expensive—world to Parker Brothers. Nobody at the company spoke the jargon, much less understood how to find the people and parts they needed to make a computerized product. And General Mills, even if it had wanted to help, didn't know a silicon chip from the chocolate variety.

The Doyles offered themselves as teachers and advisors, but Dohrmann continued to fret. What guarantee was there that this market would catch on? Heck, the average board game sold for well under $10 in those days; these electronic or computerized gizmos would have to sell for several times that much. Who on earth would shell out $30, or even $20, for a kids' toy?

There was meeting upon meeting, design conference after design conference with the Doyles—and far more skull sessions took place without their knowledge. By the end of 1975, most of the key decision-makers at Parker Brothers knew in their hearts that this would be the way the company and the industry would have to go sooner or later, particularly now that both companies and consumers could afford to produce electronic toys. Silicon chips that cost $100 at the time General Mills bought Parker Brothers were priced at about $2 apiece less than a decade later.

Dohrmann informed the Doyles that Parker Brothers intended to start gearing up for production. He offered no guarantees as to which, if any, of the Doyles' designs would be marketed, or when. "It'll take us a good two years to get rolling," he warned. "Can you stick with it?" The Doyles said they could.

While Parker Brothers was planning and worrying, however, some of the competition was already in full-fledged development. At Toy Fair in 1976, three hand-held and tabletop electronic games were introduced—one a football game, another an auto race, and the third (and most controversial) a game whose object was the nuclear annihilation of the opposition's cities, called *Missile Attack*.

An irritated Bob Doyle dashed off a letter to Parker Brothers that spring, pointing out that a case of the corporate jitters had prevented the company from getting the jump on the new market that he had promised them. When, oh when did Parker Brothers expect to take something—anything—to market?

The Doyles pressed on, offering Parker Brothers a pinball-like game for the 1977 season. It was shelved for being too expensive to manufacture, with its seventy to eighty light-emitting diodes (LEDs). Instead, Parker Brothers rather reluctantly elected to take the plunge into the market with *Sink the Sub*. It would straddle the line between the old and the new with the slogan "The board game where you match wits with a computer." If it flopped, executives consoled themselves, there was always *Riviton*. (Even prior to Toy Fair, advance orders had indicated that *Riviton* would be a hit—maybe strong enough to become the new staple that Ranny Barton had vowed to find.)

Sink the Sub was renamed *Code Name: Sector,* a cryptic appellation that was generally disliked from the moment it was mentioned. Parker Brothers toyed with the idea of keeping the game off the market—until a couple of days before Toy Fair in February of 1977, when the word from Parker Brothers's outside network of designers and packagers was that archrival Milton Bradley was

going electronic with something called *Comp IV*. It proved to be
a tabletop game in which several players tried to guess a three-
to five-digit number picked randomly by the unit's microprocessor
brain.

Word had it that Parker Brothers's competition in Springfield
was stumbling to market with little more grace or determination
than the group in Beverly. Top executives at Milton Bradley
couldn't warm up to the game—some had publicly admitted they'd
had a hard time figuring out how to play it. Nonetheless, from
the earliest tests, there was nothing lukewarm about the public's
response to *Comp IV*. After chaining the game to the bars of
several New York watering holes for a few weeks, they found it
stimulated a love-hate relationship with patrons. Either you couldn't
put the thing down, or you'd want to strangle the little gizmo
with its chain and smash it silly against the bar. A good sign,
that—a very good sign.

Parker Brothers showed up at Toy Fair 1977 ready for battle,
with a showroom motif somewhere between *20,000 Leagues Under
the Sea* and *Mr. Roberts,* complete with attendants natty in sea-
going attire. This nautical positioning was a calculated jab at the
competition. Traditionally, the naval wargames motif had belonged
to Milton Bradley, which made millions on a board game called
Battleship.

Milton Bradley got the last laugh, however. Luckily for
president George Ditomassi, his designers had already started work
on an electronic game not unlike their flagship board game *Battleship,* and quite similar to concept to *Code Name: Sector.* Buyers
were ushered to the backroom for a look at a prototype, and many
liked what they saw. It was quickly rushed to market.

Despite being outspent by about $100,000 in national adver-
tising—$700,000, as opposed to Parker's $800,000—Milton Bradley's
Electronic Battleship blew *Code Name: Sector* out of the water. In
these early days of computers—when computing phobia was the
real market battle to be won, Parker Brothers's "smart" game was
too smart. The computer usually won the game. In fact, the best
that could be said about this largely unloved game was that it
outsold its projections—as did all six of the electronic games that
entered the market that year. The market segment racked up total
sales of $21 million, a very respectable percentage of the $3.3

billion (wholesale) market for toys and games. The big seller was Mattel's *Football,* the popularity of which owed to its being an adaptation of a hit video game, the sort that had begun to transform and repopularize amusement arcades.

The big questions had been answered, and decisively so: The demand for electronics was there. With the opening of this category of plaything, no longer were customers lost at age thirteen or sixteen, and no longer did toy prices have to top out at $10. The public was indeed willing to double or triple the money it spent on a toy, particularly if that device appealed to adults and children alike, as most hand-held electronic games did. Parker Brothers invested in an electronic future by buying the Doyles a $25,000 design computer, and signing them to an exclusive design contract.

Still, the Doyles enthralled no one with their follow-up proposal, a game called *3-T.* The prototype was a strip of plywood with a grid of just eleven LEDs, each with its own accompanying switch. With the help of a microprocessor in its guts, the machine had the brains to make moves and counter-moves that would counter-act a player trying to get a row of the LEDs lit. Bill Dohrmann took one look at it and nixed it. "That's *Tic-Tac-Toe,*" he said disgustedly. Talk about public-domain games: *Tic-Tac-Toe* was literally eons old, dating back to 1400 B.C.

The Doyles were undeterred. Sure it was like *Tic-Tac-Toe,* that's why they named it *3-T.* But they pointed out that this was a far more complex version of the old X-and-O game. In this version, the computer was capable of changing strategy from game to game, and adapting to a human opponent's moves.

Dohrmann wouldn't budge. "Parker Brothers will never sell *Tic-Tac-Toe,*" he insisted. Parker Brothers had resolved itself to making only those games that wouldn't have existed without the chip. This game could be as easily played with pencil and paper, as could *Comp IV, Electronic Battleship,* and *Code Name: Sector.* Besides, those LEDs and their switches were bound to cost too much money.

But what if there were a way of cutting down the number of switches? And what if the Doyles took several more of the dozens of games they had in development and put them in the same box, with audio? Wouldn't it help justify the price to the consumer if *3-T* could make sounds? If it could play more and different kinds of games?

Dohrmann said he'd think about it.

He'd better think fast, the Doyles said to one another ruefully. It was already the fall of 1977. If the company didn't act fast, it would end up sitting out 1978. They began to think that was just what Parker Brothers wanted.

In reality, the last thing Parker Brothers wanted to do was sit out 1978. Without a follow-up entry in the burgeoning market for hand-held electronic games, the company would "end up in the cheap seats," as Dohrmann was fond of putting it. Electronic games were the biggest thing to hit the toys industry since plastic. They had changed the nature of game-playing itself. The computer chip offered random variables far beyond those of two six-sided dice rolled together. And because a player's opponent had become an "intelligent" computer chip, not a person, it was difficult even to cheat, the way a solitaire player might. In this heightened and newly sophisticated environment, there was no way Parker Brothers could go back to board games alone. It needed another electronic game.

Its best hope was something called P.E.G.S., the Parker Electronic Games System, which was invented by in-house designer Arthur Venditti. It was similar to Milton Bradley's *Electronic Battleship,* in that it was a two-sided board on which opposing players (usually youngsters aged seven to fourteen) would make moves, hoping not to bump into each other and light up the board. P.E.G.S. wasn't breaking any sales records and it wasn't vastly different from *Code Name: Sector.* But what did Parker Brothers have besides that and *3-T*? Dohrmann still hadn't really warmed to the idea of *Tic-Tac-Toe,* but if it were the only horse available, he'd reluctantly ride it.

Ron Jackson was another story. Having grown as gung-ho as anybody on electronics as a category, he was nonetheless unwilling to get behind any product that hadn't been proven to have the legs to go the distance. He pointed to tracking information that showed some toys companies backing away from the market, fearing fast obsolescence. The most notable company in that regard was Ideal, the nation's third largest publicly held independent. Recently mentioned as one of the more aggressive companies in the hand-held electronics category, the company was now pulling out of the market after having launched just two game entries. Why should Parker Brothers continue going where others now feared to tread, particularly with a product that seemed anything but a sure thing?

But there has always existed an unquestioned force in the toys and games industries that carries deserving products to the marketplace. Good ideas, no matter how bad they may seem at the time, often refuse to die. So it was with *3-T*. With little consultation between designers and marketers, and absolutely no declarations of support from management, *3-T* was gathering aid and comfort from many corners of the company.

On one of his frequent strafes of the R & D lab in search of ideas, Stearns had spied the hunk of plywood with LEDs on it. "It's just a *Tic-Tac-Toe* game," he was told. "Going nowhere. Pretty boring." Stearns was shown how the lights blinked for Xs and shined steady for the Os.

"That's not boring, that's fabulous," exclaimed Stearns. It wasn't so much the game or its flashing lights that intrigued him as its voice. *3-T* spoke not just bleeps and bloops, but whole sentences in a single sound, it seemed. Win a game, and the sound heard was a clear attaboy. Lose it, and the raspberry was a dead ringer for "Sorry, sucker." It had personality.

Stearns went straight to Jackson's office. "Why aren't we developing this?" he asked incredulously. It wasn't the first time that Stearns had waxed rapturous over a product, and given his generally impetuous nature, it probably wouldn't be the last. Perhaps just to get rid of him, Jackson told Stearns to write him a memo on it—which the young assistant product manager did, quickly and persuasively.

Meanwhile, the engineer who had shown Stearns the *3-T* prototype had developed a so-called soft switch—a mylar sheet that could take the place of all of the individual circuits that powered the LEDs. All you had to do was press it anywhere on its surface and the nearest light would light. It was much cheaper than placing individual switches.

Bob Doyle, for his part, had learned that Texas Instruments had developed a new and more capable silicon chip, one that could power the multi-game machine he envisioned. It began to look like Parker Brothers could, indeed, get twice the play value for half the price.

In October of 1977, the Doyles went back to work in earnest, picking each other's brains for all the computer games they had played or seen played over their years in science. They came up with about fifty that could be adapted to smaller computers and less sophisticated users. By the time Dohrmann called and gave them the formal go-ahead for what they were doing, the pair had already spent weeks closeted on the third floor of their Cambridge triple-decker, trying to decide—with the "expert" advice of their older son and his playmates—precisely which of the long list of games would be programmed into *3-T.* They chose four: "Echo," a game in which you try to replicate a pattern of lights and sounds generated by the machine's brain; "Blackjack 13," a version of a casino game; "Mindbender," a numbered code to decipher much like *Comp IV;* and "Magic Square," another puzzle.

Then Doyle had a brainstorm: Why not make *3-T* play music? Stearns, who had been appointed product manager of the project, and Dick Dalessio, the newly appointed marketing manager for electronics, enthusiastically agreed. And if it could talk, why shouldn't it sing? Others at Parker Brothers failed to see the need to complicate an already complicated project, but they let the zealots have their way.

For three months, Doyle, Dalessio, and in-house developer Venditti had shuttled back and forth from Texas Instruments in Houston, getting the chip programmed to Parker Brothers's cost specifications. Wholesale margins were not to slip below 55 percent. On their sixth and last trip, they asked the chip engineers to make *3-T* capable of memorizing sixteen notes.

"No sweat," said the engineers.

"Well then," said Doyle and Dalessio, "how about thirty-two?"

The engineers hemmed and hawed, but after pulling an all-nighter they came up with the extra memory.

Doyle and Dalessio had burned some midnight oil of their own, however, and had realized that most musical phrases are longer than thirty-two notes. "How about forty-eight?" they asked. "Can we do forty-eight?"

The Texans were losing their tempers, so the Parker Brothers delegation broke for lunch. On return, they found that engineers had found room for the extra sixteen notes.

By Christmas of 1977, *3-T*'s final prototype was ready. When it was presented to company brass, the engineers had a whole group of *3-T*s singing "Frere Jacques" in rounds, with "Twinkle, Twinkle, Little Star" and the theme from the movie *Close Encounters of the Third Kind*—which had just opened in movie theaters— as an encore. There were triumphant grins all around.

But even the best products seem to develop glitches and hitches in the last feverish rush to Toy Fair, and *3-T* was no exception. Parker Brothers tested the product by showing a group of children film clips on *3-T* and eight other competing electronic games. To everyone's dismay, *3-T* flunked. It came in dead last, with a measly 2 percent interest level. But it was flat-out too late to do anything about it; who could conceive of it? There was no longer anyone inside Parker Brothers who hadn't put heart and soul into this mass of circuitry. To hell with marketing and research, said the unspoken concensus. If the test didn't support the prevailing bias— which was by then instinctively and almost unflaggingly positive— then screw the test.

The last item of business was to select a name. Everyone who had enjoyed even slight involvement with the project had been adding monikers to a growing list, as was the practice at Parker Brothers. Gradually it had been winnowed down. Nobody wanted anything so technical as *3-T*, that was for sure. Dalessio liked names like "Adversary" or "Challenger" names that others in marketing and advertising deemed likely to exacerbate the public's fear of computers.

Stearns took it upon himself to spend some time with a thesaurus in the hope of finding a more genial name. He tried a couple of outerspacey categories. Nothing thrilling there. Then he tried "magic." "Hoodoo, voodoo, abracadabra, mumbo jumbo . . ." No, what he needed was a proper name, not a synonym for the noun. "Aaron's rod, Aladdin, Aladdin's lamp." Nope. He skipped down to "magician." "Sorcerer . . . wizard, witch . . . Merlin, Comus. . . ."

Wait a minute—how about *Merlin,* the electronic wizard? Perfect, he thought. Everybody else, including Parker Brothers's hard-to-please ad agency, agreed. The gizmo would be tabbed *Merlin,* and positioned as a programmable music-player that also featured five "ingenious" games of logic, strategy, skill, memory, and chance.

But to further avoid any hard or cold connotations, Stearns and the ad agency opted for commercials with the soothing sound of nursery rhymes: "Where's *Merlin,* where did he go? He's out with Jenny playing *Tic-Tac-Toe.*" Bill Dohrmann, *Tic-Tac-Toe*'s nemesis at Parker Brothers, no doubt winced when he heard it.

Still, in a year full of challenges and setbacks, physically getting *Merlin* to market proved to be the toughest. The blizzard of 1978 blew into the eastern seaboard, wreaking havoc in New England. Hit with more than a foot of snow, battering winds, and ruinous tides, Massachusetts came to a standstill. Roads couldn't be cleared for all the stranded cars that cluttered them. Invoking a statute that had been established to deal with the aftermath of nuclear war, Governor Michael Dukakis banned travel for days, ordering that violators be arrested.

What was Parker Brothers to do? Part of the sales staff was already in New York, but the big guns were stuck at home, and the displays—including a six-foot, fully operable model of *Merlin*— were sitting snowbound at the plant. Three days after the storm and just one day before Toy Fair opened, Ron Jackson managed to charter a plane for the equipment and a few essential people. Everybody else made their way to the airport as they could. Stearns avoided the ban on cars by using a hotel limo. One of Parker Brothers's key ad agency men hitched a ride with some physicians who were exempted from the travel ban. A few staff members feigned their own medical emergencies to gain access to the roads.

For the next ten days, Stearns stood in the Parker Brothers showroom at Toy Fair eight hours a day, pitching buyers. Sure, actors had been hired to conduct the demonstrations—many of them trained spokespeople who knew how to talk all day without losing their voices, all of them ready and willing to suffer sore feet and aching backs for a fee of several hundred dollars a day. But Stearns was a man with a mission, determined to personally sell each buyer on this toy. In most cases, it wasn't a tough sell; the trade had come to New York City clamoring for electronic games. The only problem faced by Stearns or anybody else manning the Parker Brothers display was how to convince those buyers to pick *Merlin* over a competitor named *Simon*. As usual, Milton Bradley was running apace of Parker Brothers, with a similar game.

Merlin was priced at $19.95, Simon $19. *Merlin* was smarter, more sophisticated—almost coldly so. *Simon* was more engaging, more eye-catching, but not as bright (it could only play one game). Parker Brothers had been looking down its collective nose at Milton Bradley's entry, derisively dubbing it Simple *Simon,* but it proved a formidable competitor. Both *Merlin* and *Simon,* in fact, sold out in their first seasons. Each company had sorely underestimated the size of what turned out to be a $500 million market for electronic games.

Near the end of Toy Fair, at the close of a particularly grueling day, a diplomatic breakthrough was achieved. Ron Jackson went to Bill Dohrmann with his hand outstretched in a gesture of conciliation. "We did it," he said, beaming as Dohrmann accepted his handshake. *Merlin's* chip alone was worth more than all the plastic, cardboard, and paper in any board game, and Parker spent eight times more money developing Merlin than it did on its top board game of the year, a zany three-dimensional affair called *Bonkers!* But in the flush of success, nobody could seem to remember feeling it might not be worth it.

In a mere eighteen months, Parker Brothers had transformed itself from a company that dealt with four basic commodities— plastic, paper, ink, and glue—to one that knew its way around the high-tech world of silicon and circuits. For better or worse, Parker Brothers had grown up. It had gone from the children's world of the Toy Fair to the decidedly adult atmosphere of the annual Consumer Electronics Show (where the exhibitors included distributors of pornographic movies, to the amused surprise of some staffers). All struggle and internal strain aside, it had been a team effort that had paid off richly for the company.

In 1978 Parker Brothers produced more than seventy-five toy and game items and reached sales of just over $82 million. The company was the seventh-largest games and toys company in the United States, following Mattel, Fisher-Price, Milton Bradley, Kenner, Hasbro, and Ideal. It had gained an image as an industry leader without tarnishing its impeccable reputation for quality, innovation, and fair play.

Then, tragically, the company's lucky streak came to a halt. Reports reached Ranny Barton's office in April of 1978 that an eight-year old Wisconsin boy had suffocated on a *Riviton* rivet that he had placed in his mouth.

For a company that had staunchly supported safe-toy initiatives in recent years—and prided itself quality toys well made—this was a shocking blow. Never before had Parker Brothers seen a product cause a serious injury, much less a fatality. Marketing director Ron Jackson traveled to Minneapolis to consult with General Mills's medical director and quality-control staff, both of which supported Barton's conclusion that this had been a freak accident.

If anything, *Riviton* had been more thoroughly examined than other new products, because Parker Brothers recognized from the start that this toy could become a staple of the magnitude of *Nerf*, and maybe as reliable a seller as many of its board games. The rivets in the sets had undergone particular scrutiny, being small and very ingestible. The company had been reassured by research showing that the inhalation of food or objects was rarely a cause of accidental death in the product's target age group. When the Consumer Product Safety Commission conducted a hazard evaluation of *Riviton* after the boy's death, it fully supported the company's research and cleared Parker Brothers of any wrongdoing.

Still, Ranny Barton decided to take no further chances. He ordered R & D to find some way of deterring children from putting the rivets in their mouths. The application of a bitter-tasting chemical called Bitrex was under consideration when the phone rang again in November. A second child, a nine-year-old New Jersey boy, had similarly suffocated to death on a *Riviton* rivet.

Now Barton and Jackson faced an ethical conundrum. Here they had two deaths on their hands, a mere seven months apart, each apparently due to product misuse. They could pass the incidents off as horrible flukes, but both men felt the moral tug to take action of some kind. The question was what kind of action to take: Issue a warning statement or label? Redesign or modify the product? Or, launch a total recall?

Warning statements and labels seemed halfway measures. A redesign proposal was rejected as too costly, and more important, too slow to be of any use in salvaging the sales of the product. With General Mills's approval, the decision was reached on November 24, 1978, the day before Thanksgiving, was to recall the entire line, domestic and European, and issue refunds for as many of the 900,000 sold units as could be found. Anything less, said General Mills's quality-control staff, would be "cosmetic and inadequate."

Parker Brothers employees gasped when the decision was announced. During the previous two years of development, they had shot the rubber rivets at each other and playfully stuck the suction cups on their tongues and cheeks. To have children die from similar horseplay was appalling. As much as it hurt to abandon a popular product long in development, few wished to see it stay on the market.

The recall was a long and painstaking process that lasted well past Christmas—a time when Parker Brothers should have been, by rights, sitting back and watching the sales figures rise. Instead, Barton was forced to inform General Mills and its stockholders that an $8.9 million loss would appear on the ledger for the fourth quarter. That represented only the cost of the buybacks and disposal of the more than 450,000 sets turned in—not the time and effort spent on orchestrating the recall, or the lost future sales of *Riviton.*

General Mills, upstanding and consumer-conscious as ever, was completely in accord with Barton's handling of the recall. But the millions of dollars lost couldn't help but leave Kinney, Atwater, and Swanson uneasy. For a conglomerate that had grown accustomed to the autonomous success of its subsidiaries, the *Riviton* incident was an eye-opener, particularly since it came so hot on the heels of *Merlin.*

In a single year, General Mills had seen for itself the awesome volatility of the toys business. Through *Merlin,* it had seen the glorious potential for growth and change. With *Riviton,* it had also seen how quickly disaster could strike. Thanks to *Merlin,* and some equally successful product introductions at Kenner, the Toy

Group grew 23.8 percent, to sales of $610 million in fiscal 1979. But operating profits dipped 4.8 percent to $60 million, clipped by the $8.9 million pretax charge related to recall of the *Riviton* construction toy. The recall had broken an eight-year string of steady group profit growth. Once again there were questions deep in the food side of the business about the arm's-length management of the Toy Group and all of its divisions.

Still, awful and disruptive as it was, *Riviton* was history within a year of the recall. At Christmas of 1979, with better supplies, *Merlin* became the industry's number-one toy. Thanks to that product alone, Parker Brothers's revenues were within shooting distance of $100 million by fiscal 1980. In dozens of interviews, an enthusiastic Ranny Barton predicted that soon half of Parker Brothers's business would be in electronics. He was fairly safe in saying so; already, the new market segment represented almost 40 percent of revenue. For a company that had long relied on a handful of board games for more than 90 percent of its revenue, the metamorphosis was nothing short of amazing.

How long would the boom times last? The projections were undauntingly hopeful: Electronic toys were predicted to be "here to stay." The toys industry as a whole grew by just under 13 percent, but the hand-held electronic games segment bounded up more than 300 percent, from $112 million to $375 million, spurred by the category's unprecedented appeal to teens and adults. Now at about 10 percent of industry sales, electronics was projected to contribute at least 30 percent of what would become an $8–9 billion industry by 1985.

Still, nobody who knew the cyclical ups and downs of the toys industry doubted that the category was headed for a shakeout. Inventor Bob Doyle had predicted in 1976 that 1980 would be the year it would arrive, and by the time 1979 was halfway through, it certainly began to look like he'd be right.

All the signs were there: First, there was the recessionary economy, which traditionally meant better sales for staples—such as *MONOPOLY,* dump-trucks, and dolls—than for the year's newfangled gizmo. Second, there were signs of saturation in the market: Almost overnight, this seller's market had become so crowded with entrants that it tipped the balance toward the buyer. It seemed everybody and his brother was making hand-held electronic games.

The number of products in the market had skyrocketed from only four items in 1976 to nearly 250 in 1979. Unfortunately, after just two years, there seemed to be more me-too'ers than marketers of new, innovative ideas. Customers were beginning to get bored. They were less and less willing to pay $20 or more for different versions of games that they'd already played to their hearts' content, so discounting was becoming heavy. The toys business was known for its "hula-hoop mentality," and most astute observers could see that this electronic fad was about to fall off the industry's hips.

Who would survive? The early betting was on the strong, well known, and well financed companies—which put Parker Brothers near the top of a list that included bigtime crest-riders such as Mattel. Like the Big G on a *Cheerios* box, the very knowledge that General Mills stood behind each Parker Brothers product seemed the next best thing to a sales insurance policy.

Still, prudence dictated that it was time for Parker Brothers and its competitors to begin cushioning themselves against the probability of at least a slowdown in sales—first by cutting back on inventory, and second, by developing new or complementary products.

Ideal Toys had already made the shift admirably, having introduced a box-shaped puzzle called *Rubik's Cube* to counterbalance its comparatively modest participation in hand-held electronic games. The brain-teaser was a sales monster—much to the chagrin of Bill Dohrmann, who had been using one as a paperweight for more than a year before the product was introduced in 1979. *Merlin* co-inventor Bob Doyle had brought one back from a European toy fair for Dohrmann, suggesting that Parker Brothers buy the license. Dohrmann, considering it a conversation piece at best, had taken to showing it off to visitors. "Isn't it just the damndest thing? It's a big deal in Europe, apparently." And so it was in the U.S., after Toy Fair in 1979.

As General Mills watched, open-mouthed, Parker Brothers began revising its electronic-games sales forecasts downward in steps, then in jumps. Almost as quickly as it had ballooned, the burgeoning market was deflating, threatening all $60 million of Parker Brothers's new-found revenue.

Most nerve-wracking of all, the company had nothing that could even begin to make up the loss. True to his goal, Jackson had held the company's line down to fewer items than the company had featured in about fifty years. What's more, idea traffic from the design community had slowed. The contract with the Doyles had been allowed to lapse, Parker Brothers deeming itself to have secured sufficient in-house design and engineering talent to support its lines of business. And most of the other leading freelance designers were busy with video games, a one-time fad that seemed to be cropping back up again.

Back in 1972 Magnavox introduced *Odyssey,* the first home video game. Nearly 100,000 were sold at a whopping $100 apiece. Maybe it was sticker shock, or maybe it was the fact that the Odyssey machine lacked long-term play value, but video games—at home or otherwise—didn't attract much attention with buyers until 1975, when *Pong* became a national pastime in the arcades. Executives at many toys and games companies found *Pong* boring. At Parker Brothers, it completely flunked the play-value test. Nonetheless, the trend couldn't be ignored. *Pong* buyers were obviously spending money they could have spent on board games.

Parker Brothers was keeping close watch on the evolving trend, but only from the sidelines. The Doyles had acknowledged and rejected video technology back in 1974–1975, preferring the simpler and therefore cheaper format of electronic games. Because the technology was more versatile, it would leave "more room for more companies to be more creative," as Bob Doyle had put it (erroneously, as it turned out), and would therefore discourage the knockoffs and copycatting that often kills hot business segments.

There was no further discussion of video at Parker Brothers until 1977, when a California newcomer of astounding speed and strength, Atari, put out the first home video game. Still, when the production of similar machines was proposed by marketers in Beverly, again the answer was no—the market was proliferating too fast for Jackson's taste. Already Mattel, Atari, and Coleco were into it, and the technology was moving so quickly that any Parker Brothers entry would be late, even obsolete, by the time it hit the market. Parenthetically, it was also seen as a significant drawback that the games still tied up the TV set, and lacked the complexity that allowed players to hone their skills. Parker Brothers's research indicated that mastery, or the hope of it, was more important to players at home than to those in the video arcades.

Parker Brothers congratulated itself for its caution a year later, when some forty companies jumped on the video bandwagon and crushed it to death. Coleco, for example, was stuck with $15.2 million worth of inventory.

Still, by 1978–1979, some insiders were predicting that when the cost of the hardware fell below $100—probably within a couple of years—there would be a big revival in video games. Everybody knew that *Merlin* and *Simon* were underutilizing the capabilities of the new chips that had been developed. Increasingly, hand-held electronics seemed to be just a transitional technology, one that gave the industry time to mull over the changing market without the huge investment of tackling it head-on, while also giving the consumer a chance to become comfortable with computerized playthings. Even the most stubborn of skeptics, at Parker Brothers and elsewhere, agreed: The question probably wasn't whether the video age would arrive, it was when, and in what form.

4

TEAM PLAY

*F*iscal 1980 was one of the best years the General Mills Toy Group had yet had. Kenner topped $100 million on *Star Wars* revenues for a second year in a row, while Parker Brothers achieved new highs in sales and profits, led by growth in *Merlin* sales and a record volume year for *MONOPOLY*. The Toy Group achieved a sales increase of 10.8 percent, for a total of $647 million. Operating profits rose 7 percent to $60.1 million.

Still, as Parker Brothers stared deeper into the coming through of the hand-held electronics wave, Ranny Barton informed General Mills that his company would probably have trouble achieving its revenue and earnings goals in fiscal 1981. Barton held his breath and waited for reply. As a rule, General Mills expected all measures of corporate performance to travel the up escalators; as far as management was concerned, the other direction didn't exist. But the response to Barton's bad news was taken well in Minneapolis. If that was the way it had to be, came the message from Don Swanson, that was the way it had to be. The vice chairman in charge of the non-food operations told Barton he appreciated the advance warning.

Grateful for the corporation's indulgence, Barton's glad-handing instincts took over. He couldn't say enough for his corporate parent.

In a centennial edition of the *Salem Evening News,* Barton credited General Mills with Parker Brothers's stunning success in hand-held electronics. "Certainly the company, had it remained a family business, could not have taken the risks, taken advantage of all the opportunities we have been able to take with General Mills," he gushed. "If we had been a family business when the electronic games had come along, I think it would have been too scary for us to get into. We just could not have done it." Barton termed the marriage to General Mills, now having cleared its first decade and then some, a happy one.

The reporter wanted to know what regrets Barton had, if any, over the twelve years since the merger. Barton took one of his long, blank pauses, mulling over the question. The sheer growth of the company, combined with the employee horse-trading that is always a feature of a boom market, had combined to make first-name conversation and low turnover levels things of the past. "I don't know everybody in the factory anymore and I couldn't tell you what game is on the presses today, the way I could before," Barton replied.

But if Ranny Barton felt he somehow knew less about Parker Brothers as it grew, General Mills knew more. The conglomerate had a new chief president now, Bruce Atwater, and with him came increasing attention to the company's non-food groups, which had grown in importance to the General Mills's quarterly income statement. The Toy Group, for example, now represented 15.2 percent of sales and 19.9 percent of operating profits. Initially concerned about the risks of projects such as *Code Name: Sector* and *Merlin,* and shaken by the almost overnight rise and fall of *Riviton,* General Mills was asking more questions these days, and requiring more reports. Quarterly tallies of various kinds became monthly, or even weekly. Annual planning exercises that were once completed in several fortnights of hard work now stretched over a full three months.

Research and development man Bill Dohrmann was among those increasingly vocal in their concern over General Mills's growing influence on Parker Brothers. He suggested to Barton, not totally facetiously, that the company had quit the toys business somewhere along the line. "We seem to spend a helluva lot of time on marketing studies, on meetings with product managers, on trips to Minneapolis and calls to New York City—but not very much on making toys," Dohrmann said, his long legs splayed under a coffee table, his hands locked behind his head in a gesture of relaxed certitude. He urged Barton to consider the toll that change—indeed, success—was taking on Parker Brothers.

Dohrmann felt that the new bureaucracy had cost Parker Brothers something unique and intrinsically important—its sense of fun, for lack of a better term. But Dohrmann was referring to much more than the laughter that less frequently echoed down the hallways. What he missed was the grand guessing game that Parker Brothers once played with its customers and its competitors—what to make, when to make it, how to sell it, when to get out of it. Now, gut instincts and experienced guesswork took a back seat to an ever-rising stack of paperwork, and it didn't seem that anybody outside of New York or Minneapolis could make even a simple decision without quantitative backup. This tendency to seek managerial justification, vindication, and exculpation in the numbers—it was "a chicken-shit way of doing business," Dohrmann said.

Barton well understood Dohrmann's complaints, but he staunchly defended the newly regimented Parker Brothers. Certainly the company had changed in significant ways, but, painful as they may have seemed to some employees, the changes were for the best. Indeed, Barton bluntly stated that those who found it necessary to criticize the company's progress had simply reached their level of incompetence, and were no longer qualified to work in such a fast-growth operation.

Still, none of that was to say Barton lacked gripes of his own. He had plenty, and they all boiled down to the presence of one man: Bernard L. "Bernie" Loomis, a former Kenner president who had taken over the management of the entire General Mills Toy Group in 1978, at the height of the hand-held electronics boom.

After years of loose-reined management and mutual respect between Beverly and Minneapolis, Barton now found himself under the whip of a man who had recently been his professional equal. To Barton, Loomis and his newly established Toy Group office in New York City represented a new and unwelcome level of governance within the conglomerate. Loomis had taken an active role in strategic decision making throughout the Toy Group, pushing the divisions hard for growth and expansion. In so doing, he had elbowed Parker Brothers into ever closer product-development cooperation with Kenner and its trendy toys. It seemed both Barton and Parker Brothers had lost rights to self-determination that might never be regained.

Nonetheless, Barton was a company man, and he may have tolerated the changes if he had found Loomis personally enjoyable to work with. As it was, Barton loathed Loomis almost as much as he feared him. "Every time it's him on the phone, I get this pit in my stomach," Barton admitted to close colleagues.

The conflict that Barton felt with Loomis was an all-out clash of personal and professional style. In fact, if ever there were a personification of the differences between the slower-paced, almost courtly games industry and the frenzied glitz of the mainstream toys business, the increasingly fractious relationship between Barton and Loomis was it.

As much as anything else, Barton hated the fact that Loomis flaunted his taste for the best in everything—from clothes to food to office furnishings—and drove what Barton considered to be a most ostentatious car, a Cadillac. By contrast, the unassuming Barton drove a station wagon and ate his lunch at the counter. In his Kenner days, Bernie had bragged of his political end-runs; Ranny was a great believer in corporate protocol. As a manager, Bernie was hands-on; Ranny was hands-off. Where Barton sought consensus, Loomis seemed determined to foment creative conflict. Barton motivated; Loomis, by many accounts, humiliated.

Even before taking over the reins of the Toy Group, Loomis had seemed to hold Parker Brothers in disdain. He was heard to disparage the company as a bunch of dilettantes and amateurs, and to ascribe Parker Brothers's success to four lucky breaks: *MONOPOLY, Instant Insanity, Nerf,* and *Merlin.* Most observers in Beverly attributed Loomis's scorn to rivalry, if not jealousy. Despite Kenner's vaunted revenue growth, Parker Brothers was still the profit leader. The smaller company was making money hand over fist. Now it wasn't Kenner that got first mention in the annual reports. It was Parker Brothers.

Loomis made no secret of the fact that he disapproved of Barton's style and strategy as a manager. He considered Barton laid-back at best; ill-prepared and gutless at worst. With Barton's reliance on consensus, Loomis found he couldn't necessarily depend on Barton to exhibit the managerial control Loomis expected when higher-ups came calling. While Barton didn't consider it embarrassing if he couldn't answer a question put by the brass in a meeting, Loomis seemed to. Barton's close associates winced at how hard Loomis pushed Barton, with his barked orders and sarcastic questions.

It all added up to be one of the most painful and personally unrewarding periods of Barton's career. He had always considered himself a sensible, mannerly man, and here he was, reporting to someone that he regarded as a streetfighter. It seemed neither right nor fair. "The man is abusive, and I resent having to deal with him," he told managerial colleagues and subordinates alike.

Bernie Loomis wasn't known—in 1978 or ever—for his managerial patience, tact, or steady-handed leadership. He has never been anything but hard-driving, outspoken, and as mercurial as they come. But few deny him his status as one of the toys industry's true geniuses, not Barton, and certainly not Loomis himself. He is a man "untroubled by false modesty," as one reporter put it. His colleagues go at least that far. "Name any successful toy, and Bernie'll claim to have had something to do with it," is a common refrain among friends and enemies alike.

If the origins of today's toys are traced far enough, however, there is truth to be found in the purported boasting. Loomis is generally credited with strengthening the ties between toys and television, with putting toymakers on the creative end of character licensing, and, by combining the two tactics, introducing some of the biggest-selling, longest-lasting, and industry-altering toy concepts of his day. By anyone's measure, Bernie Loomis's ideas were (and are) a *bona fide* asset to a toy-making operation.

Still, when General Mills went shopping for a new vice president for its Toy Group in 1978, Loomis's was not an obvious name to find high on the list of candidates. He hadn't come up through General Mills's ranks and, therefore, he didn't know or appreciate the many structural and cultural idiosyncrasies that made the company tick. He was neither a WASP nor a preppie; he didn't even have an MBA. Worst of all, Loomis seemed to wave his differences like a red flag in General Mills's face. "MBA," he loved to taunt, "means CYA." He also pointed out that he was then the only Jewish executive at or above his level among General Mills and its divisions, sometimes venturing to predict that his creed would limit his career. None of this enamored him with headquarters.

But Loomis had worked wonders during his years at Kenner. And as the Toy Group had grown too large and unwieldy to fit comfortably among Don Swanson's ever-increasing non-food responsibilities, Loomis began to look like Minneapolis's man. Who knew toys better than Bernie? Then-president Bruce Atwater flew to Cincinnati and offered him the job.

At first Loomis balked. He sure as hell wasn't going to move to Minneapolis, he said, professing to be no fan of snow and cold. But if the Toy Group headquarters were moved to New York City, and Loomis were given a free rein to apply the strategies that had been so successful at Kenner to the entire Toy Group, perhaps something could be arranged. Atwater readily assented.

The news of an impending change in Toy Group management hadn't shocked Ranny Barton. He had been among those who had told Don Swanson he needed to trim back his responsibilities. Initially concerned when he heard the man tapped for the job was the headstrong Loomis, Barton nonetheless warmed to the idea after a meeting with the man. They shared a congenial drink at a New York hotel, over which Loomis seemed to go out of his way to assure Barton he had everything to learn from him. "I want you to teach me games," Barton recalled being told. "We're going to be partners." But the honeymoon didn't last a month.

Money was one of the sore points. It piqued Barton, and others among General Mills's divisional management, to hear rumors of Loomis's purportedly princely compensation package. Loomis had gotten stock options and incentives that were, according to the gossip, on a par with those at the highest echelons in Minneapolis. It galled Barton. "The man thinks he's God and king, never mind boss," Barton muttered.

But Barton also reserved some ire for General Mills. As he saw it, the conglomerate had allowed Loomis to bully his way into the promotion by the sheer force of his accomplishments at Kenner. Far be it for Barton to deny Loomis's talent, or his energy, or his success in turning around Kenner. But there was little in the man's background to suggest that he could be a good manager for the Toy Group, as Barton saw it. He thought General Mills ought to have recognized that.

Bernie Loomis came from a hardscrabble background. He was born in the Bronx, the son of Russian emigrants who dabbled in both show business and fashion. Unlike many in the toys industry who trace their interest in the business to early childhood, Loomis received few true playthings in his modest upbringing. But young Bernard prized his Lionel train catalogue and used it to build fantasy train sets in his mind. As he neared his teens, his fertile imagination led him to "play" a full season of American League baseball with just a deck of cards. According to his elaborate system, some cards were designated balls or strikes, while others represented doubles and pop flies. He tracked not only each team's supposed scores, but the pitching records and batting averages of individual stars throughout the league.

Dead-end sales jobs paid Loomis's way through night school at New York University—swimming pool sales, hardware sales, and paper-supply sales among them. By the late 1950s he had become a toy manufacturer's sales representative, for no other reason than it paid better than his previous jobs.

At the 1961 Toy Fair he began what was to be a decade-long association with Mattel and the couple who had bought the company from founder Harold Matson, Ruth and Elliot Handler. The Handlers were big guns in toys, having invented the perennially popular Barbie and Ken dolls (which were named after their own children). But Loomis saw no reason to demur or defer in their presence. By his own recollection, he started an argument with his new bosses on the first night the three met—some inconsequential flap about the merits of a particular sort of product testing.

Loomis became a key marketing figure at Mattel. There he made competitors sit up and take notice with his innovative use of television as a promotional vehicle. Loomis and some of his cohorts reasoned that if the industry could advertise toys on television and make toys based on characters and ideas licensed from television shows, why not give toys shows and cartoons of their own? The idea bore fruit in 1969, when Mattel developed and launched a thirty-minute show on ABC. Its story line centered on Mattel's new line of miniature cars called *Hot Wheels*.

Jealous toymakers were the first to complain about the show and its obvious sales pitch. They argued that the show violated

Federal Communications Commission regulations concerning the separation of programming and advertising. The FCC agreed. Television stations were told to log part of the show as advertising time—a cumbersome and, because advertising minutes were limited by law, costly requirement that seemed likely to keep broadcasters and toymakers out of bed in the future.

Loomis left an ailing and embattled Mattel in 1970. The company had grown bloated and spendthrift with its success. When a factory fire and a strike combined to interrupt shipping, its overhead nearly sunk the company. In the meantime, relations worsened between Loomis and his bosses, the Handlers. Walking papers in hand, Loomis's first inclination was to leave the toys business and get a business degree. But first he made sure everybody knew where to find him, just in case.

One of those who came looking was Craig Nalen, the harried head of General Mills's then-toddling Toy Group. Nalen had an unusual and slightly sheepish request to make: Would Loomis consider taking over Nalen's job?

The offer was made around the time that Don Swanson was moving in on Nalen's turf, though Nalen didn't mention the particulars of the management shuffle to Loomis. Rather, Nalen simply said that the Toy Group needed someone who could stand up to the brass in Minneapolis while catering to the interests of a diverse group of companies. For credibility's sake alone, that someone should well understand the toys business. Nalen pointed out that Kenner was in particular need of Loomis's experience, drive, and creativity. The Cincinnati company had been languishing since it had been acquired; it couldn't seem to find its direction. Nalen, in truth, was looking for a savior. Far from oblivious to the anti-diversification rumblings surrounding him at General Mills, Nalen felt that both he and Kenner would be history at General Mills if things didn't change soon—though, again, he shared none of the reasons for his urgency with Loomis.

Loomis nibbled on the bait awhile, feigning interest in the Toy Group job. When he was certain that he was Nalen's fish, he jerked the line hard. Loomis would "be damned" if he'd wind up in "that glass palace in Minneapolis, playing those corporate games." But if Nalen wanted to give him Kenner, Loomis continued, he'd see what he could do to get the company back on its feet.

Nalen heaved a huge sigh that gave way to a belly laugh. "Thank God," he said. "That's what I wanted in the first place!"

Loomis turned Kenner around with a string of hit toys, most of which were derived from licensed properties. He hadn't invented such character licensing—the practice was virtually as old as toys and games themselves, and had changed little over the decades: In exchange for certain hefty royalty fees, Kenner or another licensee was granted the right to use a legally protected name, graphic, logo, saying, or likeness in conjunction with a product, promotion, or service. But Loomis took the use of licensing to new heights as a toy-development technique. The beauty of the strategy, as he saw it, was in its high visibility. The already-high public recognition of the licensed character increased retail traffic in the toys stores and, thereby, virtually guaranteed impressive sales on a relatively small budget for advertising and promotion.

Loomis's first big licensed hit was an "action figure" (in other words, a doll for boys) based on the TV series *The Six Million Dollar Man.* To General Mills's initial consternation, Loomis went ahead and negotiated the license without mentioning his plans to headquarters, much less getting approval. But nobody stood on protocol when the money started rolling in in the millions. Then, all anybody wanted to know was how he had known it would sell. Where had he gotten his research? What study had told him it would strike such a responsive chord?

Research? Study? Loomis snorted with laughter. It just seemed "toyetic," he said, coining a word that became part of his design vocabulary. It just looked like something a kid would play with.

Other licensed properties came and went at Kenner during the 1970s, most of them from television series: *The Bionic Woman, Nancy Drew,* and *The Man from Atlantis,* to name three. Each was an expensive proposition for Kenner that sold well, but lasted scarcely a year.

Loomis recognized that he was contending with one of the hard facts of licensing: While licensed characters and their built-in visibility made toy development less risky than starting from scratch with new ideas, they weren't dependably profitable. High licensing fees were the leading factor, of course: Rarely could a manufacturer get away with making the same licensed gizmo long enough to earn back the investment. Unlike either staples (whose sales and profits tend to build with time) or trendier toys (whose production costs are held down to cope with their quick rise and fall in popularity), licensed products sold long enough to turn a profit only if they were updated or accessorized every several years to keep the license current in the eyes of the buying public.

Loomis decided to be more picky. Spending what he had been spending, he didn't figure it worthwhile to develop any property that wasn't extendible—that is, anything that by its nature couldn't produce accessories and ancillary characters to milk the trend for four years and more.

Loomis found such a property in *Star Wars.* In April of 1977, a month before the Steven Spielberg-George Lucas movie opened in the theatres, Twentieth Century Fox Film Corporation sold the "galaxy-wide" rights to the name and images of the movie's characters—Darth Vader, Luke Skywalker, Han Solo, and the others—to Kenner. Other toymakers, including Mattel, had declined the opportunity to bid. They complained of holes in the screenplay. But Loomis professed not to care about the plot; the toymaking potential was what had caught his eye. He planned to bring out the first of a long line of *Star Wars* merchandise a year after the movie's first Christmas in the theatres.

But when the movie became a box office smash months in advance of the planned introduction of the merchandise, what to do? Loomis wasn't at a loss for long. He hit upon the idea of selling certificates of ownership—a little something for the kids to show off while waiting for the production lines to punch out the real thing. The ingeniously simple solution worked. *Star Wars*-related toys generated revenues of $100 million for Kenner in the first year. Loomis had built Kenner from a $50 million company with losses of $5 million, to a $200 million company with a respectable profit. Not bad for less than six years of effort.

After *Star Wars,* Loomis became even more selective. He rejected the *Ziggy* license, saying there were already too many tie-ins to the famous comic strip character. Instead, he told executives at American Greetings Corporation to come back when they had something that would get him "in on the ground floor." Loomis now wanted to take on the dual role of licensor/licensee. In other words, not only did he wish to acquire licenses from other entities, he wanted to develop his own characters and license them to yet other merchandisers.

What Loomis proposed was no minor change in tack. If it caught on, this double-edged approach to licensing would put Loomis and other toymakers in the driver's seat in ways they hadn't enjoyed before. No longer would they be paying outrageous royalties for characters from movies like *Star Wars* or TV shows like *The Six Million Dollar Man.* The shoe would be on the other foot: The toy companies would come up with the characters, and the networks and the production companies would come to *them* with checkbooks in hand. Loomis, like most industry insiders, reveled in the prospect of the role reversal.

As Loomis was settling into his new Toy Group office in New York, he chose *Strawberry Shortcake,* a little girl with fruit and flowers on her bonnet, as the character to try out his strategy. The stories differ as to whether Loomis picked the little girl out of a stack of greeting cards himself, or whether American Greetings selected the figure and brought it to Loomis for development. But the story ends the same, with Loomis declaring himself about to make "toymaking history"—not just with the strawberry-scented doll, but with an entire cast of friends (dolls such as *Lime Chiffon* and *Raspberry Tart*), potentially hundreds of toy accessories, and unprecedented television support.

In early 1980 the first *Strawberry Shortcake* television special aired, called "Welcome to the World of Strawberry Shortcake." It was as much an hour-long ad for Kenner as Loomis's *Hot Wheels* cartoon had been a pitch for Mattel, but there was nowhere near the protest. With a more permissive mood prevalent in Washington, D.C., what little hew and cry arose came from children's watchdog organizations. Licensed toys left nothing to the imagination, charged the critics, adding that the television shows built around these toys had no value but to the toymakers.

Loomis and others countered by saying that the substantial cost of creating toys and television shows had encouraged toy companies to favor licensed products that were indeed well conceived and designed. Anything less would be a fad at best, and fads didn't earn back multimillion-dollar television investments.

General Mills stood clear of the controversy, but it admired the Loomis strategy. Suddenly, toys didn't seem to be such a strange, volatile industry anymore. With *Strawberry Shortcake,* Kenner had engaged itself in a style of marketing that closely resembled the General Mills's own, wherein popular products were supported by strong advertising, plus spinoff or flanker products that boosted market share within a single category, or as it was sometimes called, a "brand franchise." Hamburger Helper begat Tuna Helper begat Chicken Helper, and so it went. Licensed toys, with their new products pushing the popularity of the original concept to new heights each year, were "product franchises." Just as children demanded that parents buy each new cereal that came out, so did they clamor for each successive expansion of the *Strawberry Shortcake* line. These annual additions to the product line were the toys industry's equivalent of a "new and improved" banner across the cereal box.

General Mills wasn't alone in believing that the toys industry had at last found in licensing its Holy Grail—its key to achieving longer and broader product cycles, with better volumes and profits. Financial analysts and toys-industry experts alike sung the praises of licensed toys. True, development costs had zoomed exponentially higher with the popularization of licensing, boosting the barriers to entry in the toys industry to the proportions of a Great Wall. It now cost $10 million, even $20 million, just to talk about developing a property—and, of course, the required television show to go with it. Still, for all its expense, the licensed approach to toymaking was far more preferable to starting from scratch with unproven concepts year after year, never certain that any one would be as successful as the last, much less a hit.

But improved stability was not the only aspect of licensing that enticed General Mills. From the beginning, the licensing gambit had also appealed to General Mills's penchant for seeking new efficiencies and interdependencies among its many and varied toys divisions. When Loomis suggested early on that his licensed properties become mega-franchises, manufactured and promoted "wall-to-wall" within the entire Toy Group, executives in Minneapolis agreed. Why shouldn't Parker Brothers help milk the popularity of *The Six Million Dollar Man* or *Star Wars* by making games to accompany Kenner's action figures? Why shouldn't Fundimensions do the same with crafts? These realizations played no small role in getting Loomis his group vice presidency.

But the implementation of this more cooperative approach required an intra-Group cohesion that was increasingly hard to come by. Kenner and Parker Brothers still had trouble tolerating each other's presence in the Toy Group; how could they now work together? The crux of the conflict was simple: Each company believed itself to be the superior organization. Parker Brothers saw Kenner as somehow less genteel, and prided itself in maintaining a consistently higher return on investment. Kenner, on the other hand, thought it worked harder for its profits, since margins were traditionally higher on games.

The historically strong rivalries between Cincinnati and Beverly had become cold war during Loomis's tenure at Kenner. Where product development was concerned, both companies began paying less attention to the strength of their ideas than to the size of their respective turf. Each seemed determined to expand its influence in the Toy Group, even if it meant doing what the other did best.

At Parker Brothers in particular, the new crop of bright and ambitious product managers wanted desperately to break out of the old board-game patterns. It was frustratingly difficult to achieve growth and, more important, to keep the creative juices flowing, on a restricted diet of paper, plastic, ink, and glue—especially since board games was a market in decline. It was inevitable, perhaps, that the two companies would begin trying to steal each other's marbles. When they did, neither Minneapolis nor New York made more than a half-hearted attempt to intervene.

As adamant as General Mills was on planning and the establishment of clear lines of authority, it had never developed an explicit policy on who could do what in the Toy Group. There had been only the general assumption that Kenner, with its Play-Doh, its dolls, and later its licensed characters, would be the more traditional *toys* company. If it were a fad, or made of mostly plastic, it was Kenner's. Fundimensions, meanwhile, was responsible for *crafts* and its Lionel line of toy trains. And Parker Brothers's raison d'etre would remain, with few exceptions, in *games*. The trouble was, more and more games contained plastic playthings or molded forms instead of traditional game boards.

(*Nerf,* for example, was much more a toy than a game.) And quite a few plastic toys were marketed with elements of game play.

The dilemma for the design and marketing troops of both companies was: What should they do if they came up with a particularly good product idea, something that looked certain to push up earnings and boost bonuses, yet didn't really mesh with their company's calling? For the sake of their own pocketbooks as well as the company's income statement, they went after it. Like smart-alecky kids, both Kenner and Parker Brothers tried to see how far the parent could be pushed. It didn't really matter in these one-upmanship contests whether the gains really bettered the company; what was important was to beat the other team at its own game, sometimes literally.

Back at Kenner, Loomis developed a *Star Wars* board game, gleefully thumbing his nose at the dividing line between toys and games. Sales were lackluster at best. Parker Brothers then stepped into the action-figure category that Kenner knew so well, with a $25 doll called *ROM.* Ten inches tall, *ROM* could hold an assortment of weapons in his hand and fly with rocket pods strapped onto his back. Most interesting for the designers and marketers in-house, *ROM* made breathing sounds that made for great intra-office obscene phone calls. But the public never seemed to find any sex appeal in the doll (though a leading comic book publisher licensed the rights to the character). Subsequently, Loomis's attempt to encroach on hand-held electronic game territory with an entry called *Red Line Hockey* was hip-checked out of the market by other, more popular sports-oriented games.

But the Parker/Kenner rivalry reached its peak when Loomis gained control of the entire Toy Group and institutionalized the sharing of licensed concepts. During his tenure, it became the practice of the Toy Group to gobble up the rights to any given license in all available or conceivable formats—electronic game, board game, dolls, crafts, you name it—and farm them out to the appropriate division to "really make the character explode," as Loomis was heard to enthuse. Parker Brothers found itself saddled with trying to devise board-game versions of Kenner licenses such as *Strawberry Shortcake.* As time went on, Kenner, too, found itself assigned the task of making playthings to support and augment Parker Brothers products.

With the enforced alliance at the product-development level, the companies seemed to cling all the more tightly to anything that would differentiate one company from another. For example, Kenner staffers noted that Parker Brothers designers bent over backwards to use different terminology to describe the various stages of product development, as if deliberately creating confusion within the group.

Still, one of the bigger factors in keeping a chill on relations between Kenner and Parker Brothers was Loomis himself. His abrasive style, combined with what Parker Brothers staffers assumed was his bias toward Kenner, became a Maginot Line between the companies. They may have been working on similar concepts for the same man, but not even the mandates of Loomis's marketing strategy could make the two companies work like a team.

By 1980, the seeds of a managerial mutiny were sprouting in the Toy Group. Several times a week Ranny Barton received exasperated telephone calls from managers in various corners of the far-flung organization seeking consultation and commiseration on what was increasingly termed The Loomis Problem. Dislike wasn't strong enough a word for what people were feeling; some professed to hate Loomis. And not even the man's closest aides and associates knew quite how to contend with him. When Barton asked their advice for how to deal with Loomis, the only response most could offer was "carefully."

No longer was it a question in Barton's mind of how Loomis was managing him or Parker Brothers, or the enforced cooperation between Kenner and Parker Brothers. He feared for the future of the entire Toy Group. In pursuit of his goals, Bernie Loomis had splintered, gutted, or alienated the various divisions of the group.

The trouble had begun back in 1978 in the European subsidiaries of the Toy Group. Together these European operations were losing $20 million a year, with an even larger negative cash flow. Loomis was determined to whip them into shape and "get them on the team." He spent the better part of his first year in office revamping the European operations, convinced that they were badly organized, lacking coordination and leadership, and not nearly so healthy as they had made themselves look.

"You're reporting profits that aren't there!" Loomis accused managers in London and Paris. The business overseas was "a lie," as he angrily put it to anyone who would listen stateside. At Loomis's insistence, three or four layers of management were completely replaced in some companies. Not a single general manager survived the Loomis purge.

Few within the Toy Group disagreed that the European operations were a mess, and mostly because each division insisted on going its own way. Widely admired by other toy companies for having been independent and successful in their own rights prior to being acquired by General Mills (most toy manufacturers had been forced to spend the considerable time, talent, and money to start their own international divisions from scratch), these companies were even more fiercely self-interested than the American companies. Many of them licensed products from Mattel, Hasbro, Ideal, and other American competitors of the Toy Group, while turning up their noses at products developed by sister companies Kenner, Parker Brothers, and Fundimensions. They also kept their own counsel where accounting practices were concerned and, as Loomis saw it, blatantly pumped up their volume figures to please Minneapolis.

Some of the problem in Europe was structural, dating back to the early days of the Toy Group. The domestic companies had been given little incentive to help the European operating companies do well—Kenner or Parker Brothers had no stake in the profits of a sister company in France or England, for example. The only way they could share in any success overseas was to collect royalties on the sales of their own products. So the practice of the domestic companies became to dump anything and everything they could on the Europeans, including the products that didn't move stateside.

The result? The Europeans got burned a few times too many, and retaliated by taking their business to American companies other than those within the Toy Group. The Americans then counter-punched: Rather than selling *MONOPOLY*'s European rights to Palitoy, the newly consolidated General Mills subsidiary in Great Britain, Parker Brothers stuck with Waddington, another British games company that they deemed better equipped to sell the product.

Even when the domestic and international companies did manage to do business together, there was often needless chauvinism and duplication of effort. It wasn't rare to see a European company spending $100,000 to tool up for the manufacture of the same product made in another European operation or American division.

Instead of reconsidering the basic relationships among the American and the European companies in the Toy Group, Loomis focused on the outward symptoms of product development and distribution. His dictum was simple: The European companies would exist as foreign sales outlets for the Toy Group. They would sell what the Americans were selling when the Americans were selling it. No longer would they be allowed to buy Ideal's latest hit, or wait until Kenner's most recent licensing coup had proven itself before adding it to the line. Loomis demanded complete and total loyalty to his strategic changes, and those who didn't deliver to his satisfaction became International Division history.

Loomis's insistence on fealty had two unfortunate side effects: When the European companies put less emphasis on finding and developing their own products, the domestic companies lost a fertile source of ideas and experience for their own development. (The British games company Waddington, for example, was the source of Parker Brothers's hit game *Clue.*) And, by locking the Hasbros and Mattels of the world out of General Mills's foreign subsidiaries, Loomis forced competitors to build their own distribution networks. Critics predicted that someday a revenue-hungry General Mills might need the Europeans to renew their old relations with Toy Group competitors, and it would be General Mills's turn to be locked out.

General Mills approved of Loomis's unification strategy, but not his methods. By turning over rocks, churning up policies, and changing managers, Loomis was not only offending General Mills's sense of decorum in his handling of the European problem, he was threatening to cause a much wider managerial exodus. The scuttlebutt reaching Minneapolis was that a growing number of executives in other divisions would prefer not to be working for the man. Still, nothing in Atwater's public comments or actions suggested anything but unflagging support for Loomis.

Loomis, meanwhile, seemed alternately pleased and concerned by the growing enmity surrounding him. As pressure grew for his replacement, he seemed to become more incorrigible. For example, Loomis told colleagues that he thought he had General Mills figured out where getting funds and decisions were concerned: If you were afraid to be wrong and wasted your time with paperwork to try to make things happen, you were more likely to get in caught in a bureaucratic quagmire. It was a batting average game, he figured—and one he'd rather not play. "Every time I want to tool a toy, they want it to be a committee decision!" he thundered.

Annoyed by the red tape and politics ploys of General Mills, Loomis simply stopped telling Minneapolis what he was doing. He side-stepped policy and procedure, and flat-out ignored orders— or what passed for orders, anyway. "What orders?" he would say, mocking General Mills's well-known reluctance to spell out its displeasure. "There are things you're supposed to interpret as gospel if it comes from the right people, but they're not orders."

"He's pushing General Mills's face in the mud," Barton fumed of Loomis. But to whom could anybody complain? As Barton saw it, Loomis had made himself an impenetrable wall between the companies and headquarters. In the past, Barton and the other general managers had been able to speak freely with General Mills executives, from the chairman on down. Ranny's back-channel conversations with staffers in Minneapolis had never fazed former boss Don Swanson, for example. But when Bernie heard about them, he confronted Barton with angry incredulity: "You've been talking to *who*?"

Barton's long-smoldering anger with Loomis all but came to blows in the winter of 1980, when Parker Brothers held a gala celebration commemorating its achievement of the $100 million mark for annual revenues. It was an elegant, candlelight dinner at Castle Hill, an old, Italianate mansion on the sea in nearby Ipswich, Massachusetts. For days in advance, Loomis, neither comfortable with nor tolerant of Barton's affinity for the Yankee style, protested the fact that the party was "to hell and gone"— namely, on Parker Brothers's native turf instead of in New York.

On the day of the celebration Loomis swept in with his entourage for an operations review—in essence, a product-review session. These were the times that Loomis was most enjoyed and valued by his subordinates in the divisions. For all his bluster, the guy knew his stuff where product development and marketing were concerned; virtually nobody questioned his genius. It proved to be a typically cordial session.

But afterward Loomis made the rounds of the offices of many of Barton's key managers, verbally roughing them up for lack of energy, diligence, or ingenuity. Some were given the disheartening news—not always true, it turned out—that Barton had no intention of promoting them in an upcoming reorganization. In fact, Bill Dohrmann was handed a *de facto* demotion. Dohrmann had "too much on [his] plate," Loomis told him, saying Dohrmann's research and development duties would be limited from that time forward to design and product acquisition matters only, not development tasks as well.

Co-workers, seeing the ashen faces of Loomis's victims, streamed into Barton's office, asking what on earth was going on. More important, they wanted to know what Barton was going to do about it. "What *can* I do?" Barton spluttered in reply. "Every time I try to interrupt he throws me out!"

By the end of the workday, Barton had lost his customary cool. "Keep me away from him or there's going to be a fight," the usually unflappable blue blood told his associates. When it came time to board the bus that would ferry employees to the dinner, Barton hung back. Once Loomis had seated himself, Barton walked stiffly past him to the back of the bus.

On arrival at the castle, there seemed to be no pleasing Loomis. The drafty stone building was too cold, it was aggravating his head cold. Whose idea was this? How much executive time and talent had gone into planning this overblown shindig? Twenty minutes later he went into a rage because nobody had remembered to bring the coat he had forgotten back in Beverly. When Parker Brothers staffers heard the fracas, some volunteered to retrieve the garment. Barton blew a gasket. "If you or anybody leaves for that reason," he snapped, "I guarantee you won't have a job." He sent the bus driver back instead.

What followed that night was a long multi-course dinner for 150. The atmosphere at the head table was noticeably tense, and Loomis left long before the evening's finale—the cutting of a huge commemorative cake. Barton, obviously relieved by Loomis's departure, loudly ordered that two bottles of champagne be brought directly to his table. *"Now,"* he declared to his amused dinnermates, "the party begins!"

The next morning, Barton tracked Loomis down by telephone in New York to register his disapproval.

"As far as I'm concerned," Barton said, "your behavior was totally unacceptable yesterday, start to finish." How could Loomis berate and insult Barton's staff? What had compelled him to conduct performance reviews with them, when the purpose of the session was *product* reviews?

"Ranny, you didn't understand what I was trying to do for you."

"Well, I would like an apology."

"No need for that. You misunderstood me. And I had a cold."

After an awkward silence, it was Loomis who abruptly ended the conversation. "I'm sorry you misunderstood," he reiterated. Then he hung up.

Barton kept dialing, apprising personnel in Minneapolis and key members of Loomis's staff in New York of the incident. The Parker Brothers president found plenty of commiseration. "Bernie loses control," said staffers and corporate administrators alike. Barton came away convinced that he was not alone in viewing Loomis as a loose cannon that ought to be tied down or removed altogether. Barton kept his fingers crossed for the latter.

Several months went by. When General Mills still hadn't taken any action against Loomis, Barton telephoned Don Swanson, the head of all of General Mills's non-food operations. It was time to see how much muscle Barton had built up, and how readily it could be flexed.

"Don, you said if I ever needed to, I could go over my boss's head," began Barton. "Well, I'd like to sit down and talk with you." The two made plans to meet in New York that week.

On the appointed evening, after drinks and pleasantries, Barton put his glass down, faced Swanson, and sighed heavily. "I had to tell you face-to-face. If six months from now Bernie Loomis is my boss, I'm out. I don't have to put up with this. I don't need the insults or the aggravation." Barton stopped Swanson before he could interrupt. "I'd feel better if you didn't say anything right away. Just think about it."

But Swanson did speak, leaving Barton assured that General Mills backed him to the hilt, and furthermore, that help was already on the way. Barton gathered from what he heard that others had gone to Swanson with complaints, most of the general managers in the Toy Group it seemed. But Barton recognized that only he, with his family riches, had the financial wherewithal to threaten to quit and mean it. Maybe his move would prove the decisive one. He could hope, anyway.

Nothing happened for several more months, however, until General Mills's annual management meeting in October of 1980. Barton arrived at the conference, held that year in the colonial town of Williamsburg, Virginia, to find a series of unscheduled meetings in progress. The rumor was that Bernie Loomis was going to be "seeking new career challenges," as the news releases usually put it.

After dinner that night, Don Swanson confirmed the buzzing in the hallways. He called Barton and Kenner president Joe Mendelsohn aside to inform them that Bernie Loomis would soon be leaving Toy Group management to start an elite design and licensing strike force intended to serve all of the group's divisions. It would be called Marketing and Design, "or M.A.D," Swanson said, prompting snide grins all around. Nothing was final yet, Swanson stressed, but it appeared the new head of the Toy Group would be a headquarters import named Jim Fifield. "I'm telling you now because Jim's here, and I thought you might want to take advantage of the opportunity to get close to him."

Fifield, like most of the up-and-comers at General Mills, was a veteran of the brand-manager system. His big break came in 1973, when he was appointed to head General Mills's venerable Golden Valley Group, the largest of the food divisions. In 1976 he moved to the smaller New Business division (considered a fast-track proving ground), where he was party to the acquisition and development of *Yoplait,* a highly successful French-style yogurt. Then he hopscotched back into the company's basic business, becoming group vice president for consumer foods (with special responsibility for developing participation in new grocery store categories).

There Fifield distinguished himself by having the guts to stop an apparent marketing juggernaut. In 1977 he nixed a highly touted processed potato-chip brand, slated to be called *Mrs. Bumby's*. The brand had managed to pass its market test, but it failed to pass muster with Fifield. Maybe it was the test data, or maybe it was the fact that a *real* Mrs. Bumby had turned up to complain about the use of her name; whatever it was, Fifield smelled disaster. His move to scuttle the product—which no doubt reminded Bruce Atwater of his one-time decision to substitute *Potato Buds* for the older but lower-quality potato mix, *Betty Crocker Instant Mashed Potatoes*—was heralded as an example of how General Mills faced up to failure. "If you have an idea that's a reasonable thing to try, and you've gone at it properly but it fails, then all you've done is tried," commented Atwater in one publication. "If you can't stand back from your own brainchild and look at the data, you've got an awful mess."

Beyond this rough sketch of his career path, most of what anybody in the Toy Group knew about Jim Fifield was what was in *Standard and Poor's:* James Guy Fifield was born in 1942 in St. Louis and raised in Colorado. He attended Southern Methodist University and its business school, receiving his MBA in 1965. With that alone as introduction, Fifield became the subject of much curious hallway chat during the conference. What really made the guy tick? How was he likely to run the Toy Group? Was there any evidence he would be an improvement over Bernie Loomis?

Before the conference was over, it became official that Fifield was indeed taking over in New York. Everybody's schedule was jam-packed, so there wasn't much time to squeeze in an extra meeting, but Fifield managed to sit down with Barton and the other Toy Group presidents for ten minutes between sessions. He was looking forward to working with them, he said. He considered the management of the Toy Group a challenge. And he was excited to begin learning about the business from the general managers themselves—just as soon as he was able to schedule visits.

Barton, already making plans in his head to host the new executive, asked if Fifield would prefer a formal or an informal presentation.

Fifield shrugged. "You tell me."

"Well, I'll give you an hour of numbers," Barton replied, "and then we'll get you out into the various functions. Walk your tail off."

Fifield laughed his assent. "What plane you want me on?"

Barton was joyfully speechless. Bernie Loomis would never have let anyone presume to dictate his schedule, not even for the sake of first impressions.

It was a small moment, a relatively meaningless bit of banter, but it lingered long in Barton's mind. This Fifield certainly seemed to be a give-and-take sort of guy. Barton dared to hope that his company was really going to be *his* company once again, and that order would be restored in the Toy Group. In so doing, Barton felt a greater sense of satisfaction and anticipation than he'd felt in, oh, probably two years.

Bernie Loomis, meanwhile, was tossing off darker predictions from the sidelines. This was the beginning of the end, he told several close associates on separate occasions. The power shift in the Toy Group signaled General Mills's overall discomfort not with Bernie Loomis, but with the toys business itself.

Lest his words be chalked up to sour grapes, Loomis was quick to assure cohorts that his transfer to M.A.D. had been his own idea, a job change that he had suggested to Don Swanson fully a year earlier. All he had ever wanted from the Toy Group job, he explained, was one year to shape up the operations and another year to enjoy the fruits of his labors. He'd gotten both and more. Now he was glad to let General Mills do what it wanted with the Toy Group. He was going to move into his new digs across the street from the Toy Group headquarters and get back into more creative work.

No, Loomis opined, what he read in Fifield's appointment to the Toy Group job was high-level frustration in Minneapolis. CEO Bruce Atwater—soon to be named chairman of the conglomerate—neither enjoyed nor understood the volatility of the toys business, Loomis maintained. By installing one of his own number-crunching MBAs in a job that Loomis thought rightfully belonged to a toys-industry loyalist, Atwater had telegraphed his intent to monitor the Toy Group more closely, probably with an eye toward making it a steady, predictable performer, as bankable as one of his food groups.

The very idea left Loomis chuckling derisively. Down years came and went like clockwork in the toys industry, the only trick of the trade being how to take them profitably, he preached to his listeners. Mark his words: There would come a day when General Mills would recognize that it didn't know how to run a toys business and it didn't want to learn. Then the conglomerate would wash its hands of the whole blasted thing.

5

ROLL AGAIN

*T*he word out of New York in early 1981 was that Jim Fifield, the smiling appointee to the Toy Group vice presidency who the divisional managers had met in Williamsburg, was cold and stand-offish—prone to walking the halls alone and looking through people, or tinkering with the antique toys he had bought to decorate his sleek, high-tech office.

Fifield had professed wanting to build a friendly, team-like atmosphere in the Toy Group—that was presumed to be the motive behind his announced plans to take the entire Toy Group white-water rafting in Colorado, his childhood home, as part of the group's annual meeting that spring. But for every such stride he made toward organizational acceptance, his tendency toward gruff-ness and impatience cost him one with his subordinates. Talk too long at a meeting, and Fifield would act as if his time were being wasted. Call him on the phone and sometimes the uh-huhs would trail off until it wasn't clear that he was still on the line.

Fifield seemed to acknowledge the existence of his Mr. Hyde side. He had good days and bad days, he told the operating managements of Kenner, Parker Brothers, and Fundimensions soon after his arrival in New York. If the division presidents wanted to see their ideas implemented, they ought to start by selling them to his staff members. Not only could his underlings screen out any obvious policy clinkers, they'd know when and how to bring the potential strokes of genius to Fifield. Who better to know when the boss was having one of his good days?

Having heard the stories, sources in Minneapolis said they weren't surprised that the man had been slow to endear himself to the Toy Group workforce. They said Fifield had a reputation back in his headquarters days of being a no-nonsense, sometimes hotheaded manager. One story in particular made the rounds: When Fifield once became convinced that a subordinate was spending too much time letting his fingers do the walking, he had purportedly gone into the hapless victim's office to suggest a bit more legwork. To illustrate his point, it was said, Fifield ripped the telephone out of the wall as he made his exit.

It was beginning to look as though the Toy Group had landed itself another Bernie Loomis, some glumly suggested. But those on the New York staff who were veterans of Loomis's regime quickly begged to differ. Despite the tendencies they shared toward impatience and displays of temper, Loomis and Fifield were archetypes. Loomis understood toys better than Fifield ever could, but he had been totally incompatible with General Mills and its approach to business. Fifield, on the other hand, was cut of heir-apparent cloth—albeit a bolder weave than what was typically seen at General Mills.

Like Bo Polk years before, Fifield was the boss's protégé—but that didn't make him shy about saying he wanted to be president of General Mills someday. And, like Polk, Fifield had challenged the corporate establishment with new ideas at various points along his career path. Fifield was a survivor and, by definition, a master of headquarters politics. But never was he one of the guys—Fifield's reputation was that of lone wolf.

Part corporate animal and part rebel, Fifield was perhaps the ideal man for the Toy Group job. He knew how to get things done the General Mills way, but he also had a look and style that well suited him to the high-rolling club that was now toys and games. Tall, tanned, and lined across the forehead, Fifield's plain midwestern features inspired instant trust even as the rare appearance of his dimpled half-smile gave him a roguish air. His workaday uniform included embellishments such as collar pins and suspenders, but in his off-hours, he sometimes pulled on cowboy boots. In short, for all his business-school training and General Mills dues-paying, Fifield could play the role of the kid to the hilt. One-on-one conversations became sprinkled with references to his many exploits, ranging from belligerent confrontations with street characters in New York to the time he roller-skated about Central Park with a girlfriend. But even as he revealed these details from his life outside the office, Fifield retained a formal distance from his listeners. He seemed determined not to get too familiar with anyone.

However, Fifield exhibited no such reticence where business was concerned. He got up close and personal with the details of his new charges in the toys and games markets with impressive speed. Toy Group headquarters subordinates and divisional managers had to concede they were amazed by how much Fifield had learned in a few months on the job, and by how little he had complicated their lives. They may not have exactly taken him to their hearts, but the man was brilliant, they agreed—always five steps ahead of his direct reports. He would never have the intuitive grasp of the toys business that Bernie Loomis did; Fifield hadn't lived it. But, damned if the new Toy Group executive didn't pick up the rudiments, and fast.

So, when Fifield sent a memo around in the spring of 1981 calling a meeting to discuss the emerging market for home video games and how the Toy Group should address it, few were surprised. He had proven again and again that he was a man who did his homework. The memo simply acknowledged the same hypothesis that others within the divisions had reached—that video was going to be the next go/no-go decision for the Toy Group companies. Fundimensions, with its toy trains and crafts, would probably take a bye. But Kenner and Parker Brothers would no doubt *both* want a piece of the action.

Rich Stearns's new office was so empty that it echoed. Just months before, he had been lord and marketing master of *Merlin,* a $100 million product that recently had been named the industry's best-selling plaything. He had been surrounded by a score of people hanging on his every directive. Now here he was out on his own, in a tiny cubicle equipped only with a desk and a phone. My, how times had changed.

When the 1981 Toy Fair offered convincing proof that *Merlin* would not survive another season as anything but an also-ran, it had been decided that it and others of Stearns's moribund electronic games would be shifted over to Bruce Jones and his board-game marketing team. Under Jones's supervision, sales of *Merlin, Code Name: Sector,* and the other electronic playthings could die a quiet death when their sales stalled out for good. In the meantime, Stearns would be free to begin looking for the next big hit.

His was a burdensome responsibility. Parker Brothers was in desperate need of something to fill the revenue crater that the hand-held electronics implosion was going to create. But Stearns knew before he started that he'd be recommending video games. That was where the big plays were being made these days. Besides, if Stearns had to pick how he wanted to spend his own time over the next year or so, video was his choice.

Stearns considered himself an arcade-games freak from way back, having pumped quarters into *Pong* machines in Ithaca, New York, while his wife studied cases for law school. And he'd been one of Parker Brothers's proponents back in 1977 for looking into video. Now, as was predicted back then, video was back and the once-exorbitant prices of the products were down. Plus, while earlier video-game systems could play just one game, the industry's newly programmable consoles provided far greater flexibility—you changed the game merely by plugging in another cartridge. The trick for Stearns was to find the strategy that would allow Parker Brothers to attack the market in a proprietary way.

For staff the 30-year-old Stearns snared Bill Bracy, a man ten years his senior. Bracy had been among Bernie Loomis's managerial installations in Europe. When Loomis stepped down from the group vice presidency, Bracy joined Parker Brothers as manager of special projects, working out of an out-of-the-way cubicle in the purchasing department. In that capacity he had made the rounds of the company, spending time in sales, marketing, and a number of support functions. There were no high-level strings pulled to win Bracy's availability; Stearns simply called him aside during a play-testing session and told him they were going to share a mission: to get Parker Brothers into video. Bracy readily agreed.

This new game-playing genre looked to be the wave of the future. In calendar 1981, U.S. sales of video game systems and software cartridges were expected to triple, to $1.2 billion. Already some were predicting them to double again in 1982, to more than

$2 billion. By comparison, sales of all other toys and games would rise only 6 percent to $4.9 billion in 1981, and probably not much more than that in years to come.

Outrageous as it would have once seemed, a $2 billion market for video games was not at all unlikely, given their rapid proliferation. Already there were an estimated 35 million video-arcade gamesters in the U.S., and a single game, Atari's *Asteroids,* had made enough money to land the company well onto the bottom tier of the *Fortune* 500.

From the offense, Stearns and Bracy saw lots of money to be made if the projections were wrong by half. Atari had gone from zero to more than $700 million in revenue already, and seemed a sure thing to hit its own $2 billion mark within a couple of years. And look at Activision of Santa Clara, California, founded by a group of Atari defectors: It had been shipping cartridges only since mid-1980, and already the company was selling at an annual revenue rate of $50 million per year.

But Stearns and Bracy felt Parker Brothers's interest in video was really defensive. By staying out of the market, Parker Brothers could be committing corporate suicide—if it was indeed true what they and some of the rest of the industry suspected, that the cardboard of more traditional games was giving way to silicon chips forever.

Through the early stages of their exploration, marketing vice president Ron Jackson remained skeptical of Stearns's and Bracy's enthusiasm. It was already late in the game, he warned, pointing out that most of the current entrants were in the market before 1980. To go in now would be like becoming the tenth man on a baseball squad: There wouldn't be a lot left to do.

Others in-house agreed. Experienced employees, especially those on the traditional side of the company, considered video a highly risky fad—one very much like the hand-held electronics boom that had just gone bust. "I just don't see it being a long-term business," said board-game marketer Bruce Jones, shrugging off the video trend. *"Merlin* wasn't, was it?"

One of the few friends that Stearns, Bracy, and their video dreams could claim was product-development director Phil Orbanes, a 32-year-old who had been designing toys since he was a toddler and working for toy companies since the age of 16. Even before

Stearns had given up his *Merlin* responsibilities, Orbanes was doing some exploration on the sly, using company resources in ways that were unauthorized but acknowledged. Having convinced Ron Jackson to buy him a costly reverse-engineering computer, Orbanes had corralled some technical people to do research on silicon chips and circuitry. It was a time-consuming project, and gains were incremental at best.

Everything began to come together, however, as spring was budding the trees. Kenner's president, Joe Mendelsohn, informed Jim Fifield that Lucasfilm Ltd., the producer of *Star Wars,* had dangled its video license before Kenner's nose. The production company had gone to Mendelsohn as a matter of courtesy, since Kenner wasn't in the video business. It sought simply to put Mendelsohn on notice that it intended to license the property to a video-game manufacturer, probably Atari.

Fifield, like Mendelsohn, recognized the competitive opportunity as one that wouldn't keep. But Fifield was not inclined to let any one of his Toy Group companies, much less all of them, pursue the market willy-nilly. One would get the nod, just one. But whichever company it was would have to prove itself worthy. In the memo he sent out, he asked each company to come prepared to talk about how it would approach the market. Fifield would sit in judgment.

Fifield's timing couldn't have been much better, from Parker Brothers's perspective. Stearns had gone into his new-ventures job in April. He and Bracy were about ready to reveal a video strategy by the end of June. Now here was the meeting, coming up at the end of July. To top it off, Ron Jackson had announced his resignation during the same transitional period, assuming the presidency of The Talbots, Inc., a women's sportswear chain that was part of the General Mills Specialty Retailing Group. All of Parker Brothers wished Jackson well, but Stearns was less ambivalent than most in watching Jackson go. With his marketing nemesis gone, there appeared to be one less hurdle to be cleared in getting Parker Brothers into the rapidly expanding market for home video.

Now the only real roadblock that remained was Kenner. On size and swagger alone, the company had led the Toy Group since Bernie Loomis pulled it out of near-bankruptcy. Besides, Kenner

had already won "intergalactic" rights to the *Star Wars* toy line,
which for four years had equalled or exceeded the revenue volume
of *Cheerios*—$100 million per year. Possession being nine-tenths of
the law, simply having the license seemed to give Kenner the
inside track in the video race.

Still, the troops in Beverly stubbornly refused to believe that
Kenner had to be the hands-down victor. Parker Brothers had
shown itself to be no slouch of late; with the arrival of hand-
held electronic games in 1977, Parker Brothers had grown by 30
percent per year. So fast had the company grown, in fact, that
plans were on the drawing board to double the size of the Beverly
headquarters. But most of all, Stearns and Bracy felt it could
and should be argued that video games were just that—*games*—
and therefore more properly Parker Brothers's domain than Kenner's. Then again, when had turf issues been that clearcut in the
Toy Group?

Stearns and Bracy elected to take no chances. Despite the fact
that Fifield had billed the meeting as merely an opportunity for
discussion, Stearns and Bracy prepared as if it were to be a major
product-development presentation. They began pulling together a
full-fledged business plan.

Isolating the strategic options was a no-brainer. There were
only three ways for Parker Brothers, or any entrant, to go:
hardware (video consoles) only, software (game cartridges) only,
or some combination of the two. Forget any option involving
hardware, said Stearns and Bracy—Parker Brothers had enough
trouble keeping its chips together with *Merlin*. Besides, Atari and
Mattel's *Intellivision* were already scrapping over which would be
the dominant console system. The market didn't need another to
confuse the issue.

Software-only, namely cartridges: that would be the ticket.
Why should Parker Brothers design a new record player if it
could get away with just selling records? Why make the razor if
they could peddle the blades?

The next question was which "record player" or "razor"
Parker Brothers should design for, and the answer was painfully
obvious: Whichever one they *could* design them for. Each of the
systems on the market accepted only the cartridges that were
specifically encoded for their hardware. If Parker Brothers wanted

to make cartridges for somebody else's system, the company would first have to break that somebody's code.

This became Orbanes's self-appointed mission. He closeted two engineers in a back room to pore over photomicrographs of the Atari chip, which had been blown up to poster size to more easily trace its circuitry. "We've got to be clean, do all the legwork ourselves," Orbanes explained to Barton, as the older man donned his bifocals to ponder the mazes of solder on the circuit boards. Parker Brothers would run afoul of the law if it in any way copied or stole Atari's proprietary expertise. Figuring out what made the Atari system tick through reverse engineering—slow and painstaking as it was—was four-square legal.

Late nights and early mornings were the drill as Parker Brothers readied its plan. Within days of the actual meeting, all was in readiness and Stearns was typing up his marketing information. Then, suddenly, Dick Dalessio, the man who had replaced Ron Jackson as Stearns's boss in marketing, couldn't attend the session and Orbanes came down with a flu bug that laid him too low to carry the presentation on his own. Stearns would have to pinch-hit for Dalessio. It would prove to be one of the luckiest breaks in Stearns's young career.

The night before the fateful meeting, Barton found a team taut with anxiety awaiting him in New York. With Stearns fidgeting and Orbanes gray with his virus, Barton was only too glad to play the role of coach. In something of a pre-game peptalk, he admonished Stearns and Orbanes to avoid over-confidence and stay calm and gracious throughout the meeting—especially through a certain surprise announcement planned for the end of their presentation. "I don't want to see any Cheshire-cat looks," Barton said. "They'll only come back to haunt us."

The meeting convened in the more-spacious conference room of Bernie Loomis's new M.A.D. offices, located across the street from Toy Group headquarters. Still, the assemblage was unusually small at an even dozen participants. Fifield had asked each company to keep its delegation down to a maximum of four people.

Exercising his home-court advantage, and perhaps the clout of having been a Toy Group executive, Loomis and his group led off. Armed with drawings and easels, Loomis—now derisively referred to in some quarters as "the M.A.D. consultant"—described an ambitious proposal for the design and production of both video hardware and software. He called his idea Operation Leap-Frog, a self-assertive name that left Stearns and Orbanes suppressing smirks.

Loomis and the M.A.D. men envisioned a pay-per-play system whereby a satellite would transmit a variety of games to a home videoplayer. The actual selection and purchase of the game would take place in shopping-center kiosks. And, if all of that weren't Buck Rogers enough, Operation Leap-Frog featured a variety of accessories—3-D glasses, headphones, even a gun to shoot at the screen. Loomis's group seemed to garner points for creativity, but no one in the meeting rushed to support their gee-whiz notions. Not atypically, Loomis seemed to have overreached.

Kenner went next. But, to most everyone's surprise, its delegation offered no specific proposal. President Joe Mendelsohn had apparently taken Fifield's memo quite literally—his troops had come well-read, with opinions to offer and questions to ask. They mentioned a couple of hardware options. Then discussion turned to the safer suggestion that the Toy Group simply license its properties to Atari. Given the early handicapping that favored Kenner, its was an anticlimactic performance.

Fifield then turned to Barton. "Ranny?"

Barton replied by turning to Stearns, who was already assembling his notes. "Rich?" Fifield followed Barton's gaze with a look of curious interest. Stearns was the only man in the room whose face was unfamiliar to Fifield.

Stearns began the Parker Brothers presentation with a description of the burgeoning video-game market. Arcade video machines would eat almost $8 billion in 25-cent pieces in that year, 1981, and purchases of home video equipment were snowballing. Already 3.5 percent of U.S. households were video-equipped, and the most conservative projections called for a doubling by the end of the year. True, expectations were that sales of dedicated video-game systems would level off in a few years, but only as the result of a switch in preference for the next phase in the market, the introduction of home-computer video.

With the increased power and sophistication of the home computer, the game-playing possibilities seemed endless and exciting, enthused Stearns. Video represented a new and revolutionary technology for entertainment, especially in games. It could not be ignored; it had to be exploited. As Stearns saw it, Parker Brothers was like a buggy-whip manufacturer staring into the grille of an automobile: It had come face to face with the future. But this time the wheel was a semiconductor. If *Merlin* and his electronic buddies were the biggest thing for the toys industry since plastic, video was going to have the society-transforming implications of steel over stone.

Stearns acknowledged that the competition was stiff and likely to get stiffer. Atari, the company that pioneered arcade video with *Pong,* had been in the market with home video consoles and cartridges since 1980. Next in line was Mattel's *Intellivision,* followed by Activision. Atari was the monster, with 80 percent of the market, and it—like competitor Mattel—manufactured its own hardware. The new kid on the block, Activision, was piggybacking on Atari's system with impunity—though Atari had launched a lawsuit to try to put a stop to it, claiming Activision's expatriate founders had stolen the secrets to Atari's cartridge code.

If Parker Brothers were to go into this business, it ought to do it on the cartridge side, advised Stearns. To produce its own dedicated system would be foolhardy at this stage of the game, he reasoned. "Somebody will come along and make our system look like the steam engine before we know it." Fifield, who seemed impressed by Stearns, nodded appreciatively. "We could be looking down the barrel of an IBM in three or four years."

Obviously, Stearns continued, Parker Brothers had an advantage in developing cartridges, as it understood the games business as almost no one else did. But the company lacked the necessary distribution channels, and therefore would have take steps to produce cartridges that would automatically "open doors to us." Those cartridges should be Atari-compatible, Stearns said, and imbued with all the play value Parker Brothers was capable of mustering. Parker Brothers could perhaps staff up with enough technical people to begin inventing its own games, as Mattel and Activision had, but Stearns saw greater speed and success in Atari's strategy: buying up licenses to leading arcade games such as *Space Invaders, Asteroids,* and *Pac-Man.*

"We've got to aim for the rights to some of the biggest names, games, and characters in the world—particularly those that are already popular in the arcades," Stearns said. To further establish itself, and to avoid getting caught in what Stearns described as "the inevitable shakeout," the company would advertise heavily from the beginning, so as to become viewed by the video game-playing public as a premiere provider of game cartridges.

Then it came time to talk money. The market's barriers to entry were only ankle-high, asserted Stearns, as the bulk of the overhead would come from the acquisition of licenses. Pricey as those rights were likely to be, production costs would be minimal. Each cartridge consisted merely of a simple plastic housing containing a memory chip that stored the game program, plus a few small springs to hold the plug-in cartridge in place. All told, the material would cost less than $4. But the finished product would retail for four or five times that much. Stearns pegged the anticipated first-year revenues for Parker Brothers at "$10 to $15 million, no sweat."

By then, everyone in the room was clamoring to know how Parker Brothers intended to design around the patents on Atari's exclusive software. Obligingly, Orbanes rose to provide the afternoon's magic act. Parker Brothers, he announced, had cracked the Atari code. By reverse-engineering the California company's own game cartridges, the design team in Beverly had discovered how to make Atari-compatible cartridges without courting the $20 million patent lawsuit that Atari had filed against Activision. "We're clean," proclaimed the still-ailing Orbanes, in the most expansive tone he could muster. There was no possession of inside information; the coup was strictly the result of reverse engineering. Orbanes presented a listing of the codes with which the cartridges had been programmed, and pointed out the patterns within them that revealed their meaning and function.

The reaction to Orbanes's announcement was subdued. But there didn't have to be cheers or gnashing of teeth to know that Parker Brothers had blown the meeting wide open. Amid the shrugging shoulders, shaking heads, sighs, and chuckles around the conference table, little needed to be said. Certainly there was no decree necessary from Fifield. Parker Brothers had gotten the Toy Group's video go-ahead by acclamation.

One of the few who spoke was a surprisingly magnanimous Bernie Loomis. It seemed to him, he said, that Parker Brothers was the company best equipped to take the Toy Group into the video market. Afterward, that moment was all Barton wanted to talk about. "Did you see Bernie's face? Did you?"

Ecstatic as they were with the outcome, there was to be no post-presentation celebration for Barton, Stearns, and Orbanes that day. Barton had more meetings to attend before flying home. Orbanes repaired to a friend's house to nurse his flu, where he spent the next four days in a headachey haze. A tired but excited Stearns flew home.

"How'd it go?" Renée Stearns asked her husband as he slumped into a chair that night. Not bad, not bad at all, he replied. Parker Brothers had, indeed, gotten the video nod. And *he* had been tapped to head a marketing and development SWAT team on the project. A small, weary smile spread across his face. "I think our lives changed today," he said. He committed the date to memory: July 28, 1981.

General Mills wasted no time in getting the word out. The news was ballyhooed in the fiscal 1981 annual report, released just weeks after the July meeting in New York: Parker Brothers would be the Toy Group's entrant in the video-game market. It would introduce its first game cartridges the following June.

Fiscal 1981 had been another year of enviable progress for the General Mills Toy Group—now the leader in a worldwide toys market that totaled $11.5 billion in sales. Operating profits grew 17.5 percent, to a record $70.6 million and sales reached $674.3 million, a gain of 4.2 percent. General Mills proudly reported that the Toy Group's operating profits had grown at a compound annual rate of 12.4 percent over the previous five years.

But the video announcement allowed Parker Brothers to save face in what otherwise would have been an embarrassing annual report for the Beverly gamesmakers. Despite having achieved sales growth of 35 percent in its electronics category for the year just ended, the company had been forced by market conditions to project declines for fiscal 1982. Now there was at least hope of picking up the slack with video. At the annual meeting in September, shareholders applauded the news.

The emergence of General Mills and its Toy Group as a player in the video market only served to compound the growing esteem in which the Minneapolis-based conglomerate was held. General Mills's overall revenues now ran to a tidy $4.9 billion, roughly a third of which came from ten subsidiaries in food, toys, and fashions. The percentage of profit that came from these non-food divisions was just as impressive—something more than 50 percent. As diversifiers went, General Mills was regarded as among the best.

In December of 1981, *Dun's Business Month* honored General Mills as an "All-American Marketer." The magazine lauded the company for having demonstrated an uncommon ability to "identify potentially dynamic new businesses and develop them through aggressive marketing and astute competitive positioning." Commented CEO Bruce Atwater, "The nature of our consumer businesses means that innovation and risk-taking are the critical skills. That just means competing better than the next guy, and I think we've done pretty well."

Indeed, General Mills was gaining a reputation as a big company with an entrepreneurial flair throughout its operations, certainly not just within the Toy Group. Sales zoomed from $1 million to $50 million in the first three years after the company acquired *Yoplait* yogurt and expanded it to include *Yoplait Custard-Style Yogurt.* Noticing a surge of interest for the *Izod* sportswear line it acquired in 1969 and added to its Fashion Group, General Mills put the distinctive alligator logo on virtually everything the company produced—and the line's revenues grew from $30 million to $300 million.

Still, even as the financial press was crowing over the fact that General Mills's next fearless foray would be video—and the admiring hoopla continued over General Mills's ventures in food and fashion—a more cautious strategy was coming into focus through the squarish horn-rim glasses of Bruce Atwater.

The onetime product manager of *Potato Buds,* who had recently moved up from the presidency, sized up his conglomerate with apparent concern. Although General Mills's revenues and earnings had marched ahead "with the precision of a well-drilled Marine platoon," as *Financial World* put it, the company's stock had been "marching in place" for almost a decade. Seven times since 1972 the share price had broken into the low to mid-$30 range, only to retreat. It was always something: If it wasn't the lousy stock-market of the 1970s that was the culprit, then it was the more recent competition of sexier energy and technology stocks.

Atwater considered it a particularly opportune time to try again to break the jinx. Consumer stocks, particularly food shares, were gaining in shareholder popularity. Many investors were once again gravitating toward General Mills for its stable growth and bankable yields. Still, while the company's return on equity had hovered around 17 percent, well above average, the shares hadn't yet commanded top dollar. Even at a price of $35, the shares were at a meager eight times projected earnings, and nine times current earnings.

Eight or nine wasn't enough for a company banking on annual sales and earnings increases of at least 15 percent over the next five years, in Atwater's opinion. Something was wrong. When asked for their assessment, analysts said they thought it was the company's non-food business that was depressing the ratio. After all, General Mills's was a blue-chip stock, and blue-chip buyers were more insistent than most in seeing good returns coupled with steady growth. Steadily as they had grown over the last few years, there was always the potential for volatility in trend-oriented industries such as toys, fashion, and specialty retailing—one had only to look at the *Riviton* debacle to see that. The non-food companies seemed to be dampening investor ardor for General Mills shares.

Atwater understood and shared the concern. He hadn't made it any secret that he was among those who believed General Mills had diversified too widely. From the mid-1970s on, certainly since Atwater had succeeded Jim McFarland in 1977, General Mills had quit seeding new business and begun weeding out poorly performing lines in each segment. Aside from some expansion in the Restaurants division, there was a *de facto* moratorium on new acquisitions. Some of the earlier purchases, in fact, were being revamped. There were even rumors that some might be sold or restructured.

Seeking to put renewed emphasis on profitability, Atwater committed the company to a highly ambitious goal: General Mills would hike its average return on shareholder equity to 19 percent by 1984. Surely such stellar performance would be rewarded with a higher share price. To aid in pushing the additional dollars to the bottom line, Atwater set out to consolidate some of his operations. After more than a decade of decentralization, General Mills would be managerially centralized once again.

By 1980 two vice chairmen with small staffs divided responsibility for the organization. One, F. Caleb "Cal" Blodgett, headed Consumer Foods, Commercial Foods, the International Division, and many functional support divisions. The other vice chairman, former Toy Group executive Don Swanson, headed Restaurants, Direct Marketing, Specialty Retailing, Toys, and Fashions.

Within this new configuration, Atwater scaled back operations to focus on five core divisions: Consumer Foods, Restaurants, Toys, Fashion, and Specialty Retailing. He then began trying to build market share in these segments, usually by identifying and pursuing one key consumer trend. Restaurants, where the Red Lobster chain was booming and producing record earnings, now launched another chain called The Good Earth to address the health-food craze. Fashion increased the *Izod* line to capitalize on its popularity as part of a preppie uniform. *Yoplait* yogurt and the *Nature Valley* line of cereals were the vehicles for Consumer Foods. In the Toy Group, of course, the great white hope was video.

These many changes set the stage for the 1981 announcement that any savvy division head had seen coming: The days of managerial autonomy, long on the wane, were now over. Each division would have to live up to a series of hard-and-fast financial goals and restrictions, the overall intent of which was to keep General Mills aware of even the most incremental changes in company performance. Working-capital loans, for example, would now cost 13 percent instead of 7 percent, and those companies that exceeded working-capital guidelines to build too much inventory would face hefty financial penalties. Some tracking reports would become weekly instead of monthly. "We can deal with problems, but we don't like surprises," commented Don Swanson.

There was even talk—apparently never implemented—of putting chief executive officers through an interpersonal training program that stressed delegation, succession planning, and other skills that they were judged to lack. "You've got to do things differently when you get to a certain size, or you're going to suffer," explained Atwater.

Some of the fashion companies, including Izod-LaCoste (the sportswear manufacturer), Footjoy (shoes), and Lark Luggage complained bitterly—and in the latter two cases, publicly—about what they said were already formidable reporting chores and tight purse strings. Nonetheless, Ranny Barton, always one to support the home office, was broad-minded. "They seem realistic," he told *Business Week* of the new rules.

Barton had reason to sound content in the face of change. Business had been relative bliss for him since Jim Fifield had been installed in Bernie Loomis's place. Though some of Barton's colleagues and subordinates still feared Fifield, and the man's own staff in New York seemed to regard him respectfully but warily, Barton had nothing but admiration for the rigor and discipline Fifield had restored to the Toy Group. Never had he quaked in Fifield's presence as others had; all Barton felt was excitement, and the heady euphoria of possibilities.

Now that Parker Brothers had become the Toy Group's standard-bearer in video, Fifield made the company and its emerging product line his project, spending a large percentage of his time either in Beverly or on the phone with people in Beverly. Fifield devoted hours to conversing with Barton on matters of strategy, making sure the Parker Brothers president understood both how to implement the plan and why it was important. In so doing, Fifield had seemed to go out of his way to win Barton's allegiance.

Fifield's unblinking attention on Parker Brothers served to put plenty of pressure on Barton—probably no less than Loomis had. But Fifield applied it far less oppressively. He rarely issued orders, for example. Instead, he would gently point out some perceived omission in Barton's planning, or cite some error in his reasoning, and then muse aloud about an alternate approach. If Barton seemed too willing to capitulate to Fifield's suggestion, Fifield pulled him up short. "Just go home and think about it. Call me in the morning."

By the next day, Barton would have taken the solution as his own. When Barton then called to thank Fifield for his valued perspective, the young Toy Group executive would lean back in his chair, his usually somber mask relaxing into that half-grin

of his. "Hey, don't forget, I'm here to be used," he would demur.
"You challenge my thinking, too, you know."

Fifield reassured the games company president regularly, in
dozens of small gestures, that it was truly Barton—the last remaining Parker family member—who was running the show.
Barton, describing himself as "all fired up" by his new sense of
participation, went on to reach the apogee of what still had been
a fairly unremarkable managerial career. His enhanced role was
a credit to Fifield's considerable motivational skills, and Barton
acknowledged it: The Toy Group executive had virtually taken
Barton by the hand and led him into a more aggressive managerial
game—one which allowed Barton to feel like the indispensable
character he'd always hoped he'd be.

At Fifield's direction, it was Barton who became the keeper
of a corporate checkbook with a $5 million credit line. Instead of
tapping some rising young executive for the duty, Fifield made
it Barton's job to negotiate many of the foreign game licenses
Parker Brothers would acquire, particularly those originating in
the Far East. It proved to be a near-perfect match of personality
and job description—that is, once Barton got the hang of it.

Barton's first trip to the Orient was an unmitigated flop. On
arrival at the design company, he was ushered by a young woman
into a sitting room spread with tatami and low couches, then
joined by five to eight men—only one of whom acknowledged any
fluency in English. Together they drank green tea, and presently
the English-speaking executive asked Ranny his purpose in visiting.

"Gentlemen," Ranny announced, in his most measured tones,
"I wish to purchase the American home video rights to one of
your very popular video arcade games."

The men spoke together in Japanese for two minutes, five
minutes—then, to Ranny's consternation, they all smilingly stood,
bowed, and walked out. When the young woman returned a
moment later, it was to accompany the befuddled Barton to the
door.

Barton went straight to the executives in General Mills's
Asian operations for advice. They listened to Barton's story and
laughed gently. Barton had made the mistake of stating his

business too soon. "You must make many trips before you divulge the nature of your trip," he was told. "Four trips at least."

Once he got the protocol straight, Barton was a hit with the Japanese. Not only had he the good breeding of the North Shore aristocracy to recommend him, he represented the family behind the company—which brought to the negotiating table a sense of tradition that the Japanese seemed to appreciate. To them Barton was the shōgun, the ceremonial presence, the very embodiment of the Parker Brothers's tradition. Barton also had in his favor a natural sense of diplomatic timing. Unlike some of the impatient young tigers under him, including Rich Stearns, Barton knew when to push negotiations and when to hang back and drink tea. He had a knack for guessing what cards the other side was holding, and a sixth sense for how to play his own.

Barton shuttled back and forth from Japan eighteen times between September of 1981 and the end of 1982, meeting manufacturers and hobnobbing with the other American toys-industry executives he met in airports or company lobbies. So frequently was he in Tokyo, in fact, that employees began calling him "Barton-san." Even Fifield joined the good-natured ribbing, referring to Ranny as "Lanny."

As Barton courted the foreigners, Stearns and Bracy worked the domestic licensors. In contrast to Barton's studied diplomacy, their approach was direct, to say the least. Without so much as a letter of introduction, one or the other would simply call the company, ask for the president, and request a meeting. Seldom did they get in, however, without having to offer a long and detailed introduction of their company and its video strategy. To most video-related companies, Parker Brothers was an unknown in 1981. "It's just like Carter in '76," quipped Stearns. "Jimmy who?" Or, in this case, "Parker what?" More than once they were asked if theirs was the company that made the fountain pens.

Licensing success came slowly. Parker Brothers offered $250,000 for *Donkey Kong,* one of the most popular Japanese-designed arcade video games of the day, only to lose it to Arnold Greenberg and his samurai from Coleco. Other deals arose and were clinched before the company even got wind of them. But, just as the most addicted video-game player always tended to be the one who was losing, failure only strengthened the company's resolve. Just one big license was all it would take to gain Parker Brothers admission into all future bidding sessions, Stearns, Bracy, and Barton told themselves—just one.

The license that Stearns most coveted was *Frogger,* Los Angeles-based Sega/Gremlin's most successful game. Like *Pac-Man,* the game was cute and simple enough to appeal to people who didn't ordinarily cozy up to a video game, but challenging enough to present an interesting contest for the accomplished player— someone the trade increasingly referred to with a straight face as a "video athlete."

Unlike most video games—which were predominantly shoot 'em down, eat 'em up, knock 'em over, or blow 'em away endeavors— *Frogger* was a rescue game. The frog's job was to rescue a froggy maiden—without getting hit by a car, bitten by snakes, or drowned. With its colorful graphics and its engaging audio personality, the game left Stearns positively smitten. He waited impatiently for it to be put out for bids.

In the autumn of 1981, soon after *Frogger*'s arcade debut, Parker Brothers made an offer of $250,000 for the home video rights, with an almost heart-stopping royalty guarantee of 8 percent. The highest royalty guarantee that Parker Brothers had even considered to that point was 6 percent. The deal, like most of its day, also tied the designer's potential take to the success of the game's arcade sales. This sort of structure was created to make sure that manufacturers such as Parker Brothers didn't pay big bucks on something that turned out to be a flop in the arcades. Arcade popularity, after all, determined which home games were also popular in the stores.

After presenting the bid, Stearns stayed close to the phone all afternoon. Finally the call came, and the tone of the voice on the other end of the line told him all he needed to know. The Sega/Gremlin representative said he hated to be the bearer of bad news, but somebody else had won the license. Stearns tried to sound nonchalant in defeat, but after hanging up he went to Ranny Barton's office in the mood to suggest ritual suicide.

Barton looked at Stearns quizzically on hearing the news, as if he weren't certain what Stearns was telling him. "We needed this one, right?"

Stearns nodded glumly.

"It's get-it-or-forget-it for us?"

A shrug and a nod.

"Well, would half a million do it?"

Stearns, brightening, said it damn well should.

Together they called Sega/Gremlin and asked for twenty minutes to confer on a new bid. Dialing again, Barton caught Fifield going out the door for the day and asked for a consultation.

With his watch unstrapped and laid before him on the desk, Barton sketched out the details of the situation for Fifield as quickly as he could. "They gave us twenty minutes to consider another bid, Jim," Barton concluded, "and now it's down to nineteen. What do you think?"

There was a long silence.

"About eighteen minutes left, Jim."

More silence, punctuated with the sounds of shuffling papers and an occasional sigh. Finally Fifield spoke: "That's a lot of money. What are you *doing,* Ranny? What am *I* doing?"

Barton still hadn't heard a clear answer. He was getting nervous, flicking at the strap of his watch. "So are we off or on, Jim?"

"You've said it yourself," Fifield replied with finality. "We gotta have it."

Without stopping for so much as a triumphant smile, Stearns disconnected the line for Barton and re-dialed. He handed the receiver back when he got the right party on the line.

"We're prepared to go to half a million dollars," Barton told the Sega/Gremlin representative. "Will that change anything?"

It might, came the response. The board of directors would re-assemble and get back in touch.

That night, at home, Stearns received a call telling him that Parker Brothers's revised offer had been accepted. "We're in business," Stearns advised his marketing cohort, Bracy.

As expected, winning the license to *Frogger* proved to be the watershed event for Parker Brothers. Now, not only did these Yankee gamesmakers have a *Star Wars* title to offer the trade at the 1982 Toy Fair, but also this new arcade hit. Neither game was actually ready to sell, but each was well into development. That was all that was necessary to be taken seriously in the market. Based on favorable preliminary reaction from the trade, a cautiously optimistic Stearns bumped his sales projections up to $20 million.

Then came end-of-the-year figures showing that the top American manufacturers—led by Atari and Mattel—sold every home video console and cartridge they could manufacture. Almost overnight Stearns's first-year forecast of $20 million was obsolete. So obsolete, in fact, that he could have spoken of $100 million in revenues without feeling foolish.

As the market became larger and more lucrative, companies of every description swooped in, hoping to make a quick killing on a modest investment. CBS set up game-licensing agreements with arcade video king Bally Manufacturing Corporation, and snapped up Ideal Toy Corporation to bolster the distribution network for its home video cartridges. Quaker Oats Company entered the market by acquiring game designer U.S. Games Inc.

Meanwhile, the only major toys companies that hadn't become key players in the video market were Hasbro and Milton Bradley. Hasbro's non-participation, decreed by a beleaguered board of directors that forbade management from taking the risk, came as little surprise. Since 1979, when Hasbro failed to join the rest of the industry in marketing hand-held electronic games, Wall Streeters had dubbed the company "Has-been."

But Milton Bradley's was the cautionary tale, fraught as it was with bad luck and lousy timing. Back in 1978, the company had developed a TV-connected game only to scuttle it, concluding that video technology was an overpriced fad. In 1981, as Parker Brothers shifted to home video, Milton Bradley continued to place its bets on hand-held electronic games—and watched its sales in that category plunge by one-third. The company then tried to enter the cartridge market with video versions of *Yahtzee* and *Hangman,* but tied them to what proved to be the wrong console— Texas Instruments's short-lived *Gamevision* system. The games-makers pulled their cartridges off the market in 1980 and announced that they were looking for a new-generation video system. But it was widely acknowledged that Milton Bradley was simply marking time and hoping its luck would improve.

Through the first half of 1982, as Parker Brothers's first game cartridges were entering the final glide path, the video games business continued to grow "beyond anybody's wildest dream," as an unusually enthusiastic *Business Week* put it. Not even the recession seemed able to slow it.

With just weeks to go before the shipment of the company's first video cartridges, Stearns and Bracy called all managers together to talk seriously about what Parker Brothers was getting itself into. They had to be sure the company was behind them all the way.

"We've got to do this right, or not do it at all," said Stearns. "The competition is making big commitments of dollars and personnel. We can't do video the Parker Brothers way," he said, taking a jab at the company's traditional conservatism. "We've got to talk bigger royalties—millions of dollars—and lots of people. Sure, we've got ten or fifteen people on staff, but we're going to need fifty." He asked for everyone's solemn pledge of support to this all-out effort, and he got it.

But, between the lines, Stearns was also asking for a personal vote of confidence. That would not be as easily won. He was bucking for a promotion that seemed frustratingly out of reach.

The issue wasn't skill; nobody at Parker Brothers refused to pay Stearns his due as a marketer. By anyone's measure, the guy had a knack for picking a winning game. Singling out *Frogger* from all the dozens available in both the U.S. and the Far East was lucky, if not inspired. Nothing he'd learned at Wharton about strategic planning or marketing research had much to do with it, either; Stearns was a natural. Like any successful toy designer or marketer going back to time immemorial, Stearns possessed that combination of love and lunacy that allowed him to take the right flyers.

Total immersion had something to do with it, too. Stearns and cohort Bracy spent their lunch hours going mano-a-mano with the pimply-faced 14-year-olds at the local arcades in the North Shore and Liberty Tree Malls. At first, they passed off their $5-per-day expenditures on *Centipede* or *Galaxian* or *Donkey Kong,* as marketing research. Later on they dropped even tongue-in-cheek attempts to portray the forays as business-related. After all, the two of them had racked up so many points on their favorite machines that they had practically turned them over, like a ten-year-old Chevy's odometer. It became an in-house joke that their expense vouchers should be reimbursed in rolls of quarters.

Financial and advertising executives who traveled with the pair watched with amusement as the two would run for the nearest video arcade at each airport, ties and briefcases trailing behind them. Video had become their vice. Other men may have gotten their jollies from reading *Playboy,* but these guys got theirs from *Playthings,* and the official arcade video-game mag *Play Meter.* It said a lot about the times that Stearns and Bracy were then regarded as among the five or ten best-versed video-game marketers in the country. Marketing experts were being made almost as fast as games designers were becoming millionaires.

But to his higher-ups at Parker Brothers, Stearns's youthful exuberance sometimes seemed less than discriminating, and his outspokenly opinionated style fell just this side of rebelliousness. Talented as he was, Stearns bore keeping an eye on.

Stearns thought the caution was unwarranted after his success with *Merlin.* Already he had gotten job feelers from competitors, some of whom had dangled v.p. titles before his nose. Why shouldn't he be accorded the same recognition at Parker Brothers? Particularly now, when the job he wanted was open?

Stearns's boss, marketing vice president Dick Dalessio, had been dismissed just weeks before. It was a move that was generally assumed to have been inspired, if not directed, by Jim Fifield—who had made it clear he was no fan of Dalessio's fairly laid-back management style. He was another Jackson where developmental caution was concerned.

It was Dalessio himself who had informed Stearns of his impending departure and, interestingly enough, he who advised Stearns to seek the job. "They won't give it to you; you're too young," said Dalessio. "But it would be good for you, you know, to be aggressive enough to ask."

Dalessio proved right. Even as his responsibilities grew and his stock rose with headhunters, Stearns remained only the *de facto* boss of what had become known as the "electronic side" of Parker Brothers. No title was forthcoming.

Laser lights of various hues played off CEO Bruce Atwater's eyeglasses as a throbbing disco beat pulsed from a bank of huge audio speakers. On a room-sized screen above the crowd played the graphics from Parker Brothers's first game cartridge, based on a battle scene from the movie sequel to *Star Wars*. It was called *The Empire Strikes Back*.

General Mills formally introduced the Parker Brothers line of video-game cartridges in June of 1982, at a Minneapolis reception that was uncharacteristically glitzy in all respects. Customers were flown in first class (*first class?*). After a series of product presentations, the sessions adjourned to cocktails and dinner, which were followed by the laser show (*lasers?*) and an appearance by comedian Alan King (*Alan King?*).

Flashy and exorbitant as the event seemed for General Mills—and seemingly all the attendees were commenting that it was both—the purpose of the fete was to remind the trade that Parker Brothers was part of the Big G family. It went into this new and exciting video market with the full faith and credit of the conglomerate standing behind it.

As well it should: Parker Brothers's video unit was off to a smashing start, reporting $60 million in orders almost immediately. *Frogger* contributed $40 million, while the *Star Wars* entry was responsible for $20 million of the total. By the end of the calendar year the new video category would rack up sales of $74 million for Parker Brothers, on which the company stood to earn $20 million.

The atmosphere at Parker Brothers was as much one of relief as excitement. True to expectations, the company had missed its program, fallen short of its revenue goals for fiscal 1982, and suffered a decline in profitability—all thanks to the final and thundering collapse of the hand-held electronics market. Family, word, and card game categories also declined, affected by the surge in video items. Without the introduction of the video line to take up the slack, Parker Brothers would have lost half of its $115 million in revenue. The timing in making the switch to video was as close as anyone would have wanted to cut it. "We almost missed the boat by at least a year," as Stearns later assessed it.

Stearns and Bracy began making tentative plans to expand the company's video line to twenty cartridges over the next two years, an expansion that they expected to generate cumulative sales in the $200 million range once the now-exclusively domestic distribution was expanded overseas.

But that was not the only change occasioned by the successful introduction of the first video cartridges. As if recognizing the legitimacy of the new line of products, Jim Fifield reached down into Ranny Barton's company to split the once-unified marketing group in half. Stearns, now obviously Fifield's fair-haired boy, was made vice president of consumer electronics. Having made *Frogger* an $80 million phenomenon that was said to out-play even the arcade version, he had been awarded managerial control of the entire video division. In other words, half the company, and about three-quarters of its marketing, design, and engineering talent now came under his joystick-calloused thumb. Bruce Jones took on similar oversight of the traditional games side of the business.

With this change, old chains of command were formally obliterated in recognition of the new ones that had developed. Everything had turned topsy-turvy with video, and it was Stearns who ended up on top. For some time now, Ranny Barton had been more Stearns's colleague than his superior, working together as they had on obtaining foreign and domestic video licenses. And since Stearns was the idea man, the one whose instincts selected the most desirable properties, Barton at times seemed Stearns's subordinate.

Even when Dick Dalessio had stood between Stearns and Barton on the corporate pyramid, Stearns had routinely reported up two layers—past Dalessio, past Barton, straight on to Fifield at Toy Group headquarters in New York. Since the video meeting in New York in July of 1981, the only man Stearns answered to as more than a courtesy was Jim Fifield, and the Toy Group executive kept the reins loose enough to let Stearns have his head. Unlike Bernie Loomis, Fifield rarely had the interest or the patience to sit through a product-review meeting. Nor did he seem inclined to pay attention to the politics at the divisional level, or even who did what and why. Fifield was well acquainted with Barton, Stearns, controller Denny Miller, and board-game marketing vice president Bruce Jones. Still, Parker Brothers to Jim Fifield was far and away Rich Stearns. Because of Fifield's interest in the new video market, and the corresponding closeness of the reporting relationship he established with the young video marketer, he saw the company largely through Stearns's eyes.

It would be too much to say the two men became friends, or even really friendly; aside from an eight-year difference in age, there were obvious differences in style separating them. Stearns, for example, was more frenetic than Fifield ever was, even in his Minneapolis days. And Fifield was more comfortable with life in the fast lane than was Stearns, who identified himself as a born-again Christian. Yet the traits they had in common were the most important. Among them were energy, ambition, and a willingness to stand out among workforces made up mostly of corporate wallflowers. Thus feeling they had something in common, an alliance had developed between Fifield and Stearns over the year since circumstances had introduced them. It virtually made Stearns's career. The two men talked on the phone regularly, and Fifield accompanied Stearns to several foreign trade shows.

Years later Stearns would join a chorus of people who said they had never truly gotten to know Jim Fifield. But Stearns was afforded an earlier and fuller perspective on this starched and suspendered fellow who headed the Toy Group than perhaps anybody who didn't work at his elbow in New York.

In their travels, Fifield spoke of how he loved being out of General Mills's line of sight after sixteen years of corporate rung-climbing—and of running "a $500 million company," the Toy Group, to boot. He still envisioned presiding over General Mills one day, but increasingly, he worried aloud how he would ever leave New York and the almost jet-set lifestyle he had established there. Despite these bits of revelation, Stearns's main impression was of a man who was almost an automaton where business was concerned. Fifield was one of those people for whom winning wasn't the best thing, it was the only thing. He let nothing stand in his way, be it an opponent, a rival colleague, or an inanimate object.

Fifield could walk into a trade show, looking corporate and acting senatorial, then step up to a pinball machine and play for a half hour, sparing no sweat, grunts, or body English, and refusing to move until he'd either beaten it or tilted it. When Fifield made good on his goal of taking the Toy Group whitewater rafting, he plainly got less of a kick from the roiling water than from the accompanying roughhousing: the water fights, the paddle duels, and the ultimate prank, stealing the opposing raft's bailing buckets.

Although Fifield had smoothed the rough edges from his office persona since his Minneapolis days—there were no phones yanked from walls anymore—the stories that circulated showed he had a long way to go to become a shrinking violet. At one cocktail party, he mirthfully told several Kenner staffers and their spouses how he had once settled a tipping dispute with a New York hack by kicking a dent in the side of the cab.

Most who knew him observed Fifield with a mixture of open-mouthed fascination and amusement. If there was one thing Fifield's rough-and-ready image drove home to Stearns and others at Parker Brothers, it was a sense that former no-no's, such as personal spontaneity and flamboyant intramural competition, were not only okay, but desirable.

As a result, Parker Brothers loosened its collective tie and began to take itself a little less seriously. Once known for giving fairly buttoned-down presentations at Toy Group meetings, Parker Brothers—after being egged on by Fifield, who hated the snore and drone—began to produce dog-and-pony shows that resembled a vaudeville routine in their scripted frivolity. Nowadays it was the Kenner delegation that showed up wearing pinstripes and carrying clipboards.

6

THROW DOUBLES

*T*he video craze reached its frenzied peak in mid-1982. Pre-teens who formerly hung out at the drugstore or along the downtown drag strip reconvened their cliques in the arcades of the local shopping mall. Children didn't race to the television to watch "Captain Kangaroo" anymore; the program that had been a childhood fixture for more than a generation went off the air the year before, the victim of low ratings. Parents howled over the loss, but their children didn't. Instead, they beat feet to the warm and waiting home video joystick.

But video was far more than child's play. While the typical demographics of a toy or game fell between ages four and twelve, this category probably ran closer to ages four to sixty. According to a survey reported in *Electronic Games,* about half the video-game players in the arcades and elsewhere were over the age of twenty-six. Executives on lunch hour tucked their ties in their shirts, rolled up their sleeves, and hunkered over a glowing machine, preferring a few rounds with *Defender,* or *Galaxian,* or *Pac-Man,* to the three-whatever lunch. Video jargon began showing up not just in the schoolyard but in the boardroom. Marketers, salespeople, and product designers spoke of "jiggling the joystick" on a project that was slowing, of "zapping" an adversarial person or idea, and of the need to "hyperspace it" when the competition— or the press, or the opposing lawyers—turned too ugly.

Meanwhile, books and magazines reported the latest in video etiquette (always wait to be invited to play doubles) and video music (the best tunes to shoot aliens to). Health professionals began documenting video-related maladies. In one survey of 142 arcade players, 65 percent complained of calluses, blisters, sore tendons, or numbness. Several rheumatologists advised that repeated button bashing, paddle twisting, and joystick jerking could cause skin, joint, and muscle problems, sometimes referred to as *Space Invaders*'s Revenge or *Pac-Man* Elbow. Far be it for the head-shrinkers to be left behind: The *Journal of the American Medical Association* reported a curious new psychiatric disorder that the authors termed *Space Invaders*'s Obsession. According to the research, some grooms-to-be increased their game-playing fourfold or more in the weeks preceding the wedding ceremony. One man even insisted that the honeymoon be postponed for a few hours so that he could get in a few more games.

Few crazes in America come or go without controversy, and the inevitable backlash against video took hold in 1982 as well. For every expert lauding video technology there was at least one who labeled it the scourge of society. Video games and their insatiable appetite for quarters were reviled as a cause of petty crime even as they were being exhibited in museums as folk art. City planners banned video arcades from school zones. Psychologists debated the impact of video violence on already aggressive teens and adults. And educators weighed the pros and cons of video in the classroom, some saying video technology would help teach multiplication tables and verb conjugation, others predicting that boys, with their stronger interest in video games, would step ahead of girls in so-called computer literacy (much as they already had in math and the sciences). Among the experts who passed judgment on the value of video games was the U.S. Surgeon General, Dr. C. Everett Koop, who claimed they produced "aberrations in childhood behavior." But Isaac Asimov, one of the nation's most respected science writers, predicted the games would pave the way for a new age of computerized learning and discovery.

The one thing that most everyone did agree upon was that video games, adored or reviled, were here to stay. This was no fad, expert after expert asserted; the popularity of video games represented a major social and technological shift. When skeptics suggested that video might be just another blip on the social screen, they were virtually laughed out of the room. Video technology would improve and evolve so quickly that consumers wouldn't have time to become bored. It was just as pervasive and momentous a development as television.

In this white-hot environment, makers of home video cartridges bid up the prices of arcade licenses to levels that no one would have considered sane a year earlier. For example, Atari flabbergasted the industry when it paid more than $20 million for the license to *E.T.*, the character from the Steven Spielberg movie of the same name.

"Sirens! Tie me to the mast," Stearns joked to his marketing colleague, Bracy, on hearing the news. He certainly didn't want to be seen as "chicken" by other, more spendthrift competitors, but he was determined to find the line between "going for it," as he had urged earlier, and going broke. He figured it to be at about $5 million per license, royalties included, and he resolved that he would go no higher. Stearns felt a little silly in his caution—there were those who were offhandedly suggesting that video might lead Parker Brothers to annual revenues of $1 billion before the end of the 1980s. But Stearns found support from the level-headed and equally literate Bracy, who paraphrased Kipling to argue for prudence: "If you can keep your head while others about you are losing theirs. . . ."

Still, spending limits notwithstanding, neither man advocated slowing up the pace. On the contrary: As the video market gathered speed and momentum, it attracted competition in greater numbers and higher intensity. As a result, it set the role and philosophy of once-stolid departments such as marketing and marketing research on their respective ears.

During the days of *Code Name: Sector* and *Merlin,* marketing vice president Ron Jackson had kept a tight leash on development decisions and costs. Each product was made to justify its worth, not just in the initial design phase, but in each stage of development and manufacturing. Since Jackson's departure and the concomitant rise of video, the company's grip on such spending had loosened considerably. Decisions costing $2 million, such as whether to plunk down an advance on a license, were made overnight. Five-million-dollar expenditures, such as those devoted to marketing and promoting *Merlin* and *Frogger,* were made in a week.

If video marketing were investment banking, Stearns and Bracy were now futures traders. While once they had pledged

themselves only to those well-known licenses that were deemed
pre-sold, now they were buying sight unseen. Instead of betting
on the horse—the game itself—they were betting on the jockey,
its designer. There was scarcely time to *play* the game, much less
to research the market for it or test consumer reaction to it. Parker
Brothers was flying by the seat of its marketers' pants, buying
licenses on rights of first refusal, with only drawings and crude
prototypes to suggest the final product.

It became a highly speculative game. Some properties were
acquired and produced simply to win a shot at later and more
desirable licenses. Ranny Barton authorized the expenditure of
$150,000 to buy the rights to a game called *Skyskipper,* for example.
Neither he nor anyone else within the company evinced much
faith in the game. They bought the rights strictly to win future
opportunities with Japan's Nintendo, the company that designed
the current monster hit *Donkey Kong.*

The breakneck speed of the market had regressed product
development at Parker Brothers to the early 1970s. Back then, if
sales said "Let's go," Parker Brothers would go—and they'd know
how far and how fast to go not through computerized regression
analyses, but by comparing what they heard on the telephone
with what they saw in their order books. Now it was the key
marketers who were negotiating the licenses who called the shots.

For all his General Mills training, Fifield made it clear that
he didn't mind if decisions were made without research—particularly if it meant Parker Brothers getting a jump on the competition. Stearns, ever a man in a hurry, agreed. His argument
was, if *Frogger* was a success as an arcade game, why bother
testing it?

As a result, Stearns found himself in running battles with
the marketing research department, whose staff felt Stearns had
kicked them out of the R & D process. Stearns knew they had a
point. He *had* started bypassing research on his way to negotiate
licenses. The brutal fact was, the popularity of the average arcade
video game peaked within weeks of its introduction and then
collapsed in a virtual free-fall. Within six to eighteen months,
even the home video versions of the games were history. Any
market research attempted in such a fast-paced market would no
doubt prove inaccurate, Stearns pointed out.

The marketing researchers agreed: Tracking market trends was largely futile in such a short product cycle. But they maintained that if they could only do some product testing on the licenses as they came into development, they would be able to at least identify which of the proposed new entries had the best shot in the marketplace, and therefore, which should receive the strongest promotional thrust. "Don't you want to know what the consumer thinks?" market researchers beseeched Stearns.

"We already *know* what the consumer thinks," Stearns repeated. "They're voting in the arcades."

As the once-conservative Parker Brothers became among General Mills's fastest-growing and most glamorous divisions, the conglomerate began giving it the star treatment. Almost from the day it declared itself a video-cartridge manufacturer, Parker Brothers welcomed a continual stream of visiting General Mills executives and members of its board of directors. Corporate planes arrived virtually weekly carrying one or two pooh-bahs seeking "just a peek" at a sort-of creative frenzy rarely seen in the food business. Larger delegations of headquarters brass began showing up every three to six months—in friendly defiance of a corporate rule that limited such major presentations to one every eighteen months.

It reminded oldtimers of the *Instant Insanity* invasion of 1968. These visitors, like those of the merger year, never offered criticism—what was to criticize? Nor did they attempt to suggest strategy. They just asked questions, lots of questions. As a result, there came to be three or four Parker Brothers employees who spent much of their time in the basement data-processing center to provide the answers.

Part of the draw to Beverly was the work Parker Brothers was doing to try to plot the future of electronic entertainment in the home. Several of the company's market researchers—who had been more or less twiddling their thumbs since the product-management system had proven too slow to keep up with the market—had been assigned to the busywork of determining just what role home video games, computers, and other futuristic devices might play in the toys business and what ramifications these innovations might have on General Mills as a whole. The team had set up an exhibit of gee-whiz gizmos that was a real crowd-pleaser among the visitors that some Parker Brothers employees had come to call "grain grinders."

Up on the semi-secure fourth floor—the only place in the company where one had to show a badge to be admitted—there was one conference room known as the arcade room and another called the computer room. Each was set up with a couple of goals in mind: to keep Stearns and Bracy closer to the office (i.e., out of the arcades) at lunch time, and to give visiting grain-grinders something to do after hearing their formal presentation. Their hands-on experience with the technology sometimes lasted for hours.

Parker Brothers's video marketers thrived on the attention they were paid in these visits, but the research and development stalwarts—and anybody still working on traditional board games—complained about the time the visits cost them. For any semi-serious presentation there was data to gather, charts and slides to make, and scripts to write. Dress rehearsal time had to be scheduled so that Ranny Barton could see a dry run before the real thing. All in all, it generally took a week to put together even a half-day presentation.

When he got around to running some figures on it, marketing vice president Jones figured that he had been spending 20 percent of his personnel's time on various ways of servicing General Mills and its hunger for data. Sure, all of this planning and packaging and reporting had its administrative purpose, but it didn't exactly move the ball down the field. It didn't bring anybody on his side of the business, the traditional toys and games side, any closer to introducing a new product.

"You'd think we were in the presentation business instead of the toy business," grumbled Jones, along with another perennial critic of General Mills, R & D man Bill Dohrmann. And what did Jones, Dohrmann, and their toilers get for their trouble? Not much, particularly not in the way of money, talent, respect, or even elbow room.

Board-game people were literally being evicted from their offices to make room for the continuing influx of video designers and engineers. At first, video marketing had one bank of offices on the second floor. Then it became the whole second floor of the first wing, displacing a number of R & D's board-game designers. Try as they might to shrug it off, most evictees considered the shufflings personal affronts. They were experienced people—people who were accustomed to being regarded as the heart and soul of the company. Now here they were, not even sure of having a place to sit from day to day. Some were shunted around so frequently that they saved their boxes. The most militant refused to unpack at all.

Money was even tighter than space. The front-end costs of the video business drew heavily on the company's revenue, particularly the nearly $60 million in gross revenues that poured in from *MONOPOLY* each year. Jones couldn't always be certain of getting funding for his ideas, no matter how much he thought he needed it.

It was irksome: Jones and Stearns were supposedly equal in stature, each in charge of—well, not half of the company, because video was already bigger than that by most measures—but of one of the company's two main marketing efforts. It was Stearns's side of the company that got all of the attention, however. Nobody referred to "video" on one side of the company and "traditional games" on the other; it was "video" and "*non*-video." Jones had the orphan side, the one without the big price points or the internal respect. Jones's and Stearns's departments were different sides of the company, different sides of the corridor—they might as well have been the dark and light sides of the moon.

Video games were always the first item on any company-wide agenda—indeed, for all intents and purposes, the *only* item on the agenda. "And Bruce, what are you guys doing?" the executives would say, as if it were an afterthought. At such meetings, when his report was once again relegated to twenty rushed minutes at the end of a session already well past schedule, Jones would rise and sardonically refer to his remarks as those reflecting "the *real* Parker Brothers"—not the "transient" one.

Anybody who walked into Jones's office could judge the depth of his rebellion. There was a picture prominently displayed on his wall, a magazine illustration, that showed a family playing *MONOPOLY*. In the foreground sat an abandoned video-game machine, its yanked cord wrapped around its neck like a noose.

This was not a particularly new vendetta for Jones. Since *Merlin*'s day, Jones had charted electronic and traditional games and their respective progress—not in terms of revenue growth, which electronics had won hands down, but in terms of profit contribution. "You'll never beat us," he'd said, gleefully tracking each quarter's figures. He had been right where hand-held games were concerned; they had never measured up to the per-unit earnings performance of traditional games. But, increasingly, his gloating was false bravado. Video was dominating the charts, even the per-unit earnings measures, and it bugged the living daylights out of him. Eventually the charts disappeared—certainly by the time he became a vice president. But the picture of the throttled video-game console remained front and center, where it couldn't be missed.

Jones was jealous—everybody knew that. Even Jones owned up to it. Sure, he and his charges envied the wheeling and dealing the video guys were doing. Who wouldn't be a little green-eyed? But Jones saw himself fighting a larger and more philosophical battle. He believed the company was being led astray by a Pied Piper in silicon chips. He had made it his personal mission to keep video from leading Parker Brothers off the cliff.

By way of comparison, Jones pointed to rival Milton Bradley and its still-burgeoning business in traditional games. Sure, maybe things would have been different if the Springfield company had been more successful with its video entries. But as it was, Milton Bradley stood as an example of a company that hadn't forgotten its original calling. While Jones had been forced to fight for every inch, body, dollar, and minute of attention, the competition in Springfield seemed to be maintaining or even stepping up its traditional-game efforts. It smarted to watch: For years, Milton Bradley had defended itself against the fact that it had turned down *MONOPOLY* those many years ago, by saying of Parker Brothers: "Sure, they've got number one, but we've got the next nineteen." The saying was always laughable in its exaggeration until lately. These days it seemed *MONOPOLY* was all Parker Brothers had to offer, aside from video games.

Stearns listened patiently to Jones's complaints, but he didn't understand them. As far as Stearns was concerned, the company wasn't "competing with itself," or "ignoring one side of the business for another," as Jones and others put it. Rather, Parker Brothers was *protecting* the board games by keeping them separated from the video hoopla. As for the attention and the resources that video was siphoning from traditional games, Stearns thought it only made sense that Parker Brothers should "go where the dollars are."

But where were the dollars? Somewhere between half and 70 percent of Parker Brothers's unit volume came from traditional games—it was only the margins and the selling price of the video side that were higher. Video-game sales had been scarcely better than equal to those of traditional games in the first fiscal year, and it didn't appear the actual sales gap would significantly widen in the second—unless the neglect of board games continued.

Jones maintained that Parker Brothers was gravitating to video mostly because video was sexy to General Mills and its shareholders. In days gone by, shareholders had been strictly a headquarters concern, and, in that setting, there was never any question but that the company's investment in its staples had to be protected, no matter what hot gizmos might be competing for the spotlight. Times, however, had changed. Nowadays the attitude emanating from Minneapolis was, worry about this year this year— we'll worry about next year next.

After more than a year of this, Ranny Barton, Rich Stearns, and Jim Fifield all tended to dismiss Jones's rantings as those of a crank. He was putting too much energy into fighting a psychological war instead of building product, they said. He was creating his own self-fulfilling prophesy. But they couldn't climb in Jones's shoes, or those of his subordinates, and listen to themselves talk. They couldn't parse their own subliminal messages, which were subtle but demoralizing.

For all the lip service given to preserving and continuing to promote the traditional games that had long been Parker Brothers's bread and butter, everything done and said above the vice president level told Jones and his troops that they were bygones—that traditional games were washed up, and that soon they would be sold only as nostalgia items. Stearns continued to liken them to buggy whips. And although Fifield was not the first to coin the term, the Toy Group executive seemed to enjoy calling them "bored games."

Jones and his team tried to push forward with new ideas. Still, they knew that new ideas alone weren't going to be enough to win anyone's support, inside Parker Brothers or out. Like it or not, they faced the formidable task of trying to match the excitement of video. Without that excitement, sales figures weren't the issue; the games wouldn't even get in the stores. Retailers had shelves stacked high with video games with bigger appeal and higher price points, so why should they make room for fuddy-duddy games made of cardboard and plastic? Most stores had cut the shelf space for traditional games in half. Jones clucked and shook his head each time he thought of it. He was convinced that retail buyers had underestimated the comeback power—if not the continuing popularity—of the traditional board game. But he had sales goals, and convictions weren't going to help him meet them.

Searching for salvation, Jones went to the now-under-employed marketing research department seeking signs of new trends in traditional toys and games. Fantasy games were hot, particularly those that had to do with the sort of role play that had made *Dungeons & Dragons* a cult favorite. Jones considered adapting the role-play approach to the *Star Wars* board-game license, but that idea was soon shelved. Role play didn't work when your target audience had already been to the movies and seen how the story ended. He switched his focus to staples—finding new ones and building the market for the old ones.

Jones and Dohrmann spent considerable time and effort trying to acquire Whammo, the *Frisbee* manufacturer, but while the higher-ups in New York and Minneapolis were considering the merits of the deal, Hasbro beat them to the bargaining table. Too bad, too: *Frisbee,* with its summertime appeal, would have run counter-cyclical to the winter sales that were still the predominant part of Parker Brothers's business.

Another acquisition target was *Pente,* a backgammon-like game played with translucent glass pebbles. *Pente* was attractive for its distribution channels—which included upscale department stores, specialty shops, gift catalogs, and other venues that Parker Brothers hadn't infiltrated. Acquiring the game would give Parker Brothers a foothold in these new markets. Perhaps the company could begin selling deluxe versions of its staples, or using these smaller market segments to try out new products that weren't ready for mass-merchandise, chain-store marketing. Gary Gabrel, the man who invented *Pente,* was interested, in turn, in having Parker Brothers take his game into the chains that he hadn't been able to reach. Talks began in the fall of 1982.

In the meantime, Jones was attempting to revive interest in Parker Brothers's old standbys. Games such as *MONOPOLY, Clue,* and *Risk* returned to the magazine pages and airwaves—but this time they weren't sold exclusively to children. Instead, they were promoted as a social experience for entire families. Jones's had researched parents' views on video games and found that they largely concurred with his own: The games were seen as unwholesome, as just another excuse for the kids to "veg out" in front of the TV. In response, Jones and his team assembled a campaign called "People Together," hyping the fact that Parker Brothers's more traditional games were shared activities for the whole family, not the solitary experience of the video game. Jones credited the new campaign with boosting board-game sales by 12 percent.

Ever conscious of maintaining Parker Brothers's reputation as a product leader, not a follower, Jones avoided developing games based on arcade or home video concepts as long as he could. It was a matter of pride, of course, but also of play value. The basic concepts that made video games and traditional board games fun to play were almost mutually exclusive, they were so different. "You wanna put out crap or a good game?" he challenged all comers. Jones specifically refused to do cardboard and electronic versions of *Frogger.* Anybody who could play *Frogger* on video would be bored to tears with a board-game version, Jones reasoned. But Jones was forced to eat his words when Milton Bradley bought the board-game rights to that very same game, and made a bundle on it. Then Coleco bought the tabletop rights and similarly cleaned up. Jones yelled uncle.

From then on, Parker Brothers negotiated global rights to all formats on every license it acquired. Jones's group designed a one-size-fits-all case into which video games could be converted to tabletop electronics with minimal effort. They also began to seek board-game rights to video licenses held by other manufacturers.

For example, when the *E.T.* license became available, Dohrmann and Jones dropped everything and went after it, along with dozens of other development teams. They could have avoided the stampede if they had bought the license on the first pass—the original script had been passed to Parker Brothers early in the film's production—but Dohrmann and company had rejected it. Back then it was argued that the property wasn't extendible enough—*E.T.* didn't have enough little alien friends with which to expand the line of toys and games. Nobody was thrilled with the plot line's potential as game play, either. But one of Jones's product managers saw the movie that summer and was excited enough about it to convince the others to reconsider. The traditional side certainly could use the volume, she pointed out. So why not?

Parker Brothers won the license and set a breakneck schedule for itself: Develop and ship the game by the fall of 1982, a mere eleven weeks away. The schedule was met. Almost nobody who bought into the thinly sliced rights on the character made much money—the market was overloaded with *E.T.* merchandise. Even Atari took a bath on the video game. But Parker Brothers managed to eke out a $10 million volume on the board game—which wasn't bad for a company that opted out until the last minute.

Still, Jones and his staff remained dissatisfied. They were growing weary of products that were derivative of something else—usually a licensed property held by Parker Brothers or somebody else in the Toy Group. They persevered in their efforts to find or create a new franchise. Despite having lost people, resources, and respect to video, it gradually dawned on Jones that now, as his side of the business continued to fly under company radar, was the perfect time to take some risks. "We may not have cash or much else," Jones peptalked his employees, "but, hoo boy, have we got leeway. Nobody's looking over our shoulders!"

Jones started holding long and almost euphoric skull sessions over major product departures that had been batted around for years, involving categories such as children's books and phonograph records. Was it possible, he wondered, to use toys-industry marketing techniques to sell items like these? Could Parker Brothers force a new system of distribution into existence?

His research said yes. Bill Bracy had been conducting market studies on the children's publishing business in 1981 when Stearns pulled him off the project and offered him "a real job" marketing video games. But enough of Bracy's work was done to recognize that books could be a huge and hungry market for a toymaker like Parker Brothers, and better yet, one that had almost ludicrously low barriers to entry.

There were about 40,000 children's titles on the market, with about 4,000 new ones joining the list each year. Amazingly enough, few of them were marketed with anywhere near the panache of a typical toy campaign. By the end of 1982, the entire children's book industry would reel in about $265 million at retail, yet the publishing trade would spend no more than $3 million in advertising. Parker Brothers figured it could practically buy the market for an initial six-title release with a mere $1 million investment in advertising.

But the pluses weren't exclusively financial. Books seemed a natural product line for a company that had long regarded itself as a publishing entity at heart. Jones rather fancied the idea of himself in an editorial role. Surely he could handle writers and recording artists as easily as game designers.

He would never get the chance. To maximize the publicity on the book rollout, Jones agreed to let the books become yet another vehicle for the Toy Group's licenses—at least to begin with. He ordered that stories be written to depict and promote *The Care Bears,* Kenner's followup to *Strawberry Shortcake.* The new line consisted of ten stuffed bears representing ten different emotions.

Going with the license was more an opportunistic decision than an artistic one. *The Care Bears* had legs to walk the books off the selling floor. The initial flight of books, described by the company's P.R. as being about "love, caring, dreams, happiness, friendship, wishes, and feelings," would be introduced at the February 1983 Toy Fair, along with the rest of *The Care Bears* merchandise: Kenner's toys and accessories, Parker Brothers's games and books, and Fundimensions's hobby and craft items.

From then on, all illusions of coddling authors and their ideas into children's classics were gone. It became a marketing-man's version of the creative process, and one that editorial director John Keller was proud to describe to the press. "The old way was to give authors their head. We, on the other hand, make up a list of, say, thirty interesting plot ideas, and then we do consumer testing . . . Once I have the rankings, I call up my pool of authors and give them a plot to work with, and a style sheet explaining the characters. And then I say, 'Please write 2,500 words filled with verve and excitement.' "

Almost simultaneously, Jones was preparing to take Parker Brothers into phonograph records—and once again, he opted for a licensed subject. This time it wasn't one of the Toy Group's own characters, however. Jones bought the recording rights to Coleco's *Cabbage Patch Kids.* "We're now really the keepers of the [*Cabbage Patch*] story," Bruce Jones told reporters at the record's introduction party. And what story was that? Jones furrowed his brow and did his best to capsulize. "In the magic valley, the bunny bees sprinkle crystals on the cabbage plants, and that's where the kids come from. It's sort of a biological oddity." But, straight-faced, he went on to emphasize that Parker Brothers's goal in both books and records was to sell stories for kids that weren't kiddie stories—in other words, "books and records that adults can stand."

Both the children's books and the phonograph album were successes far beyond the financial. Parker Brothers won the admiration of its industry for what the trade publications called an unusual, almost revolutionary marketing approach—particularly in its decision to develop not single volumes but entire book lines. Fifield, Jones, and others chuckled as the magazines gushed. The approach was different only to the toys industry. It was simply the systematic, product-by-product approach common to packaged goods, such as food or cereal. Did they think Parker Brothers could be associated with General Mills all these years and not learn a thing or two?

Fall was always planning time for Parker Brothers. With pre-Christmas shipping virtually done by Labor Day, it became a time to put a finger in the air and see which way the wind would be blowing for the coming fiscal year. In late calendar 1982, therefore, plans began being made for fiscal 1984, which would begin in the spring of 1983.

Parker Brothers had every reason to be upbeat. Spring shipments had been terrific. Video games remained hot, with industry-wide factory sales levels nudging $2 billion, as predicted. Coleco's *ColecoVision* was sold out. Rainchecks were being offered for Atari's new and more powerful game machine, the *5200,* in several western states. And the doldrums in some segments of the traditional toys marketplace bore witness to the continuing strength of the video category as well: Fisher Price, maker of pre-school toys, experienced its biggest layoffs since 1975. Tonka, with its toy trucks of steel and plastic, saw sales slide nearly 30 percent. The ever-burgeoning popularity of video cartridges and their programmable consoles threatened to overwhelm the rest of the industry.

So popular was the video-console category, in fact, and so consistently had the sales records been smashed, that gradually the entire video marketplace had come to assume that this was not just the first phase of a second and larger craze. Now it was taken as gospel that video-game machines could coexist indefinitely with the incoming market for computer video. This was new wisdom. From the beginning it had been assumed that the programmable video consoles, with their limited applications, would become obsolete when consumers were psychologically and financially ready to step up to home computers.

But computer sales had yet to kick in at the rates the market had anticipated, and video-game consoles and cartridges had continued to arch into uncharted territory. Atari—which had a foot in both sides of the market—had taken the expedient but ultimately fateful position that home video and computers were and would always be two separate and distinct markets. Instead of moving up to computers, Atari believed consumers were just as likely to seek out a more sophisticated home video console—even as they picked out their first home computers.

With much ballyhoo, Atari introduced a souped-up version of its video-game machine. At a retail price of $350, it sold at only $400 below Atari's least expensive home computer. Most of the marketplace considered it a supremely self-confident move on Atari's part. Apparently the company fully expected its customers to buy both machines.

The rest of the market quickly adopted the Atari view—that video consoles were complementary to the coming computer revolution, not preliminary to it. "The video-game business will never be replaced by the computer," said Ranny Barton. "There will always be people who want a game machine separate from a computing tool."

And why shouldn't the rest of the video market parrot the Atari view? Its stance effectively doubled the amount of product to sell, particularly for makers of video cartridges and software. New manufacturers stampeded the cartridge market, all but two of them turning out Atari-compatible games. Even Mattel, which pioneered its own *Intellivision* system in 1979, was now bowing to the superior market share of the Sunnyvale, California, company and producing Atari-compatible cartridges.

Here and there, voices crying in the wilderness warned that the video-game market was on the verge of loving itself to death. "You've got a bloodbath coming in cartridges," *Business Week* quoted Milton Bradley's president, George Ditomassi. But there were more optimists in the crowd by far. Said Raymond E. Kassar, the chairman of Atari: "For the video game, there's a past, present, and future. It's a ridiculous notion that it is going to burn out. Video games have become a very important part of entertainment, and of the lifestyle of this and future generations."

Huddled over graphs and sets of figures one day in the fall of 1982, Rich Stearns and Bill Bracy quite suddenly realized that the cynics were ones who were right—and probably a lot more right than they themselves realized.

The two men were poring over a study of video demographics that Bracy had completed in the wee hours of the previous morning. The hardware-penetration forecast he had developed clearly indicated that the market for programmable consoles would hit the wall sooner than expected, perhaps within months. Then the growth rate would slow to a crawl more accurately referred to as a replacement rate—but only for a few more months. Then the whole hardware market would crash.

"Wait a minute," said Stearns, sounding shaken and confused. "What exactly were we looking at here?"

"Just a breakout, by household, of all the people most likely to buy and play video games," explained Bracy. The maximum penetration, he figured, would be somewhere between 23 and 27 percent of the population—and, according to his calculations, it had already reached 20 percent.

Stearns fell back into his chair, shaking his head slowly. "The jig's up, and nobody knows it," he said. Bracy shrugged and nodded. The two men agreed it was no time for panic, but that Parker Brothers should begin tapping the brakes.

Within weeks, Stearns was asked to sit in for Jim Fifield at a video-game symposium for financial analysts held by William Blair & Company, a Chicago investment-banking firm. Scrambling for speech material, the young marketing vice president decided to use snippets of Bracy's study, just to see what sort of reaction he would get. Retailer Charles Lazarus, founder of Toys "R" Us, would be there. So would Emanuel "Manny" Gerard, the man in charge of Atari at its parent conglomerate, Warner Communications. There were no more powerful men in the industry than these. Gerard represented the leading manufacturer in the market; Lazarus, its number-one retailer.

That day, when Stearns went to the lectern and began predicting the imminent demise of the hardware market, hundreds of eyes looked up at him as if he were a creature from outer space. All the cognoscenti had been tossing around maximum market-penetration figures of 50 percent and higher, predicting that video hardware would take its place alongside the family TV. Yet, here was Stearns, using numbers half as high.

Stearns took care not to come off totally cynical in his remarks. He could afford to be bullish on the continued sales strength of video cartridges, as they would continue to sell to the installed base of video hardware owners even as total public demand for the hardware began to wane. He also spoke optimistically on the prospects for home-computer video becoming a factor in the market before the end of 1983, supplanting the expected falloff in the sale of dedicated home video machines. Still it was his first set of figures that stayed with the crowd. A decline in hardware penetration? Was Stearns nuts?

Atari's Gerard took the microphone and implied, with some apparent derision, that Atari had dozens of market researchers who would love to check Stearns's math. But when the man finished his own talk and sat down again, he leaned over and asked Stearns to send him a copy of the study.

As the bright, crisp days of September and October gave way to the gloom of November, so the internal planning effort connected with the spring program's forecasts went from data gathering to pencil pushing. Stearns began to consider modifying his early optimism. After all, it was year number two for Parker Brothers in video, but industry-wide, it was year three at minimum, and for some companies twice that. Stearns knew that shakeout time was overdue.

But there was more than industry history and gut instinct behind Stearns's thinking. Big-time investors had begun taking profits on their video stocks the previous spring, even before Parker Brothers's first video cartridges had hit the market. Some, like leading Atari investor Gene Tremblay, of Wellington Management in Boston, took his sell signal from a concerned arcade operator at the local commuter rail station. Jingling coins in his pocket as he spoke to Tremblay, the operator complained that his "take" was down for the first time in three years. Other investors keyed in on Europe, where slumping video-arcade traffic had softened share prices on European exchanges.

Arcade activity was a key indicator of the health of the home video market, and not just because it tended to indicate how enamored the public was with video game-playing of any sort. When arcade activity was down, it had a depressing effect on licensing agreements with home video manufacturers, because some royalty agreements were based on the number of arcade versions of the game that were sold and installed.

Having considered the generally cautionary signals he saw on the horizon, Stearns decided to play it safe in fiscal 1984. He went to Fifield suggesting that the electronics side of the business—essentially video cartridges and software—could produce about $150–200 million in revenues for the Toy Group and General Mills in fiscal 1984.

Fifield looked at Stearns for a moment, then began to chuckle. He was thinking more in the ballpark of $300–350 million, he said. "After all, you're at $132 million with two video games, and you're going to have twenty next year? Rich, *c'mon!*"

Stearns disagreed, but he didn't argue. He simply took the message as he saw it being delivered. Clearly Fifield was determined to set some ambitious goals for 1984. With Ranny Barton's support—"Never forget, General Mills is the boss," the older man had always counseled—Stearns decided to wait and see what the Christmas selling season would bring before taking his case to Fifield again.

Christmas proved to be disappointingly sluggish from the start. The Midwest was hard hit by foul weather, the East suffered from unseasonably warm temperatures, and the entire country was languishing amid a listless economy. The supposed blockbusters in licensed lines, *E.T.* and *Raiders of the Lost Ark,* were no better than moderate successes.

Then came an announcement that shook the video industry to its core: On December 8, 1982, Warner Communications, owners of Atari, revealed it had experienced a downturn in its sales of arcade video games and home video cartridges. It had been forced to lower its earnings projections, as some retailers were already cancelling orders for cartridges.

The news proved so devastating that it dragged the entire stock market down nearly thirty points. Trading in all video stocks was suspended. When the investment community shook off the shock and video shares returned to the tickertape several days later, Warner's shares had fallen from $51 to $35. Imagic, Inc., an up-and-comer among video-game manufacturers, was forced to postpone a public offering.

Few if any observers took this to mean that the video era was over; on the contrary, many retailers were still saying they couldn't keep up with the customer demand for video games. Instead, it was seen as a sign that the market was changing, even slowing in growth, perhaps. Competition had at last caught up with Atari, that much was clear. Amid the ever-expanding revenue volume of the marketplace, Atari's once-overpowering market share was getting squeezed. What had been 60 or 70 game titles supplied by 5 manufacturers in 1981 had now become 150 or more titles from 16 companies. The frenzy of competition was eating away at profit margins as manufacturers sought to grab a toehold in the market through discounting. "Atari's feeling the bite of all us little gnats," was Stearns's almost buoyant public assessment. In private, he was far less flip about it. Things weren't going to get any easier from here on in—for anybody.

As Christmas of 1982 passed and Parker Brothers's revenues became a sure thing to hit the $200 million mark, Stearns and others at Parker Brothers became certain that they were feeling those same old rumblings, the ones that always foretold painful change. As fabulously exciting as the video-game business still seemed on the surface, it was underlyingly clear that all the hoopla, all the growth, and all the profits were someday going to collapse. Maybe soon.

Accordingly, Stearns was more pessimistic when he went back to Fifield in January of 1983. His revenue projection for electronics in fiscal 1984? "Flat to 175." In other words, either the video side of the business would make no revenue gains whatsoever from the $132 million expected in fiscal 1983, or they would gain a relatively modest $40 million from the previous fiscal year.

Fifield accused Stearns of sandbagging. "Look what you did with *Frogger*," he chided, "and think of the licenses now in development." He shook his head, as if trying to fathom where Stearns's caution was coming from. "I still say I'm letting you guys off easy."

Thereafter, setting the spring program for fiscal 1984 became a friendly but earnest game of push and shove, with offices in Beverly and New York arguing over whose reading of the market was closer to reality. The optimistic projections Parker Brothers had been making as late as November were on Fifield's side; history and the new forecasts were on Stearns's. Stearns stood pat at a target figure of $175 million in revenues, which was delivered to Fifield in New York. But when the paperwork returned to Beverly some weeks later, Stearns' figure had been replaced by Fifield's final compromise of $225 million. The spring program, which contained the financial objectives for the fiscal year that would begin after Toy Fair in 1983, also called for $105 million from traditional games, for total company revenue projection of nearly $330 million.

Fifield's willingness to step in and amend divisional decision making left Barton, Stearns, and Bracy open-mouthed. Up until now, they hadn't an inkling of how important the video market had become to Jim Fifield. "Video's his ticket back to Minneapolis as president," opined Stearns, with the sound of revelation in his voice, "and Parker Brothers is the horse he's gonna ride."

After the 1983 Toy Fair, Fifield announced that Parker Brothers was readying sixty new video game items for introduction in 1984 (some of them the same game in as many as five different hardware formats). He nodded to the tightening retail market, emphasizing that the General Mills Toy Group was not going to be tossing out just any product that might tickle a designer's fancy, but rather, stressing the "development of franchises over single-item proliferation." In other words, there would be more video games of *The Care Bears* ilk than like *Frogger.* The former was deemed safer in a market that seemed teetering on the edge of shakeout. Noting that dolls had been Christmas's big-selling item in 1982, Fifield acknowledged that traditional toys and games were in the midst of an impressive comeback. But he clearly didn't want anybody writing off video: Home electronics would increase from 13 percent of the industry's sales to 24 percent, he predicted.

Ranny Barton's shuttle diplomacy came to an end in 1982. Arranging some Japanese souvenirs of his journeys on shelves and walls, he settled back into his office and took stock of his company.

Barton was immeasurably proud of his workforce and its accomplishments, and unflagging in his optimism for the future. But he felt a growing tension within the Toy Group. It was as if Parker Brothers and the other divisions were in the testy early stages of a tug o' war. General Mills or Toy Group headquarters would yank, then Parker Brothers and the rest of the divisions would yank back—all sides insisting they were merely checking the strength of the rope.

Not only were Barton's subordinates having difficulty charting the company's destiny without Toy Group interference, Parker Brothers and the other Toy Group divisions seemed in danger of losing their independent right to procure and produce. Corporate management was making moves toward a takeover of all Toy Group sourcing and manufacturing through what might well become a consolidated operations division.

The wheels had begun turning back with Fifield's arrival in 1981. At that time, General Mills's new chairman, Bruce Atwater, was in the early phases of his corporate belt-tightening program. Up and down the corporate pyramid the message to group and divisional managements alike was: synergy. Minneapolis was advocating any and all moves that would improve the speed, efficiency, and cost-effectiveness of its diversified operations.

In apparent response to the drive, Fifield established a task force to study manufacturing excesses and redundancies within the Toy Group soon after his arrival. He asked all four general managers to serve on it: Joe Mendelsohn of Kenner, Art Peisner of Fundimensions, Ranny Barton of Parker Brothers, and Vic Rado, representing the European operations. But he asked Rado to chair the task force. Rado's background was in operations, and as Bernie Loomis's hatchet man in Europe, he had been ruthlessly effective in coordinating and centralizing the overseas operations. For all intents and purposes, it was Rado's study and Rado's research from then on in—the operating managers only served to answer questions about their own companies.

Rado delivered the resulting report at the annual Toy Group conference of 1982, a reprise of the whitewater-rafting event held in Colorado the year before. Standing before the assemblage, Rado said he had, indeed, found an abundance of overlap in the production functions of the various companies of the Toy Group. None was a paragon of efficiency.

For example, each company in the group operated its own plastic injection-molding plant, none of which was running at capacity. At Fundimensions headquarters in Mount Clemens, Michigan, there were thirty-seven such injection-molding machines, fewer than half of which were used on more than a sporadic basis.

Then he turned to Parker Brothers. Running at only 40 percent of capacity, the output of Parker Brothers's plastics plant at Taunton, Massachusetts, by Rado's estimation, was costing 130–150 percent of what the company would pay an outside contractor to do the work. In the meantime, Kenner didn't have enough facilities to get its work done and, therefore, was enduring production delays at the hands of Oriental factories that served regular customers first and put Johnny-come-latelies like Kenner at the end of the line.

Rado recommended centralizing the Toy Group's sourcing and manufacturing not in the Orient, but in another low-cost labor region: Mexico. He was quick to stress that this was not an emergency; the *status quo* could be tolerated awhile before it would cause any noticeable red ink on the books. But he warned that all three domestic Toy Group companies were going to find it harder to compete as they continued growing, and it would be to their advantage to streamline and consolidate away the inefficiencies as soon as possible.

That had hardly been the end of it. Pressure continued to build through the summer and fall of 1982, not only to share production facilities among the various operating companies of the Toy Group, but to give up production duties altogether, leaving each company to concentrate exclusively on marketing and selling. The Toy Group was really but one company with differing marketing strategies, Fifield reasoned whenever the topic came up, and it ought to operate as such.

Soon production and operations managers within the operating divisions, the main targets of Fifield's and Rado's evangelism, were embracing the idea with religious zeal. After one of Rado's hortatory meetings with such staff members, Bruce Jones made the mistake of making a smide remark about Rado and his efficiency ideas to one of Parker Brothers's operations managers, while the two sat waiting for a plane with Barton. The otherwise mild-mannered employee turned red with anger and chastised Jones for not being a teamplayer.

The question he asked during his diatribe against Jones was the same one that Rado and Fifield were asking the operating managers—Barton, Peisner, and Mendelsohn. Why *not* coordinate production? Why *not* go even further and create a full-fledged coordinating entity at the group level? It could work just like the operations division that coordinated production among General Mills's food groups. In Minneapolis, it was pointed out, the brand-management groups invented the products and then handed them through the wall, in a manner of speaking, to a free-standing operations division. That division had total control over where the product should be made and when. Why shouldn't the Toy Group have its own operations division—a T-GOD, for wont of a better term?

This wasn't the first time a more ambitious scenario than mere overseas sourcing had been suggested. As time went on it had become less and less clear whether Fifield, Rado, and their followers were talking about establishing a full-fledged T-GOD, or simply an offshore centralized production facility. Most of the operating managers assumed the latter, based on what they had heard from Fifield while dining at a restaurant in New York's Greenwich Village during the 1983 Toy Fair.

The discussion pivoted on how to go about moving various parts of the Toy Group's respective manufacturing operations south of the border. As it was left at the end of the evening, the senior operations officer in each division was to coordinate his activities through Rado, who would, in turn, consolidate domestic and offshore production in Mexico and establish centralized manufacturing facilities as needed. Fifield was convinced the system could be up and running within a year. What's more, he predicted it would save the Toy Group $20 million a year, right off the bat.

None of the general managers was jumping up and down over the idea. With the possible exception of Mendelsohn (with his production problems in Japan), these men hadn't considered manufacturing a problem until Fifield and Rado told them it was one. But as a group, they took a deep breath and said yes, they'd cooperate with Rado in any way they could. Ambivalent as they were about it, this seemed to be the sort of move a savvy manager didn't criticize. It was textbook business strategy, after all: Where there exist disparate groups doing the same general things, it pays to consolidate to reduce wasted effort and squandered resources.

There were questions of timing and logistics that contributed to their half-hearted endorsement of the program, but the big unspoken concern had to do with control. Everybody was reluctant to lose even a small measure of his managerial control. What did a presidency mean without that? Still, nobody wanted to complain about it. It would look to Fifield like just what it was: turf protection. As good corporate soldiers they would accept the changes in the name of progress. They left that night consoling themselves with the understanding that Rado's recommendations, coming from someone with only staff ranking, wouldn't carry the clout of a direct order.

When Rado was subsequently notified by Toy Group headquarters that, yes, he was moving back to the U.S. to head up the new Toy Group Operations Division, Rado reminded Fifield that he didn't want to be relocated from his beloved London for a losing proposition. "Jim, you know this thing won't work if the general managers aren't backing me," he said. "They have to be ready to let me do what I have to do." Fifield laughed off

Rado's concern. "Vic, they're the ones asking for *you*. They're totally behind this thing one-hundred percent, don't you worry about that!"

Rado learned otherwise when he arrived stateside and found himself in a tussle with Ranny Barton almost immediately. Rado wanted to move Barton's *Nerf* production to the soon-to-be established manufacturing facility in Mexico, but Barton refused. He pointed out that it only made sense to put labor-intensive work in a low-wage region such as Mexico, and *Nerf* was virtually automated. Rado continued mentioning product lines for possible relocation, and Barton continued to nix each one.

As Barton saw it, most of Parker Brothers's manufacturing consisted of printing. It was being done economically enough at the 190 Bridge Street plant in Salem. The savings of bringing the 10 percent of Parker's production that was video cartridge assembly to Mexico was miniscule—not enough to make the cost of a move pay off. Besides, 90 percent of that cartridge assembly was being done in Salem. Any wage savings that might be realized from moving elsewhere would probably shave only cents off the unit cost, most of which would probably be lost in the cost of the move itself. What's more, with its own plant, Parker Brothers was in control of its production schedules. Whether offshore or merely off-site, subcontractors would no doubt require higher minimums, which would reduce the company's flexibility.

Rado disagreed with Barton on most counts: Parker Brothers was losing small but significant amounts on its printing operations, it often ran its plastics plant at considerably less than full capacity, it had what Rado considered a superfluous distribution center in Iowa, and as for its video-related production tasks, he argued that they were likely to become more technical, more numerous, and less cost-effective with time.

Barton won that battle, but he lost the next. Rado flatly announced that he intended to shut down Parker Brothers's plastics facility in Taunton, Massachusetts, along with another plant he deemed under-utilized, the Fundimensions plant that made toy trains for its venerable Lionel unit. All 450 union employees on the manufacturing payroll in Fundimensions's hometown of Mount Clemens, Michigan, would be out of work by the end of the fiscal year in May. A second Fundimensions plant in Toledo would become T-GOD's, responsible mostly for Kenner production.

Although Rado had managed to relieve Parker Brothers of its plastics plant and its distribution center, he coaxed only a few traditional games onto the presses in Mexico—one of which was *Boggle,* a plastic word game. Barton wouldn't budge on the rest. His reason was pretty softheaded, by Rado's lights. Uneconomical and inefficient as his manufacturing system may have been on paper, he knew it, he trusted it, and he was unwilling to dismantle it. Besides, Barton was committed to the economic well-being of Salem, and he wasn't about to harm it by sending 40 or 50 percent of his production overseas. His family had already let the community down by moving the administrative headquarters to Beverly. This was the other shoe he refused to let drop.

Rado, angrily denouncing Barton's insistence on remaining independent, asked him which was more important, the community, or General Mills's shareholders? "The community," Barton said. Rado—who had by now earned the nickname Darth Rado from Barton's underlings—scorned Barton for letting his feelings get in the way of economic realities. When Fifield got wind of the flap, he telephoned Barton and chewed him out for being uncooperative.

But growth projections and production reshufflings weren't the sum total of the increasing level of frustration in and around Parker Brothers. There were other troubles in early 1983, and they struck at each tine of the company's two-pronged business, *MONOPOLY* and video.

Parker Brothers had found itself in a brief but wounding legal struggle with Atari. The video-game behemoth, apparently trying to exert some control over the influx of cartridge and software competition, had sought exclusive agreements with certain of its distributors, a move calculated to shut Parker Brothers out of 40 of its top 100 distributors and cost the company easily $20 million in sales.

In Beverly, nobody could believe it. This was America, wasn't it? Surely what Atari had done constituted unfair competition. Parker Brothers's lawyers sought a preliminary injunction, saying Atari's tactic was anti-competitive enough to threaten more than Parker Brothers's participation in the video-game business. If

Parker Brothers didn't get its injunctive relief, they hinted darkly, "[Parker Brothers] may not be around." The motion, however, was rejected in April of 1983, and Parker Brothers found itself virtually shut out of the part of the video distribution network now experiencing the most growth: the wholesalers and rack jobbers that served electronics stores and record outlets.

As if that weren't enough, *MONOPOLY* was under siege again. The U.S. Supreme Court had refused to review a lower-court ruling in the *Anti-Monopoly* case in February. By letting stand a ruling that held that the *MONOPOLY* name had become generic, the Court had also jeopardized the trademarks of many other venerable or popular products.

Gallows humor was rampant within the ranks. Not only was nobody listening to Parker Brothers's well-founded fears about an impending shakeout in the video market, General Mills was gutting the company of its identity as a manufacturer, closing down its satellite operations and continuing to reshuffle the workforce.

That spring, amid the fears and uncertainties on so many fronts, Parker Brothers gathered as a company to celebrate its centennial. The party was planned and paid for by Humphrey, Browning and MacDougall, the company's longtime local ad agency. HBM had its own reason to celebrate, having recently passed the $100 million mark in revenues—thanks mostly to Parker Brothers's business.

The party was a black-tie affair, held in the same auditorium where Harvard's Hasty Pudding Club stages its annual farces. It was as gala an affair as had ever been held in Parker Brothers's behalf. Among the few who showed up sans tux was Rich Stearns, who would later chalk it up to youthful rebelliousness. (His sportcoated attire was duly noted by many who attended that night. Many took it as further proof that video honcho was trying to separate himself and his troops from the rest of the company.)

HBM's gift to Parker Brothers that night was laughter—a full evening's revue, with HBM account executives serving as the talent. There were old commercials presented with new twists, along with a series of skits and blackouts. One skit, based on an actual incident that had achieved a certain taboo at Parker Brothers as a conversation topic, was about a rabbit who went to work at Parker Brothers as a laboratory test animal. In a letter home, the hare mournfully describes how a Parker Brothers toy, an outdoor, cousin of a *Frisbee* device called a *Skyro* flying ring, was launched into its eye, accidentally breaking its neck. "Don't worry, Mom," writes the rabbit, presumably in traction. "The next product's safe—it's called *Riviton.*"

But the crowd-pleasingest skit of all was an elaborate jab at Parker Brothers's seemingly endless bouts of personnel-shuffling and departmental reorganization. Onstage, Parker Brothers employees acted the parts of HBM account executives, trying to make an ad presentation, while HBM employees played a series of different roles as Parker Brothers managers.

Each time the "ad group" attempted to begin its pitch, it got shuttled off to another office with a perfunctory "so-and-so handles that now." And each time the scene changed, a slide projected onto the wall depicted the rearrangement on an organizational pyramid that grew ever bigger, ever more compartmentalized, and ever more precariously balanced—until the whole thing collapsed on itself.

The skit, too, brought down the house.

7

HOUSE RULES

*T*he pace had been too brutal for too long. After two years of first trying to catch, then stay ahead of the video market, Rich Stearns was dog-tired and feeling more than a little guilty for the hole that video had carved into his home life.

So, when Parker Brothers scheduled a party in June of 1983 in Montreux, Switzerland, to introduce its line of video games to the still-awakening European market, he and his wife, Renèe, happily packed their bags. They flew into Zurich and spent the better part of a week meandering through Alpine villages, with Montreux their eventual goal.

Lovely as he regarded the scenery, relaxing as he found the journey, Stearns had been unable to keep business off his mind. He had yet to get it through Jim Fifield's thick skull that Parker Brothers's video business was heading for trouble, and there were people back home rooting for him to hit gray matter with the man while in Montreux. So, alongside the sport shirts and crew socks, Stearns had packed plenty of reports, clippings, and statistics to prove his point.

As the day of his Montreux arrival drew nearer, the file folders became Stearns's bedside reading. He mustered every number, every rumor, every salesperson's sob story to his cause. And still he knew he had his work cut out for him if he expected to prove video on the wane.

The main thing working against him was how great everything still looked on the surface. Parker Brothers had closed the books on fiscal 1983 with after-tax profits of more than $25 million

171

on revenues of $231 million—more than half of which came from video. The company was in third place in the video-game industry, behind Atari and Coleco, still holding its 15 percent share of the total market for cartridges and game software. Four of the top ten video games in the country belonged to Parker Brothers.

Stearns marveled each time he thought of it: In its first full year in the business, Parker Brothers had racked up $132 million in video sales and more than doubled the company's volume. It represented the biggest product introduction in the history of General Mills history. The Toy Group lit up like an arcade machine: Operating profits jumped 32.1 percent to $104.6 million, as sales climbed 11.2 percent to $728.3 million. Return on assets reached an impressive 24.5 percent. With 7 percent of the $12 billion worldwide toys market, the Toy Group had come to represent General Mills's second-largest source of earnings.

No wonder there were yet more kudos for General Mills and what it had accomplished throughout its non-food operations. Chairman Bruce Atwater, 51, was named one of American business's best CEOs by *Financial World* magazine. The editors called him "one of the great strategic thinkers of our time," lauding in particular his skill in "enunciating and hitting goals."

Wall Street loved Atwater, too, for having doubled the corporation's per-share earnings from $2.36 to $4.81 from 1978 to 1982 and for raising shareholders' average return on equity from 16.2 percent to 19.4 percent—exceeding the 19 percent goal he had set for *next* year—in the same period. The company's scrutinized price-earnings ratio was arching toward an eventual high of thirteen.

The Toy Group had earned its share of the credit for the conglomerate's accomplishments—thanks to Kenner's licensed products, along with Parker Brothers's electronic games and, now, potentially the greatest of all of them, its video games.

Yet, anybody who read the *Wall Street Journal* knew—as Stearns most assuredly did—that the video market was "stinko." New industry forecasts gave Stearns reason to believe that not only would Parker Brothers find it difficult to sell cartridges to retailers this year, the retailers were probably going to experience inventory backups on what they had already bought.

Stearns ticked through the numbers in his head: Parker Brothers had shipped $80 million in video games from June to

December of 1982, and had struggled to move $50 million from January to June of 1983. The trend line was heading the wrong way. He'd lay money on it: Parker Brothers wasn't just going to miss its targets in fiscal 1984—the year just beginning—it could well have losses. To Stearns, it looked like the boom/bust cycle of hand-held electronic games all over again. But this time, nobody above his level seemed willing to heed the warning signs.

General Mills and its Toy Group were behaving like novice gamesters in a video arcade. In their excitement over the growth and earnings potential of this new category of plaything, Fifield and his crowd had forgotten the first priority of video games-manship: staying alive. Sure, any smart player tried to rack up as many points as possible—that was the object of the game in business as well as in the arcades. But, as Stearns knew all too well, those who got too greedy usually wound up getting eaten— or blown up, or shot down—by something they should have seen behind them. As he'd been trying to tell Fifield for months now, it was time for Parker Brothers to begin playing more defen- sively—to keep a finger on the hyperspace button.

So far, Fifield would have none of it. Since January the man's ambitious goals had kept Barton and Stearns front and center, each of them talking as if the best was yet to come. "We expect to triple our sales in calendar 1983," Barton had said in one interview, beaming, while Stearns gulped and nodded from behind him.

Within weeks of that article, a Wall Street investment-banking firm released a study showing that Atari's market share for video- game cartridges had plunged 32 percent in 1982—from 90 percent to 58 percent—a further reflection of the huge proliferation in the number of cartridge manufacturers. But the truly ominous news was that the inventory glut predicted before Christmas had now arrived. "Millions" of cartridges shipped in 1982 had not yet sold through to consumers, according to the report. Product was stacked high in the warehouses, creating a market-depressing surplus that seemed likely to touch off another round of bloody price wars.

Fifield, having seen the worrisome report, was quick to point out that an inventory glut alone was no reason to sound the death knell for a healthy competitor such as Parker Brothers. As was the case in hand-held electronics, he believed that the bigger, stronger entrants—the ones with the most popular game titles to offer the public and the strongest balance sheets to back them up—would be the ones equipped to survive the slowed sales and slashed prices. Fifield thought Parker Brothers certainly fell into that category. There were plenty of analysts and industry spokespeople who agreed with him, he pointed out.

Besides, Fifield added, computer software was still out there shimmering on the horizon—representing the even brighter future beyond the video console. An estimated five million home computers were to be purchased by Christmas of 1983. In its annual report, General Mills was already billing itself as a major supplier of what it now termed "home-entertainment software."

But more recently there had been another series of announcements that had left Stearns uneasy about how soon or how well the predicted computer phase of the video boom would kick in. Texas Instruments—one of the key players in the personal-computer market, and the one for whom Parker Brothers was designing many of its games—had announced a $119 million loss in its home computer business. Atari's computer business had posted an $18 million loss for the same quarter.

It was make-or-break time, Stearns concluded. Either he got Fifield to back down on the spring program's revenue projections, or Parker Brothers was going to be far out on a very shaky limb.

"No matter how bad the news is, tell 'em as soon as you know." Ranny Barton had long preached that one-sentence homily to underlings who feared General Mills's wrath, and now, as he boarded the transatlantic flight to Montreux, he turned the advice on himself. Jim Fifield simply had to be persuaded to back off on the sales and earnings targets he had set for video—the numbers were just too high for Parker Brothers to hit. Barton didn't know what, if anything, Rich Stearns had planned to do to address the issue, but he—as Parker Brothers's president—intended to take it up with Fifield directly, in Switzerland.

So much had changed in so little time. These days, the toys and games businesses weren't only being run *by* food conglomerates, they were being run *like* food conglomerates. Barton didn't think that was bad. He had never regretted bringing General Mills-style discipline and marketing expertise to his company. But the abrupt ups and downs of the toys-industry's product cycle—mostly the result of children and their fickle tastes—remained a huge, irreconcilable difference between food-industry parents and their toys-industry progeny. And Barton suspected that was why Jim Fifield had overreached in setting targets and projections for the video market.

General Mills tended to believe that product life cycles could be extended at will, simply as the result of innovative marketing and good management. The conglomerate had nine Big G cereals twenty years old or older, most of which had been repackaged or reformulated to bolster their popularity. When slapping a "new and improved" banner opposite the Betty Crocker logo didn't bolster sagging sales in a maturing category, the company would solidify its position by introducing so-called flanker products—*Fruit 'N Bran Wheaties* with *Wheaties,* for example. "There is no such thing as a product life cycle," a food-group executive once put it.

Toys people knew better. Despite the industry's new-found success with longer-lasting lines of products such as *Nerf* and *Strawberry Shortcake,* toys veterans knew better than to think their product could go on forever. Smart toy marketers who worried about how to get into a market one minute were worrying about how to get out with their shirts virtually the next.

Barton knew that Hasbro, for example, was already fretting publicly about the phenomenal success of its re-introduced *GI Joe* "action figure." After having been pulled off the market in 1977, the newer and smaller version of the doll was well on its way to sales of $50 million in its first year. Hasbro executives were uncomfortably aware that this single toy represented 36 percent of the company's revenue—too much for an industry where raging success usually precedes disastrous failure. They weren't going to make the same mistake that other toymakers seemed to make over and over again—expecting theirs to be the first bust-proof toy. The word was out, in fact, that Hasbro was looking for acquisitions to give the company a foothold in other market segments.

Fully half of Parker Brothers's business was video—but that was different, Fifield and the suspendered crowd in New York apparently reasoned. Video was a whole new category of product, not a single toy. And Fifield, like so many other experts, believed that video games would become permanent fixtures in the industry.

With General Mills's time-honored combination of marketing brainpower and a healthy advertising budget, why shouldn't they?

Because they just wouldn't. Barton knew the one incontrovertible truth of toys and games was that everything had a cycle. Woe to those who didn't stay attuned to it. Even *MONOPOLY* had been temporarily taken out of production a year after its introduction to allow Parker Brothers to evaluate the market. The memo, dated December 19, 1936, said "Cease absolutely to make any more boards or utensil boxes . . . we will stop making any *MONOPOLY* against the possibility of a very early slump."

Reclined in his airline seat, with nothing in sight but dusky-toned water and sky, Ranny Barton wished for the days when one memo, based on just one set of rumbling executive guts, could shut down the assembly lines. As it was, he'd have to see if he could make Fifield's guts rumble a little.

Barton didn't look forward to the conversation. What manager enjoyed admitting that business was not going to be as good as he or she had hoped it would be? Still, Barton knew that General Mills considered only one sin to be more grievous than not hitting your sales and earnings targets, and that was not facing up to the fact that you weren't going to hit them.

Back when Barton had first taken on the divisional presidency, former General Mills Chairman Jim McFarland had many times reassured him that the conglomerate understood such things as managerial mistakes and industry cycles. As much as he hoped for ever-arching growth curves, McFarland knew that once in a while a company had to retrench and perhaps even take a down year. "Without failure," as he once put it, "growth cannot occur."

Successor Bruce Atwater's attitude was perhaps a tad less forgiving, and that gave Barton pause when contemplating the effect his bad news would have when Fifield passed it up the line. But Barton also knew that Atwater, like Fifield, was nothing if not a pragmatist. How many times had Atwater said, in various ways, that managers weren't to let their egos get so tied up in their products that they couldn't recognize when things started going awry?

The afternoon before the festivities were to begin, Ranny Barton checked into his hotel, the luxurious Le Montreux Palace.

He had hardly had time to drop his sport coat on the bed before Fifield was on the telephone. "Hello, Lanny!" the Toy Group executive boomed. Barton noted the use of his nickname. It meant Fifield was in high spirits, which boded well for what lay ahead.

"Got a bathing suit in that suitcase? No? Well, maybe you can get into one of mine. Anyway, come on up for a drink."

Fifield's penthouse suite had a sprawling view of Lake Geneva, the shores of which were lined with alpine villas and gardens. A panorama of the Alps cut a jagged line into the blues and greens of the horizon. With a bottle of native white wine and a platter of cheese before them, Fifield and Barton settled back on the balcony to scan the countryside for the chalets of their dreams.

Presently, Fifield asked Barton what he thought of the spring program—the fiscal 1984 sales, profit, and inventory goals set for Parker Brothers, now two weeks in effect.

Barton saw no need to pull his punches. Unlike the way things had been with Bernie Loomis, who bit his head off at the least discouraging word, Barton had always felt he could tell Fifield anything, knowing he'd respond in calm, reasoned fashion. Why should it be any different now, in this casual, off-the-record setting? He shielded his eyes against the sunshine, turned to his boss, and told him he was glad for the opportunity to be heard on the subject.

"The program's off the wall, Jim—complete dream, myth, and fairy tale." Trouble had been brewing for months. Video was on a very steep downslide; Barton's sales troops were already having trouble coming up with orders. In fact, some retailers had been left with such an oversupply of inventory from Christmas that they were probably done buying until the next fiscal year. Barton paused, sipping his wine. "I think we should sit Atwater down and tell him we want to cut that daggoned program in half. And we should warn him that it might be just the beginning. We've gotta bail, Jim."

Barton sat and waited for the usual barrage of Fifield's questions. Where did he get his numbers? How solid were they? Fifield would also want to know how Stearns viewed the situation, of course. Granted, neither Fifield nor Atwater was going to enjoy seeing $50 million in earnings put in jeopardy. But these were reasonable men, and surely General Mills could take it. Besides,

Atwater himself had encouraged Barton to maintain a conservative outlook on video.

Back in early 1982, months before the first cartridges were shipped, an ebullient Ranny Barton had told Atwater he thought his company could do half a million in unit volume on *Frogger*. Atwater prevailed upon him to "hold it down" to make sure Parker Brothers didn't end up holding the bag on a lot of excess inventory. Just three weeks earlier, at the Toy Group's annual meeting in Durango, Colorado, Don Swanson—the vice chairman in charge of the non-food groups—had reiterated Atwater's message. He said he hoped Parker Brothers wouldn't "get carried away with too many titles, too many SKUs." With any luck, the very fact Fifield raised the issue meant that the Toy Group executive had come around to the same point of view.

When Fifield replied, however, his tone was uncharacteristically breezy. "We could never tell Bruce anything like that," he said. "That's just totally unacceptable." He had no intention of revising his projections, he said. Then Fifield verbally put the whip to Barton. "You have one objective, Ranny, and that is to take that program and make it happen. If you can't do it," he gestured in search of a name, any name, it didn't matter, "Coleco will." On and on Fifield declaimed, for ten minutes and more. He never raised his voice, yet he came down harder on Barton than anybody had since Bernie Loomis. Barton sat mute, listening mostly to his own thoughts.

It was over, Barton told himself. The hotshot deal-making, the organizational strife, and the 100 percent year-to-year growth. The hand-in-glove relationship he'd enjoyed with General Mills— that was probably history with this conversation as well. Barton didn't know whether he felt anger or relief or merely shock, so he opted for escape. Checking his watch, Barton told Fifield he needed to go unpack and dress for the evening's cocktail reception.

Shutting the door to Fifield's room behind him, Barton realized he needed to figure out if there remained any way of having a truthful conversation with Bruce Atwater. How would Barton reply if he were asked what Fifield had just asked, namely how he viewed General Mills's expectations for his company's revenues and profits? Barton had fashioned a phrase for himself by the time he reached his own quarters. If and when Atwater asked the question about the spring program, Barton would reply, "Well, it's an awfully big number." There was always the chance that Atwater might read between the lines and see that it was *too* big a number.

The evening's reception proved to be a lighthearted gathering, filled with the bonhomie of hard-won success and the anticipation of good things to come. But as the crowd thinned and dusk became night over Lake Geneva, Fifield cornered Stearns, who had arrived at the hotel not long before the cocktail party began. "Ranny's down on the program," he said. "You aren't, are you?" Unlike Barton, who could speak with the confidence of a man who wouldn't have to work another day in his life, Stearns, the golden boy, was being asked to come clean about serious trouble in his own trenches. If his most dire projections about the video market came true, there would be absolutely no reason that he should keep his job—not by corporate logic, anyway.

Stearns took a deep breath and began the speech he had rehearsed in his head. Well, yes, he and some of the others back in Beverly were still uncomfortable with the numbers. He was poised to elaborate, but Fifield stopped him short with a grin and a friendly jab to the shoulder. "Now, Rich, I told Bruce Atwater we'd hit that target, and you're turning around and saying we can't make it? I'm sure Bruce doesn't want to hear that."

Deftly, Fifield transformed the warning into a peptalk. Didn't Parker Brothers still have the top four video licenses in the country? Wasn't it true that it was as well positioned as possible to weather any possible industry shakeout? Wasn't it also true that the company had yet to get ahold of hard sales data for this first quarter, which was *always* the worst quarter? Fifield listed two or three rumors about competitors that gave him cause for continued optimism, and in closing, suggested that the three men take a longer look before asking General Mills to leap. Stearns agreed to crunch a few more numbers.

Stearns pressed his case a day later. In a half hour's conversation with Fifield, he tried to dangle some of the contingency plans he'd worked up. Fifield still wasn't buying. "You don't know more than you knew a month ago," the Toy Group executive said firmly. "It's premature."

Frustrated, Stearns made a conference call to Beverly, where sidekick Bracy, finance man Denny Miller, and sales vice president Bill Brett anxiously awaited the news. Fifield still hadn't caught a glimpse of financial reality, Stearns reported. "We're still on the hook for another hundred over last year, or $225 million," he said. That figure wasn't only optimistic, the three on the other end of the connection concurred—it was totally unrealistic, nearly impossible.

Barton, for his part, never met the occasion where he had to fib to Atwater about the program. The man never asked. Nor did Barton tell anyone the details of the penthouse conversation he had with Fifield, or even that it had taken place. He did, however, reveal a conclusion he had drawn from the confrontation. Pressed by Stearns and the others for his reading of Fifield's implacable stance on video, Barton attributed it to ambition. "He doesn't want to hear any bad news. Bad news isn't going to get him the top job in Minneapolis."

Back in Beverly, the show went on according to Fifield's stage directions as spring stretched into summer. Stearns was all smiles for the reporters when he announced what was called "the most intrepid marketing push in Parker Brothers's 100-year history"—the allocation of a $40 million advertising budget for the year, every cent of it earmarked for video-games. Parker Brothers's company-wide ad budget had been a mere $15 million two years before, Stearns pointed out. Why such a blitz for video? He said his company was following the tradition of its big-spending parent, General Mills. "We plan to take a very, very aggressive advertising approach on a product-by-product basis," he said.

The first campaign, for the long-awaited introduction of the home video version of an arcade hit called *Q*bert*, would break within weeks on prime-time network TV, cable's MTV, and in movie theatres. There would be print ads in consumer magazines such as *Games, Omni,* and *Sports Illustrated* as well. After *Q*bert* would come *Tutankhamen,* then *Popeye,* then *Super Cobra,* then *GI Joe.* . . . The list went on and on.

Stearns had seen *Q*bert* on a programmer's screen on a game-shopping trip back in the fall of 1981. *Q*bert* was a mangy-looking character that resembled a kiwi with a nose. His goal in video life was to leap from cube to cube, making each change color. Initially, *Q*bert* seemed to be just another pretty face as video games went, but after it got into the arcades in November of 1982, it became the number-one game, popular with youngsters and adults alike. Like *Frogger* before it, *Q*bert* was often mentioned as a candidate to succeed *Pac-Man,* because all three games appealed to people who otherwise did not respond to video games—among them, women. For example, a 37-year-old grandmother from Lake Park, Florida, Doris Divelle, was one of *Q*bert's* converts. Characterizing herself as a woman not terribly enthralled with the video phenomenon, she nonetheless played *Q*bert* in a neighborhood arcade for forty-eight hours, scoring 24,000,000 points and breaking an arcade endurance record.

In keeping with the Toy Group's wall-to-wall licensing strategy, Parker Brothers was introducing *Q*bert* not only in video game cartridges and home computer software, but as a tabletop electronic game, a board game, in *Nerf* soft-foam toys, plus children's books. There would also be *Q*bert* miniature collectible figures, windup toys, plush dolls, vehicles, a *Play-Doh* set, and craft kits. And that didn't add up to a fraction of the total exposure the *Q*bert* license would receive. *Q*bert* was to be emblazoned on about 140 different products from 26 other licensees who, like Parker Brothers, had purchased specific rights. Some of the licensees included towel-maker J.P. Stevens, Topps Chewing Gum, even Gillette's PaperMate pens.

Because *Q*bert* was the year's high-priority product, Parker Brothers's programmers were rushing to get it to market by July 1983 in every game format possible. In June, however, there arose a glitch in the engineering. Programmers had overestimated the capability of their technology to handle the game. They didn't think it possible to program it on a standard 4K chip. In a joint marketing/R & D meeting that month, the programmers said they felt they had to upgrade to the more expensive and memory-laden 8K chip, and they needed an extra two months to make the change.

This was bad news. Wholesale and retail prices had already been set at a level which would offer Parker Brothers a decent margin on the 4K chip, so the company would have to eat the extra cost if the game actually came out on higher-capacity circuitry. And, if the rollout were postponed, it might well cost

Parker Brothers some of its increasingly precious sales. There was a decision to be made here, and it could well make or break the company's already precarious financial performance for the year. "We can't afford the time or the margin erosion," said Stearns, after a moment. "We can't change horses. We've got to get it into 4K in two weeks."

Had Stearns permitted the delay the programmers sought, there might not have been a *Q*bert*. As it was, *Q*bert* was one of the last video arcade licenses that Parker Brothers would convert to home video cartridges or computer software. With the late 1982 slowdown in the video-arcade market, and accompanying cutbacks among the designers and manufacturers of the arcade games, home video cartridge manufacturers found themselves scraping the bottom of the barrel for ideas. Considering the arcade market creatively bankrupt, Parker Brothers began looking to movies. The James Bond flicks *Octopussy* and *Never Say Never Again* were at the top of Parker Brothers's list for development.

Using movie licenses had been part of Parker Brothers's original game plan—after all, a *Star Wars*-related video game was the first the company ever made. But arcade titles proved to be hotter in those early days and, unlike movies, they came with play values and principles already established. Manufacturers elected to milk that cow dry before turning their sights on Hollywood and beyond. Now it seemed that any character of any kind was considered video-game material. At one point in 1983, Parker Brothers's product managers, still suffering from having to do all the marketing legwork on video with little of the decision-making or developmental power, had a list of 237 possible game subjects or characters making the rounds. Many of the names on the list were trademarks, or mascots of the products of other companies.

Parker Brothers was thinking seriously of launching a home-computer video game based on the McDonald's character, Ronald McDonald. General Foods was doing *Kool-Aid Man* with Mattel. Both Atari and Parker Brothers were talking with Quaker Oats about the possibility of creating a *Cap'n Crunch* video game. Ronald and the Cap'n were to join *Spider-Man* and *Q*bert* in Parker Brothers's newly expanded line of computer games, with a game featuring those old standbys, *Strawberry Shortcake* and *The Care Bears* among those to follow.

What few wanted to recognize was that, like hand-held electronic games before it, the video market was languishing in part for lack of exciting play value. Oh, there were the occasional sparks of creativity: For example, Parker Brothers was pursuing a deal with Crayola crayons which was slated to result in the first interactive art software, in which a child could draw on a computer screen with a crayon-like wand. But, generally speaking, because the whole video market had been geared to the exploitation of pre-existing arcade games and movie screenplays, the resulting games were only as innovative or fun as the game designers and the Hollywood writers who originally conceived of them.

Most people in research and development inside Parker Brothers and other toys companies were merely the creative community's translators—people whose technical expertise could take a successful idea in one genre and replicate it in one or half-a-dozen others. The creativity gap was industry-wide and growing: The video programmers weren't game designers or screenplay writers, and the designers and writers couldn't program. The consumer was the loser.

Parker Brothers had tried to protect the creative spark by teaming its programmers with specially hired creative directors, but the programmers revolted and threatened to quit, insisting on total creative freedom. On the other hand, the programmers also balked at programming directly from the arcade-game licenses, saying it was tantamount to copying somebody else's work. Parker Brothers couldn't win, so it threw up its hands and kept the status quo. It was more cost-effective to spend extra money on outside consultants than it would be to alienate and maybe lose what scarce talent they had.

Not surprisingly, video games gradually became variations on a narrower and narrower selection of themes. At one point, Parker Brothers developed a family-tree market segmentation analysis, just to see who descended from what. The results were disturbing, to say the least. *Space Invaders* was found to have spawned fifteen or sixteen games; other popular progenitors were *Donkey Kong* and *Pac-Man.* How long would it be before consumers figured out that, really, they'd played these games before?

During a long, hot summer of confusion and doubt there was at last a point at which Fifield seemed to realize the gravity of the situation that Parker Brothers was facing. It came in August, when Parker Brothers was wrapping up its pre-Christmas shipping. By then, the news was in and it was not good: Industry-wide, orders through September of 1983 were going to be down 13 percent, even from 1982's depressed levels. Surely the already-iffy video market was going to be affected by the overall slowdown.

Fifield telephoned Stearns in Beverly, and in a ninety-minute conversation said he had been "doing some reading." He recognized the growing inventory problem, he said, and he wanted to do what needed to be done. How deeply did Stearns think he should cut the program [the video revenue projections]? Down to $150 million?

Stearns, flustered by what he viewed as Fifield's change of heart, stammered that it might be worse than 150. He'd look at some numbers and get back to him.

In any case, Fifield continued, he did think it wise to "ramp it down, face the music, and do what's right." Considering himself thus authorized, Stearns immediately called the purchasing department and cancelled every commitment to factory or materiel that he could. He made plans to schedule a series of damage-assessment meetings and establish an inventory reduction program.

But it soon became clear that Fifield still held a more optimistic view of the video marketplace than did Stearns. When Stearns sent down the recommendation he had promised—which called for the program to be cut not to $150 million, but to $125 million—Fifield sent it back revised to $135 million. In similar fashion, the sales forecasts see-sawed ever lower that fall. Each month it was another flight to New York City for another tracking meeting, and another—and yet lower—sales figure projected on the wall.

Through the continuing haggling over the numbers, Fifield never failed to evince the belief that, no matter how bad things got, Parker Brothers was going to be among the survivors of the shakeout, by virtue of its already-demonstrated strength in the market. He wasn't the only one so confident. Wall Street was still solidly behind "General Mills's video participation"—as Parker Brothers's efforts were often identified.

While many analysts found video increasingly skittish and unpredictable, most appeared to see the Minneapolis company's entries to be among the stronger, and presumably, longer-lasting of the crop. It was exactly Fifield's argument, and one all-too familiar to Stearns. It was the same old big-is-best philosophy that had been forwarded when hand-held electronics began to suffer from its inventory glut. Once again, the clout and the credibility of the Big G was assumed to be Parker Brothers's sales insurance policy. But this time, the analysts were going further, saying that it wasn't just size that was going to protect General Mills—and, thereby, Parker Brothers—it was smarts.

One after another the analysts pointed to the conglomerate's talent for staying on top of things, managerially speaking, and for going aggressively into new growth areas without over-extending itself. General Mills's top-flight management, they said, was unlikely to make the same mistakes that most of the over-zealous video rabble had. But most of them didn't know that Minneapolis wasn't calling all of the shots.

As the stakes had grown higher in video, and the pace more exciting at Parker Brothers, Fifield's staff grew in its influence over Ranny Barton's team. In terms of Parker Brothers's strategy and approach to the video market, Fifield was virtually managing Parker Brothers from an office in a Manhattan skyscraper.

An analogy that made the rounds in Beverly likened Fifield's leadership to a driver's education instructor teaching by car phone. No matter what Parker Brothers reported ahead, if Jim Fifield said to turn, the company turned. So far Fifield had managed to keep the wheels on the road, but a crackup seemed more and more inevitable with time. From where Fifield sat, how could he see what was really going on?

This perception of a remote-control approach to management was a source of great consternation in Beverly. Sure, there was such a thing as setting high goals and motivating your workforce to meet them. Fifield was certainly a manager of that type, and the people at Parker Brothers liked to regard themselves as equal to any task he might set before them. But Parker Brothers was being pushed far beyond what seemed reasonable. Should the Beverly management stand its ground, or should it go where Fifield seemed to want to lead and let him take the consequences?

The latter stance certainly offered the path of least resistance. Besides, Fifield wasn't paying any bonuses or granting any promotions on the basis of whose dire predictions came true.

So, Parker Brothers went into strategic contortions to try to make reality match what seemed to be the expectations on high. Market researchers crunched and re-crunched numbers, until at last sales forecasts seemed high enough to meet the levels that Fifield had communicated at the outset. For example, if the best projections for the computer video market didn't suggest enough demand to meet Parker Brothers's sales projections, the researchers would search high and low for more optimistic studies, ones that would support the number he seemed to have in mind.

When even selective data-gathering failed to produce the necessary numbers, the researchers would attempt to figure out what sorts of distortions would do the trick. Many times this meant expanding the product line or hastening product introductions. For example, by adding game software for Commodore computers a year ahead of schedule, Parker Brothers could boost its share of the market—on paper, anyway. Little or no thought was given to the stresses and strains this ratcheting-up of activity would put on the organization and its operating structure, however. There wasn't time, and until mid-1983, there had seemed to be plenty of money. Therefore, if circumstances seemed to dictate the need for more equipment and personnel, more equipment and personnel there would be—whether Parker Brothers could either find it or pay for it.

From 1981 onward, Parker Brothers had been caught up in the euphoria of the video boom. People there truly believed the company could do better and better, simply by working harder and harder. When their reach (or Fifield's) seemed to exceed their grasp, they congratulated themselves on pushing harder, taking the so-called proactive approach, and ultimately, of making the stretch. Theirs was a can-do attitude, and it was exhilarating.

But Parker Brothers could only win at this game so long as its market continued to grow. In an ever-expanding video market, the volume of the revenues flowing in tended to obscure the overhead expenses flowing out. It was only now, as the inflow slowed, that there was time and reason to consider how large the deficit might be, and how soon it might arrive. What the company saw was harrowing.

In its zeal for growth, Parker Brothers had rapidly dug itself into the same old toys-industry hole: too many products, too much production, too little planning for what might soon be too little profit. It was the old case of the company throwing too much at the wall, with a twist: Classically, trouble arrives when the company finds that what it's throwing doesn't stick. Parker Brothers actually would have been better off had that been the case. Rather, plenty did stick, encouraging the company to spend more and more of its burgeoning revenues on the throwing. Parker Brothers hired too many people, produced too many products, shipped too much inventory, and generally failed to prepare itself for the day that the revenue that had become its lifeblood would slow.

Over and over again the department heads at Parker Brothers asked themselves: Why hadn't somebody put a stop to this foolhardiness? The least self-serving answer was this: They were afraid to. Although nobody had tied or gagged Parker Brothers's managers, the team-playing dynamic at work at the time was strong, and there was little precedent for second-guessing, much less whistle-blowing. Jim Fifield's underlings felt he would brook no disagreement, entertain no skepticism, and in all cases would insist that the chain of command be respected. To so much as question the means to his end would be read as a failed loyalty test, they believed.

Perhaps eventually they would convince Fifield to retrench, they rationalized. But the clock was ticking, and already it was getting too late for Parker Brothers to protect itself from the impending disaster in video. Theirs was an industry that relied on well-timed, instinctive decision-making and, in their opinion, there had come to be too much distance between their guts and Fifield's head.

Over lunches and across desks, it became the number-one schmooze topic: What the hell was Fifield thinking? How had he so quickly changed Parker Brothers, stolen its autonomy, and most of all, gotten it into such a life-threatening mess in video? The attitude at various levels of the management pyramid seemed to be, "If we can understand what's going on, maybe we can fix it."

Everyone had their pet opinions. Perhaps Fifield himself was being driven hard to produce, it was suggested. General Mills wasn't the kind of company that screamed and yelled, but in its own quiet way, it was the sternest of taskmasters. General Mills was particularly unforgiving of those managers who threatened the corporation's cherished earnings record, which had produced steady per-share increases for more than twenty years running. There was advancement for those who worked miracles to protect these bragging rights; exit brands, or the executive equivalent, were for those whose works put them in jeopardy.

In their huddles, some Parker Brothers managers posited that perhaps sympathy was in order, that maybe Fifield was being forced to live up to his own reputation for wondrous works. After all the strokes he'd gotten for the tremendous Toy Group performance of fiscal 1983, and the repeat performance he had promised for 1984, how could he go back to Minneapolis now and say, in effect, "Oops?"

Others, however, thought Fifield had fallen victim to the belief that the video boom couldn't go bust. It seemed a little Pollyanna-ish for somebody with Fifield's smarts, but there it was: From all indications, he seemed determined to manage video games as if they were cereal, or yogurt, or even Kenner's *Star Wars* franchise—he'd keep adding to the product line and boosting the ad budget, and supposedly, racking up more revenue volume.

Then again, maybe he was pulling a Coleco, some suggested—pressing onward in the hope that something, anything, would be there to take up the slack when video finally went bust. Parker Brothers had never willingly played this sort of game with its business, but it was a time-honored tactic in the toys industry, and one employed with regularity by the Connecticut toymaker. For Coleco, it was feast or famine—megatoy or no toy. The company seemed to flirt with bankruptcy every three years, somehow emerging each time intact.

But the growing conclusion within the ranks was the same as the opinion Ranny Barton had already reached: Fifield's principal focus was his own career. As many judged it, he was running Parker Brothers into the ground by his own authorization, for his own gain. Right or wrong, most Parker Brothers executives were convinced that Chairman Bruce Atwater was too cautious a man to be calling these shots. And several of their number were certain they had seen concern in the eyes of Don Swanson, Fifield's boss, during recent discussions of the video-game market. To them, it appeared that Fifield's goal was to make the Toy Group such a success by General Mills's standards that the conglomerate would have no choice but to put him on the path to the executive suite. Failing that, he might well choose to keep it *looking* that healthy until his future was secure.

Straddling the line between reality and Fifield's expectations came to be a sadly predictable game. Each month, as the increasingly depressing sales figures came in, Parker Brothers's first move would be to try to shift some of the video shortfall to traditional games. If that didn't work—and most times it didn't, because traditional games weren't having such a bang-up season either—Stearns would take his case to New York. There he would collect his forty lashes and find out later that Fifield had telephoned Kenner and upped its commitment by the $5 million or $10 million that Parker Brothers had come up short.

Stearns recognized Fifield's contingency game to be very savvy and politically astute management—for the short term, anyway. But for the long term, he felt the better part of valor would have been for Fifield to admit to Minneapolis what was going on. Instead, Fifield elected to give Atwater and the rest of the Toy Group the bad news in gradual doses. In so doing, he was violating General Mills's cardinal rule: Thou shalt not bullshit thy manager. After each New York meeting, people would come back to Beverly shaking their heads.

Through it all, Fifield seemed relatively unconcerned. He continued to insist that things were going to be looking up, always reiterating his belief that the current rumblings in the market were merely those of a soon-to-be-ended shakeout in video-game hardware, one which would only confirm the wisdom of Parker Brothers's software-only strategy. He also saw this as the pivot point in the original scenario, at which computers would come into the market and open a brand-new market opportunity in game software. Accordingly, the slides projected on the conference-room wall in New York showed not video-game proliferation, but optimistic rates of growth in computer hardware and software. It all looked heartening when projected in a dark room, where nobody could see how much guesswork was lurking in the shadows. If somebody attempted to turn the issue back to video cartridges, Fifield was quick to cut them off. "We know there's probably more downside," Fifield would reply, "but we haven't gotten good numbers yet."

By September of 1983, it was becoming crucial that Parker Brothers turn itself around before disaster hit. General Mills wasn't in the mood to suffer fools gladly. At the company's annual shareholders' meeting in Minneapolis, Chairman Atwater announced that he would close sixty to seventy restaurants and retail stores during fiscal 1984 and sell several small, unnamed companies. He identified them as "primarily out-of-position and low-volume companies," and "small operating companies . . . not integral to General Mills's future strategy."

This was not a surprise. It had been apparent for some time now, certainly since Atwater took over and tightened the reins, that General Mills was going to pare down the size and scope of its non-food businesses. In 1982, Atwater sold several specialty food companies which were part of General Rawlings's original snack-food diversification plan. The reason given for the divestiture had little or nothing to do with performance. Distribution patterns differed from General Mills's, spokesmen said.

At no time did anyone say the Toy Group companies were on the block. Still, companies deemed to be non-performers, or out of sync with headquarters, *were* for sale—and the Toy Group's first-quarter doldrums were as well known in Minneapolis as the operational idiosyncrasies that set it apart from General Mills's mainstream food business. At the shareholders' meeting, Atwater commented that the majority of General Mills's capital would be invested in consumer foods and restaurants, which he termed "our two primary growth vehicles." It used to be *five* segments—Food, Restaurants, Fashion, Specialty Retailing, and Toys, bystanders pointed out.

It was also noted that General Mills had suddenly become reluctant to talk about its non-food businesses. At one food-oriented conference, analysts who asked questions about the Toy, Fashion, and Specialty Retailing Groups—fair-game topics in similar forums in the past—were virtually ignored. The response raised eyebrows in the room, and reminded some of how uncomfortable Bruce Atwater had seemed at that disco-like introduction party for the *Star Wars* cartridges back in 1982. There began to be suspicions of trouble in the diversified conglomerate. The Fashion and the Restaurant Groups were known to be coming off their boom times badly. Maybe Atwater and his troops were second-guessing their non-food forays?

Back in Beverly, Parker Brothers was pulling out all the stops to step up its revenue. Hopeful eyes were focused where they hadn't been in several years—on the traditional side of the company. Jones thought he had some new business possibilities that could be pulled in before the end of the fiscal year, such as a second flight of children's books and some additions to the *Nerf* line. But it would take an extraordinary effort on the part of his staff. He gathered his side of the company in the cafeteria, from secretaries on up, for a peptalk.

"For a while we've been treated like the have-nots among the haves," Jones said, pacing and rocking on his heels as he spoke, "but things are changing. The company needs us now." Then Jones outlined the key projects in greater detail than he would have ever deemed prudent before. "I want to make it clear that nobody, but *nobody,* is unimportant here. No detail is unimportant, either. I'm telling you all of this so that, if you're a secretary, and you see a memo lying around, you'll understand what it is, and maybe you'll work a little harder to expedite it."

The crowd left the meeting in higher spirits than had been seen on the traditional side of the business in some time. When pre-fiscal shipping concluded on the new line, it was clear that Jones's side of the company would go well over its targets—30 percent over, by the time the books closed. Jones, seeing the figures, punched fist to hand with delight. "We proved we could do it!" When year-end review time came around, Jones got a "mathematically impossible" bonus for his efforts.

However, just as Parker Brothers was most critically in need of controlling its own manufacturing destiny, the company had finally lost the last vestiges of control over its sourcing and production. Any nimbleness the company once had in procurement or scheduling shrank away with the increasing size and clout of T-GOD.

Soon after T-GOD boss Vic Rado came back from Europe in the summer of 1983, the Toy Group's divisional presidents—Mendelsohn, Barton, and Peisner—discovered Rado had won more clout than they had anticipated. In fact, he had come in at a level above them. The general managers scratched their heads. When the group had originally discussed the changes that led to the establishment of T-GOD, the clear concensus was that Rado's role was to be staff only. Suddenly he had a separate division, with full line responsibility. Within months Rado had forty people reporting to him out of a new T-GOD headquarters in Red Bank, New Jersey.

Ranny Barton soon found that while he had retained control of the old *MONOPOLY* plant in Salem, he had lost control of its workforce. The employees there now reported not to Barton in Beverly, but to Rado in Red Bank. Even their paychecks were signed by Rado now. The same was true of every production employee throughout the Toy Group.

No longer were Barton or the other operating managers responsible for their manufacturing profits and losses. No president could take full credit or blame for his performance. Perhaps worst of all, T-GOD cost the operating companies most of their flexibility. Shipping dates and volumes couldn't be adjusted without contending with Red Bank and its schedules. Had the assumption been that this consolidation would take place over three years, all might have worked out well. Instead, Rado's goal was, bang, full consolidation within a year. To him, it seemed an eminently reachable goal; in some European countries, he boasted, he had gotten the job done in two or three months.

However, in this instance, everything went wrong, and most of it could have been predicted from the rush-rush schedule on which these changes were made. It just wasn't possible to move people and products in real life as you would on a piece of paper.

To see evidence of the lack of planning, one had only to look at the Mexican plant that was to be the hub of the Toy Group's manufacturing effort. It was actually two plants, as Rado and company couldn't find a single, freestanding building that met all the specifications. Nor did the two structures come equipped with either the utilities or the available labor to do the kinds of production needed, so capital improvements and recruitment drives began immediately. And getting information to the three operating companies was a nightmare, as their respective computer systems didn't speak each other's languages.

Difficulties soon arose in the assembly of intricate toys, such as Fundimensions's Lionel train sets. Because all of Lionel's production runs were short ones, in which more than 13,000 different and intricate tools were used, the largely unskilled Mexican labor force didn't learn enough to handle them efficiently. Orders backed up at the factory with alarming speed. Over its two years of manufacturing in Mexico, the company posted $40 million worth of orders, but shipped only $16 million.

If the pressure of the change was hard on Barton and the other presidents, the burden on Rado's staff was debilitating. One of Parker Brothers's quality assurance people suffered a nervous breakdown trying to get the Mexican facilities on-line. Another key manufacturing manager transferred to T-GOD had a heart attack.

The three general managers of the Toy Group rued the day they gave even tacit approval to the consolidation of their manufacturing activities, each wishing he had spoken more firmly against it. Now it seemed too late. They had nowhere to go but to each other with their complaints. Minneapolis was out of bounds, as Rado and Fifield had left them feeling that complaints against T-GOD would be considered seditious. But Fifield's own staff members were willing to listen, and eventually they convinced their boss to give up the ghost on T-GOD. Fifield called a dinner meeting, at the end of which he agreed to dismantle everything either in or emanating from Red Bank.

For Fifield, this was clearly a painful decision. He had staked his reputation with General Mills on two major strategic moves—getting the Toy Group into video games, and consolidating its manufacturing operations. Both were coming a cropper. He was not pleased, and neither was Vic Rado—who accused the general managers of sabotaging the effort. Seeking to smooth ruffled feathers, the general managers complimented both Rado and Fifield for recognizing "the problem" that was T-GOD, and being gutsy enough to dismantle it within a year of its establishment. Doing

so cost the Toy Group as much as T-GOD had been touted to
save: $20 million.

To anyone who still needed proof, the T-GOD debacle stood
as a vivid example of how little General Mills—and especially
Jim Fifield—understood intra-divisional loyalties. After years of
blaming General Mills for not understanding *toys,* this came as a
revelation to some: General Mills didn't understand subsidiaries,
period. No matter how much allegiance they might be made to
feel for the mother company, acquired divisions simply could not
be made to give up their identities.

Since the day Jim Fifield had walked into Toy Group headquarters in New York, he had run the group as if it were not a
collection of companies, but one company with several remote
locations. He had changed the upper-management bonus structure
so that each executive was judged not just on his or her own
company's track record, but on the performance of the rest of the
group. These were Fifield's admirable attempts to increase cooperation between the companies and build a sense of shared identity
with the group. Still, there had been no unifying corporate theme
or strategy to back up the change beyond McFarland's vague and
seldom-promoted statement that General Mills made products that
"traveled the avenue to the home." In the absence of some clear
impetus to work with the other companies, and in the presence
of an almost virulent distrust and rivalry that grew up between
Kenner and Parker Brothers in the late 1970s, each company—
Kenner, Parker Brothers, and Fundimensions—came to view shared
activities as somehow punitive and ultimately damaging to its
own sense of self.

Few doubted that sharing licenses among Toy Group companies was a good and sensible approach to the volatile toys
industry of the 1980s, but under General Mills, the practice had
gotten out of hand. Thanks to the almost exclusive dependence on
licensing within the Toy Group, Parker Brothers, in particular,
lost a measure of its creative self-esteem. With fewer and fewer
products it could truly call its own, and amid the constant
admonition that it not set itself apart from the rest of the group,
Parker Brothers also lost some of the intense chauvinism and
pride that was a good bit of its strength.

This, however, was more than an internal problem. The outside world lost its sense of the individuality of the Toy Group companies as well. At dog-and-pony shows, analysts cared not one whit whether Parker Brothers made this toy or video game, or whether it came from Kenner. What they recognized was the single entity that General Mills endeavored to present: the Toy Group. "Parker Brothers? I couldn't have cared less about knowing which products were theirs," snapped one such analyst later. "To me, Parker Brothers might as well have been the pimple on the ass of the elephant. I followed the General Mills Toy Group, and I never cared where it did its sourcing."

But T-GOD may have represented the ultimate affront. Many of the efficiencies that Fifield and Rado sought in consolidating manufacturing operations required that the companies begin to see themselves as interchangeable, mix-and-match parts. Rado had ordered Kenner to do some of its production at the old Fundimensions plant, and required Parker Brothers to make room for Kenner's work in its printing plant. Various operations people were sent to this foreign division or that, with instructions to shape up a quality-control problem there, a marketing problem there, as if they were consultants on retainer.

As video began to founder and overhead became a concern, there were ever more attempts to reshuffle people and duties across company lines. If Kenner knew plastics design cold, for example, why shouldn't Parker Brothers be sending those projects requiring plastics to Cincinnati, instead of maintaining its own design team?

Stearns was among those at Parker Brothers "sick of hearing that Kenner could do this, could do that," as he put it not only during the T-GOD era, but over the months of cost-cutting and consolidation that followed. "Sure they can, but where will their loyalties be? Parker Brothers will always be last in line." Fifield didn't recognize company loyalties, Stearns explained to underlings who wondered why he and Barton didn't fight Fifield's policies more than they had. "Whenever we complain, we get slapped in the face for it. We're supposed to be loyal only to the group. Well, that's fine on paper, but emotions don't work like that." No matter how financially sensible his requests for cooperation may have been, Fifield was asking favors and sacrifices of groups of *people,* not mere balance-sheet entries or investment portfolios.

Wastebaskets alongside the photocopiers were soon filled with too-light or too-dark copies of somebody's rewritten resume. Conspicuous absences were assumed to be for job interviews. Parker Brothers's internal reputation for constant upheaval was undiminished by the goings-on after the company completed its production and shipping for another Christmas season.

The long under-appreciated marketing research department was at last dismantled in October of 1983, some of its human pieces pushed out the door, others jammed into some another department's puzzle. Another notable casualty of the period was Bill Dohrmann, longtime R & D and product-development man. His departure was amicable enough, but it had been apparent for some time that his influence had declined to practically nil. Perhaps the final blow came when Stearns, one of the product-management punks that had made his life so difficult in the early days of hand-held electronics, became his boss. With that promotion, Dohrmann's last good shot at top management had eluded him.

It was part of yet another major restructuring, orchestrated not by Ranny Barton, but by Jim Fifield in New York. This one would literally split Parker Brothers in two.

As video games started to founder the previous summer, Fifield tacitly acknowledged that he had been remiss in letting the traditional board game side of the business slip too far. In an apparent attempt to restore some of its presence in the corporation, Fifield drew a line down the middle of the company. Just weeks after Jones had made his impassioned speech in the cafeteria, Rich Stearns became *executive* vice president of consumer electronics, but it was not Jones who would take the other half of the company, toys and games. Nor was it given to a certain R & D man who already had one foot out the door. Fifield hired a former Minneapolis colleague named Brent Andrus from the Toy Group's operations in Great Britain to take the other executive vice presidency. Jones remained in marketing as a vice president, reporting to Andrus.

Just as the new reporting relationships were being established, the stock tickers brought news that called into question how long such a division of managerial power would be necessary: Texas Instruments had withdrawn from the home-computer market, a victim of slow sales and its own cutthroat price war against competitors. Wall Street applauded, but Parker Brothers—like many cartridge makers who were depending on a switch to software—was seriously wounded. It had been working on a compatible cartridge for the TI machine when the market for it blew up in its face. TI took writeoffs totaling $660 million and posted a net loss of $145 million (even after claiming an unusual tax credit).

It couldn't be denied anymore: Home computers just weren't catching on with the public as planned. Sure, purchases of the machines were arching ever higher, perhaps powered by guilt advertising that intimated that one's children would be academically trampled by their schoolmates if they didn't have a computer to help them with their homework. But the best that could be said about video software penetration was that it would be evolutionary, not revolutionary. Most of the toys companies in the business retrenched.

Parker Brothers's first layoff occurred in November of 1983, blamed on a "miscalculation of the software market." The vast majority of the sixty people let go were video programmers and designers, many of them people who had been working for the company less than six months.

The dismissals had been expected, and even for some of those let go, they came as a relief. The impending layoffs had taken weeks of careful orchestration. Who stayed; who would go? Who got how much severance? How would outplacement be handled? None of these decisions were made as quietly as intended. Despite efforts at secrecy, anybody anywhere near the company grapevine knew what was coming. As soon as junior financial people began seeing figures projecting a scaled-back workforce, they did what came naturally: They began playing I-know-something-you-don't-know with less clued-in coworkers. Managers found themselves cornered by subordinates who didn't care so much when the dismissals would come or who they would affect; they wanted to know why the announcement was so long in coming. Wasn't it high time the company took some decisive action to dig itself out of the deepening video hole?

As the retrenchment began, Ranny Barton was in the thick of all of these discussions—chairing meetings, coordinating activities and announcements with New York, and speaking directly with some of the unfortunates who were laid off. But, to a large

extent, he was only a ceremonial presence. The real nuts and bolts
of the company were being managed by either Rich Stearns or
the import from Europe, Brent Andrus. When Fifield created the
two executive vice presidencies, each man was given his own line
personnel in marketing, R & D, and engineering. The only functions that remained shared throughout the company were finance,
human resources, and sales—all three of which were staff departments, reporting now to Barton. By anyone's measure, Barton
had gotten crumbs.

He was not the kind of man to let a bad situation fester.
Despite his apparent discomfort with some aspects of strategic
decision making, subordinates were continually impressed by how
attuned Barton was to underlying messages and political shifts,
and how fervently he pursued things that really mattered. What
mattered to him now was his future.

For Barton, the job had lost some of its fun. Parker Brothers
was no longer the gentlemanly place it once was. There had been
too many political games of late, too much stress, and even for
him, too much change. Much as he had enjoyed his shuttle
diplomacy at the height of the video era, it was really too frenzied
to have been his idea of a good time. More recently, Parker
Brothers had lost both a factory and a distribution facility to T-
GOD, leaving him feeling that the company had been splintered
and diminished.

Much of Barton's discouragement dated back to Montreux,
when Fifield's refusal to face what Barton perceived to be the
realities of the video business left him disillusioned with the Toy
Group vice president he had so respected. Since then, Barton had
noticed himself stepping a little more into the background with
each passing month. He'd never had a year in mind to retire; he
always figured he'd stick around as long as he was having a good
time and felt happy to be had by General Mills, neither of which
seemed the case anymore. After giving it some thought, Barton
had decided that nothing could keep him working for Parker
Brothers if it also meant working for Jim Fifield.

But this time he did not take his message to Don Swanson.
Barton had decided he had gone over a boss's head once, and that
was enough. He told himself that a good executive should respect
the chain unless it commands something immoral, illegal, or

unethical—in which case, better to get off the team. To him, there was no inconsistency in his position. When he complained about Bernie Loomis to Don Swanson in 1981, he was making an issue of style, not strategy. This was different. How could Barton really know that Swanson and Atwater weren't calling every shot?

Barton brought his decision to his elderly father, who had been hinting for some time that he'd like to have Ranny take over some of the management of the family investments. "You won't fault me if I decide some day to get out?" ventured Barton. On the contrary, said Robert Barton, smiling, "I'll have a drink that night." Maudy Barton, too, professed to be pleased at the prospect of her husband leaving Parker Brothers.

So, in November of 1983, Parker Brothers's centennial year, Barton quietly submitted his resignation. Tempting as others may have found it to unload on somebody or something, Barton didn't give a moment's thought to it. His letter, just as cordial and respectful as he could make it, said he wished to make the resignation effective at the end of the fiscal year, in May of 1984. But he would certainly vacate at any earlier date that General Mills might prefer.

If Barton had expected a speedy response, perhaps a shocked phone call from Fifield, he didn't get it. For a week, there wasn't a peep out of New York, though a phone call to Fifield's secretary confirmed that the Toy Group head had, indeed, received the letter. Days after that, Fifield called him from the corporate jet, in which he, Swanson, and Atwater had discussed the resignation.

"I won't try to talk you out of your decision, but I will try to talk you into staying through calendar 1984," said Fifield, leaving Barton with the impression that his words reflected the consensus of the trio. "We wouldn't want you leaving at the end of a bad year." Having been assured that he wasn't being done any special favors, Barton agreed. His resignation would remain an eyes-only matter, not to be discussed until the company was well into fiscal 1985.

8

FOLD

*T*he crash proved to be everything that Parker Brothers had feared, and much more.

Consumer tastes underwent a 180-degree turn at Christmas of 1983. Buyers, suddenly opting for more traditional toys and games, almost unanimously turned their backs on anything that blinked or bleeped, and consequently, the market for electronic and video playthings blooped. Commerce Department figures told the story: Shipments of video-game hardware fell by 10 percent, while those of dolls and toys rose 7.7 percent—led by Coleco's *Cabbage Patch Kids,* a line of dolls that Kenner had considered and rejected. Almost 2.5 million of the adorably homely orphans had been "adopted" since their introduction in June of 1982.

Perhaps most painful for Parker Brothers, sales of previously languishing adult board games went up by 12 percent and, as was the case at Kenner with *Cabbage Patch Kids,* the company had said no to what proved to be the runaway game hit of the season, *Trivial Pursuit.* With that fateful decision, the company had chosen to pass on what would eventually become $750 million in revenue.

Parker Brothers had first become aware of *Trivial Pursuit* nearly two years earlier, at the 1982 Toy Fair. A representative of Horn & Abbott, the company representing the game's Canadian designers, caught up with a lunch-bound Bill Dohrmann in the lobby of the Toy Building at 200 Fifth Avenue and managed to press the thick, square box into the R & D man's hands. One month later, the package was returned to Horn & Abbott headquarters in Toronto with no explanation. Ranny Barton never saw it; neither did Bruce Jones.

It turned out that Dohrmann and his part of the product development team had nixed *Trivial Pursuit* for reasons similar to those that made George Parker say no to *MONOPOLY* so many years before. Like the famous real-estate game, the trivia contest didn't measure up to Parker Brothers's notions of what constituted a good, marketable game. At a retail price of more than $30, it was three times the price of a normal board game, featuring what they considered to be bad packaging and boring graphics. What's more, *Trivial Pursuit* was a game geared exclusively to adults, and as a game category, adult trivia games had been a perennial bomb.

Parker Brothers wasn't the only company not enthralled with *Trivial Pursuit;* Milton Bradley was among a handful of others that turned up their noses, executives in Springfield pausing only to offer backhanded congratulations to the game's inventors for having the gall to market such an expensive game.

Hardly anybody at Parker Brothers gave another thought to *Trivial Pursuit* until the following Christmas, when the word out of Parker Brothers's Canadian operations was that the game had become a cult favorite north of the border. The news gave Jones a momentary attack of nerves that passed when he found out who had finally bought the domestic rights to the game. "Oh, Selchow's got it? No problem," said Jones, dismissing the competitive threat with a wave of his hand. Selchow & Righter, the makers of *Scrabble* and *Parcheesi* in Bay Shore, New York, was the sort of place a games designer went when there were no other takers. For years the Long Islanders had been roundly derided in the games industry for their lack of marketing hustle.

Trivial Pursuit remained but a rumor from Canada until just before Christmas of 1983, when domestic sales of the game broke wide open on little more than word-of-mouth endorsements. Selchow & Righter easily cleared out its stock of 1.3 million games that season and sent a lot of disappointed consumers away empty-handed. Still, the industry guffawed when the company announced it was gearing up five factories to produce 20 million units in early 1984, anticipating retail sales of $600 million. The entire board-game industry hadn't generated more than $275 million in retail sales in calendar 1983! What were these guys, crazy?

To the absolute stupefaction of all, Selchow's projections proved to be conservative. The Canadian game spurred an American craze. Suddenly, the public possessed a voracious appetite for anything that tested one's memory for fun facts and useless information. Even an obscure company's also-ran entry, *Bible Trivia*—which many retailers considered iffy at best—virtually walked off the shelves.

Once again, Jones winced at the prospect of following the market instead of leading it, but what choice was there? He grabbed the trend's coattails by finding and developing Parker Brothers's own trivia game, *People Weekly,* and bought the rights to sell *Trivial Pursuit* in Europe and Australia. *People Weekly* didn't get rave reviews in the trades, but it became one of the games to buy when *Trivial Pursuit* was out of stock—which was all of the time during most of 1984. The licensing of the foreign rights to *Trivial Pursuit,* however, proved wiser in the planning than the doing. Translating or otherwise making American trivia understandable to foreigners, or finding foreign equivalents to substitute, wasn't easy.

Most years Parker Brothers had managed to shrug off missed opportunities and bum luck—it was part of the business. But the company had been losing far too many of late to convincingly feign the "win a few, lose a few" attitude that was considered sporting. Over and over it rolled in Jones's mind: If fate had been with Parker Brothers, *Trivial Pursuit* could have bailed out video as video had bailed out electronic games. All those millions in black ink could have flushed out the red in which his company was now awash. The game would have saved the whole Toy Group's year, and that wasn't the half of it. Depressing as it was to contemplate, Jones had missed his one big chance to put the board-game side of the company back in the driver's seat. The only redeeming factor in the whole mess was the fact that *Trivial Pursuit* had renewed the faith of long-skeptical retailers in board games.

Parker Brothers wasn't the only company left gaping at the reversal of fortune at Christmas of 1983. The speed and strength of the turnabout took everyone in the industry by surprise; even the victors were left slapping their foreheads in bemusement. Said

Stephen D. Hassenfeld of Hasbro, whose company saw a big resurgence in old standbys such as the thirty-year-old *Mr. Potato Head* and continuing sales of the revived *GI Joe,* "This year has absolutely destroyed the forecasting models of the last few years."

Retailers were fooled, too. They had ordered traditional toys almost reluctantly at Toy Fair, apparently expecting it to be another sluggish year in every category but video. And why not? Back then, the economic recovery the Reagan administration had promised was still regarded as political rhetoric or wishful thinking, and video games were the rage. Then, without warning, the economic indicators were up, video was history, consumers were clamoring for everything that wasn't in stock. Many of the most popular new non-video entries went to rainchecks well before Thanksgiving, and the few new shipments that arrived were sold before they hit the shelves. Shades of Loomis and the early days of *Star Wars:* Kenner, which had a very good year despite missing out on *Cabbage Patch Kids,* was posting signs offering customers free prizes if they'd just wait and buy their toys based on *The Care Bears* license next year.

The industry's reaction was predictable. Like passengers on a listing ship, manufacturers and retailers alike ran from one rail to another in early 1984, from video to traditional playthings. At Toy Fair in February it was standing-room-only in showrooms such as Hasbro's and Coleco's (where *Cabbage Patch Kids* had more than made up for the video losses associated with the Colecovision system), but no-man's land in those of Atari, Activision, and Mattel.

Speculators bailed out of the market in droves. Quaker Oats, owner of highly successful Fisher-Price Toys, sold U.S. Games Corporation, a small marketer of Atari-compatible cartridges, less than a year after it had acquired it. Twentieth Century Fox shuttered its entry in the market, Fox Games. Mattel discontinued production of its *Aquarius* computer, but denied rampant rumors that it would soon write off its entire electronics division. Milton Bradley, which thought it had sewn up deals to sell a voice-commanded game module to both Atari and Texas Instruments, abandoned development of the *Vectrex* system when both corporate customers cancelled their orders.

At the same time, the shift in the market touched off a new wave of mergers. Leading the pack was Hasbro, which banked on a continued revitalization of the market for traditional board games by spending $350 million to buy up Parker Brothers's rival, Milton Bradley, along with its very lucrative Play-skool division. The new Hasbro-Bradley became the second-largest independent power in the toy trade, with annual sales in excess of $800 million.

Like Hasbro, the relatively few toys and games companies that had resisted the temptation to get into video games—or more truthfully, missed the opportunity—began looking smart. They had been razzed unmercifully for their lack of gumption, and they were forced to twiddle their thumbs while competitors counted the booty of what became a $2 billion market for video. But they also sat out what may have constituted the biggest single-category disaster the business world had seen to date.

Video manufacturers had lost $1 billion in 1983 alone—more than they had made since the first consoles hit the market. Yet most could not shift gears and roar away from the shambles of this dying phenomenon. For the leaders in the market, attempting any sort of turnaround was akin to throwing a vehicle traveling sixty miles per hour into reverse without the aid of the clutch.

▪ Atari—which reached sales of $2 billion in 1982, making it the fastest-growing company in history—was losing hundreds of millions of dollars each quarter. By the end of 1984, losses would hit the $1.5 billion range.

▪ Number-two ranked Activision did better than most, reporting losses of less than $5 million.

▪ At Mattel, where a 23 percent decline in sales in calendar 1984 reduced the company's net worth from $275 million to first $70 million, and then to a negative sum, executives were candid in saying that if their company recovered, it would be only by the grace of *Barbie* and *Ken,* and several new but traditional toy and doll entries. Behind the scenes, the company was talking to an investor group about a restructuring plan.

▪ Parker Brothers would finish the year with three of the top five best selling titles in home-computer game software: *Q*Bert, Popeye,* and *Frogger,* for a total share of the market of 15 percent. June-through-December sales of video cartridges had been stagnant when compared to the same period a year earlier, and matters worsened considerably after Christmas. Due to a virtual stoppage in retail orders, Parker Brothers had dropped back to a pace that would put total company revenues at $150 million, with $40 million of that revenue coming from video closeouts at cost. For all intents and purposes, Parker Brothers had kissed goodbye half of its sales and nearly all of its profits for the forseeable future.

There remained optimists in the crowd, observers who saw hope for the continued health of the electronic toys business in the fact that total unit sales for calendar 1983 were only marginally lower than 1982's. But even these Pollyannas conceded that much of the traffic had been churned up by discounting so deep that retailers were virtually giving merchandise away—and amazingly, customers still seemed increasingly reluctant to buy at any price. For every *Q*bert,* still commanding its list price of $31.99, five similarly priced games were selling at 75 percent off. Retail margins were gone and manufacturer's profits were evaporating fast.

There was only one solution for any video-game maker with a lick of sense—to stop production and slash prices until consumer demand could flatten the mountains of unsold inventory. As Christmas passed and the calendar turned to the traditionally slack-sales months of January, February, and March of 1984, manufacturers wrangled and maneuvered to empty their warehouses into retail distribution channels any way they could.

The not-so-gentle persuasion bordered on coercion. Parker Brothers's salespeople, for example, went to retailers who already had 100,000 units in inventory and offered to ship another 100,000 for free. The deal would drop the retailer's average unit cost, they pointed out, allowing the retailer to run out the first batch at less of a loss. The problem, of course, was that the retailer now had to find enough customers to buy twice as much merchandise that already wasn't moving. But, with any luck, the salesperson was out the door before that realization dawned.

Still, not even this prodding and prying managed to dislodge the log-jam in the distribution system. The glut, now estimated at $30 million unsold cartridges, proved just too big. Parker Brothers barely eked out video-game revenues of $20 million in the spring of 1984—and that was considered good progress by manufacturers with less popular products.

In January of 1984, *Fortune* named General Mills the nation's most admired food company for 1983, an honor worthy of much pride and celebration.

But, in Minneapolis, consternation was growing. The business world was all agog with video's sudden crash, and executives from headquarters couldn't stick their noses out their office doors without being asked what they were going to do about the apparent crash of the highly touted category. Ironically, video—for all its publicity—was the least of General Mills's troubles. Certainly the Toy Group was having a tough go with the sudden stall of its high-flying line of cartridges and software, but the early indications were the Restaurant and Fashion Groups were doing at least as badly.

It was no doubt a troubling state of affairs for Bruce Atwater, who had long boasted that General Mills's broad product diversity cushioned it against business reverses. Since inheriting the management of the diversified company, Atwater had billed General Mills as a "fair-weather company," one whose so-called "item" business always had a sunny market segment ready to help weather the storms somewhere else on the income statement. If one line of business was down, surely General Mills would find brighter prospects to warm the shadows.

When this arrangement worked—and it had, beautifully, for quite a few years—it was classic portfolio management strategy at its best. For example, the non-food groups helped boost earnings during the 1970s, when General Mills's cereals were foundering. At the turn of the decade, strong gains in packaged foods had made up for profit declines in Specialty Retailing's two collectibles companies. (In fact, in a business in which a 25-year-old product is considered over the hill, sales of the reformulated Bisquick, which was originally introduced in 1930, soared past the $100 million mark for the first time in 1981.) Then video came along and bolstered some softness in the Fashion and Restaurants Groups in fiscal 1983. Now the Toy Group, the last holdout and best hope for buying time for the recovery of the still-ailing units, Izod and Red Lobster, was looking shaky too. Virtually all of Atwater's "items" were in decline, and despite another of the company's claims to fame—its tracking and planning prowess—General Mills seemed to have been caught totally by surprise. This sudden spate of volatility had come as a rude awakening. But it was made all the worse by the growing suspicion in the business community that some basic managerial miscues were to blame.

Amid the embarrassment and uncertainty, General Mills's executive vice president for non-food products, Don Swanson, took the lectern to speak to Wall Street analysts in April of 1984. He began with an assessment of the Toy Group, projecting a very strong year for traditional toys, particularly the licensed playthings of Kenner. Although Parker Brothers's video sales rallied from June to December of 1983—with shipments of $80 million, thanks mostly to *Q*bert*—profitability was down sharply due to heavy discounting in the marketplace. These doldrums, in a category that accounted for about 25 percent of the group's operating profits in 1983, were expected to drag down the entire Toy Group's profitability. Swanson termed the expected losses "small."

Still, Swanson insisted that General Mills continued to regard the home entertainment software market as a viable business with "attractive growth possibilities." Swanson said the company saw home entertainment software as "a low risk speculation." The category afforded very little fixed asset exposure, he assured the crowd, "and we manage our inventories very closely." Furthermore, thanks to the layoff and some related cutbacks at Parker Brothers, the Toy Group had entered calendar 1984 with "a scaled-down expense base."

The Great Shakeout of 1983 was over, Swanson summarized, without using exactly those words. The difficulties of the past six months had weeded out all but the serious competitors, of which the General Mills Toy Group was one. Video cartridge sales would continue to decline, Swanson acknowledged, but he was bullish on "entertainment software for home computers," which he said would only increase with further household penetration in hardware. That penetration, he said, would rise from 9 percent to 15 percent by 1985—a percentage at variance with Stearns's and Bracy's increasingly pessimistic assessment of the market. Already, Swanson noted, one-third of Parker Brothers's software sales—from the manufacturer to the trade, that is—were for computer formats. He didn't comment on how much of that volume had sold through to consumers.

Many analysts no doubt missed the subtext, but insiders could see what was going on: Swanson was reflecting Fifield's view of the situation—that the troubles in the video market were simply a trade problem resulting from a temporary glut of inventory, and that the survivors of the shakeout would better serve a public not only still wild about video, but ready to graduate to computers.

This video peptalk was necessary, not only to counteract the damaging post-Christmas press coverage of the video market, but perhaps to reduce the blow of the news that Swanson had yet to report on the Fashion and Restaurant Groups, which was at least as bad. Izod, whose sales had quintupled from 1979 to fiscal 1982, had fallen back to a revenue level that was but three times its 1979 volume. Earlier reports showed the division headed for a 10 percent decline in sales, and a 30 percent drop in profits—meaning that 50 percent of the operating profits for General Mills's entire Fashion Group was in jeopardy. The Red Lobster restaurant chain, bolstered by a costly expansion and upgrading program, increased its 1983 revenues—but earnings were going to be off as well, by about 10 percent.

Again, there may have been few in the audience who keyed in on it, but Swanson had to have seen similarities between the problems that had been dogging Fashion and Restaurants for the past year or two and those which now plagued the Toy Group. Like Parker Brothers and Kenner, both Izod and Red Lobster were pre-1970 acquisitions that hit their strides at the same time that the Toy Group surged, between 1979 and 1982. Taken together, Izod and Red Lobster came to account for about 20 percent of General Mills's $5.6 billion in revenues and a slightly larger percentage of its profits.

Then, over-confident managers—at whatever level—started ignoring the danger signs that foretold major shifts in their marketplaces. Despite research indicating that restaurant customers wanted fewer fried foods and more appetizers to "graze" on, the Restaurant Group resolved to see no evil until it was too late. Sales growth not only stopped, but turned south. Izod similarly overlooked a growing consumer boredom with the same old preppy polo shirt, the #2058, in the same conservative colors of navy, green, and cranberry. Izod stuck to its knits, and sales unraveled.

Both Fashion and Restaurants had behaved as if the gravy train would chug on forever. "In a changing market, we stayed with the same styles too long," commented a chagrined Izod marketing executive. To those paying attention at Parker Brothers, the statement had the strong ring of familiarity.

Back in Beverly, Stearns could practically feel the heat being turned up under his seat with each week. With both Fashion and Restaurants hurting, pressure was building on Parker Brothers to pull out of its video nosedive and lead the other groups to safety. All eyes seemed to be on Stearns and his electronic sinkhole. How had he let the damn thing open up? What was he doing to close it?

Stearns reacted defensively. There wasn't a manager alive, he said, who could have avoided getting swept away in the tidal wave that hit the video-game market in late 1983. For all the early warning signs, the boom had gone bust more quickly and completely than anyone could have projected. "Getting washed away was not the culpable act," he said to underlings, jabbing the air with a finger. "Standing on the beach was."

Stearns felt that if he had gotten the flat sales-growth target that he had lobbied for during the setting of the spring program, he would now be in a better position to come in with a profit in fiscal 1984. Instead of playing a $100 million game of catch-up, he would be looking at a shortfall of $20 million, maybe $50 million at most. The temptation to look Fifield in the eye and say "I told you so" was strong.

Barton, too, was catching his share of flak. "What's wrong?" some executives in New York and Minneapolis chided him. "Last year you were a $200 million company. Now it's going to be more like $100 million. What's going on? What are you doing about it? But Barton knew he couldn't do anything about it and, furthermore, that he wasn't really expected to. Barton was still president, as Fifield had insisted he should be—but the job was his in name only, and not for long.

Barton resubmitted his resignation in April of 1984 as planned. This time there was no lag in hearing a response. Fifield accepted the letter with the pre-agreed effective date of December 31, 1984. But Fifield had apparently grown less concerned about the appearance of having put Barton out to pasture "at the end of a bad [fiscal] year." The public announcement went out immediately: Barton, 51, had retired and would be replaced by Rich Stearns— who, at age 33, would become the youngest president in General Mills's corporate history.

Barton's decision to step aside took Stearns by surprise, but in truth, the younger man had felt an inkling of his promotion. As layoffs and cutbacks began at Parker Brothers in 1983, many of them carried out at his own urging, Stearns had gone to Barton to express concern about his future at Parker Brothers. He was afraid he would soon be forced to eliminate his own job, he said, "and then what?" Barton, ever cryptic when in possession of proprietary information, told Stearns he had nothing to worry about. "There are things I know that you don't," he said.

"What things?"

Barton smiled. "Trust me."

Stearns assumed Barton meant that somebody else, probably Brent Andrus—Fifield's European import on the traditional-games side of the business—would be axed to create a position for him when the bottom fell out of video. But it was Stearns's compatriot, Bill Bracy, who put the idea in his head that there might be bigger moves in the works.

One thawing afternoon in late March, while the pair lunched in a car outside a fast-food restaurant, Bracy folded his arms across his chest and told Stearns he'd put the pieces together. The only explanation for Barton's unelaborated assurances that made any sense, he said, was that Ranny Barton would step up to chairman and Stearns would be named president.

"Aw, get out," said Stearns. "I'm too young, and I've got a huge black eye where video is concerned." But Bracy's words stayed with him. That night, Stearns told his wife that Bracy's assessment might be out on the far fringes of possibility—and that if she didn't mind, he'd rather not speak of it again until the other shoe dropped.

It dropped within a week. Barton strode into Stearns's office one day and, peering over his bifocals, informed him that the two of them had been summoned to New York for an audience with Fifield.

Alone with the Toy Group executive in his office, Stearns
was informed by a smiling Fifield that Barton would be leaving.
Fifield gave a bit of a speech about how unfortunate Barton's
decision was, but he soon came to the point: Parker Brothers was
Stearns's to run if he wanted it.

Stearns exhibited more surprise than he really felt. Before
addressing the promotion, however, he took the opportunity to
apologize for not pulling off Fifield's game plan with video.

Numbers weren't everything, Fifield replied, brushing off
Stearns' contrition. He was sure Stearns had done his best. Did
that mean Stearns would take the job?

Stearns said it did.

Back in Beverly, Barton's "announcement day" began with
a meeting with his managers and support staff to break the news,
then more meetings in the cafeteria to make the announcement
to the entire workforce. There were gasps and tears in each session,
but Barton himself displayed little emotion. His departure was
part of a long-term plan to devote more time to family and
community interests, he said. When employees probed to find out
if Barton was being pushed aside, he hushed them with neither
a confirmation nor a denial. He had no regrets, he said. General
Mills had supported him in a way that allowed the little, family-
run company to grow from $35 million to well over $200 million
on his watch. What more could he have asked? Stearns, taking
his turn before the crowd, said he viewed his assumption of the
presidency at Parker Brothers as "a sacred responsibility."

Like many of the employees in the audience who gathered
in shocked little knots in the hallways to discuss what had
transpired, Barton had been surprised to see Stearns get the nod
for the presidency. While Stearns had been Fifield's one and only
stated choice for the job, Barton had argued for the return of his
former controller and marketing man, Ron Jackson, who was still
managing The Talbots for General Mills.

Barton liked Stearns well enough, but he was one of those
who had long believed that many of the marketer's attributes
were also his deficiencies, managerially speaking. Stearns's energy
and flair for risk-taking argued against his being able to set a
steady and levelheaded course for the company. His enthusiasm
for every aspect of a project would likely make it hard for him

to delegate responsibility. But most of Barton's arguments against Stearns boiled down to the same ones that the video executive had offered against himself: He was too young, and yes, he was somewhat crippled by his leadership in electronics. From *Merlin* to *Q*bert,* Stearns had always worked just beyond the mainstream, with only a few subordinates at his elbow. The majority of the workforce didn't know him enough to fully trust him, and Stearns's background was too narrow to prepare him for the many and diverse pressures he would contend with in trying to turn Parker Brothers around.

But when it was certain that Stearns would be the successor, Barton—ever the classy aristocrat—displayed none of his qualms. He introduced Stearns as the new president with apparent pride and pleasure, and told reporters that Stearns's "meteoric rise" of the past seven years had left him "more seasoned than people many years his senior." Stearns's "more classical marketing background" would also allow him to "take a more professional approach to the years ahead than I might have," Barton added.

Though Stearns protested, Barton wasted no time in vesting Rich with full authority. The last family member to serve at the helm of Parker Brothers was out of the presidential digs the same week. Wearing the title of chairman now, he would serve the remainder of his term in an out-of-the-way office in a less prestigious corner of the building. In the private moment when he handed over his keys, Barton congratulated Stearns on his accomplishments to date and offered what Stearns read as an apology for leaving him with the troubles that loomed ahead.

With the promotion, Stearns had inherited the fallout from the recent layoffs of sixty people—the second major personnel cut in six months, and the first to affect more than video-oriented employees. At the time, Barton explained that he had cut deeper than he'd had to because he didn't want him or his successor having to go through the ordeal again. Within weeks, however, Fifield was talking as if more layoffs were in the offing.

Then there was the problem of closing the books on fiscal 1984: Parker Brothers was unlikely to even get into the ballpark of its revenue and earnings targets unless a superhuman effort was launched to book more sales.

The end of the fiscal year was always a tense time, particularly in the last few years, when the need to play catch-up on sales became strong. But the pressure to hit the numbers was markedly more intense this year, not only due to video's doldrums or those elsewhere in the non-food groups, but because of a new and ambitious corporate earnings policy. In fiscal 1983, at the height of the video boom, General Mills had achieved an impressive 19.9 percent return on shareholder equity—again exceeding the goal it had set for itself. Playing straight to the grandstands, General Mills had announced in the ensuing annual report that the company would continue to hit or achieve the 19 percent goal for the foreseeable future. The company intended to stay within the upper quartile of *Standard & Poor's* 500 best-performing companies over the next five years. Earnings per share growth would exceed the rate of inflation by 6 percent, on average; dividends were to maintain a payout ratio of 35 to 40 percent of earnings over the same five-year period.

As a result, some found it sad but not surprising to see dozens of Parker Brothers employees manning forklifts and loading docks on Memorial Day weekend. They were hurriedly shipping out games and toys that they knew no retailer wanted, but they were going through the motions anyway—all in what they knew might be a futile effort to boost not only their own revenues, but General Mills's as well.

By "loading" or "mortgaging" or, in the vernacular, "ramming," inventory—overshipping merchandise before the end of a fiscal year—a company can book sales that it would be otherwise force to record in the following year. It is a common practice in the toys industry, and although it often serves mainly to push problems from one year to another, it had become customary at Parker Brothers since *Merlin* days to have the sales department put the arm on retailers to take extra shipments each spring. Retailers often agreed, knowing that they wouldn't have to pay for the merchandise until the following winter when they did 60 percent of their business. The practice marked quite a reversal for a company that had, back in the super-successful 1970s, impounded trucks and withheld shipments at the end of a fiscal year to do the opposite—to hold revenues down.

This year, with a huge gap between projections and actual sales yawning in Stearns's face, the inventory-loading was going to be too heavy for the shipping and accounting departments to handle alone. Disgusted by the contortions that corporate policy was requiring of Parker Brothers ("It's just not good business to ram product down your customers' throats to make your numbers," Stearns complained to colleagues), yet determined to get the job done and keep spirits high, one of his first presidential duties was to hang sign-up sheets, asking for volunteer stevedores. Virtually all of the company's managers showed up at one time or another during that Memorial Day weekend, some with family members in tow. A crew of vice presidents pulled the night shift.

Why devote their off hours to such a project? Loyalty was the answer for most, but they didn't mean loyalty to Jim Fifield or General Mills. They worked mostly out of allegiance to the name Parker Brothers and all it had stood for over the past 101 years—all they hoped it would stand for in as many years to come. For top-echelon managers, it was also a pocketbook issue, however. Their bonuses depended on making the numbers that Fifield had set.

During a similar but smaller year-end drill in 1983, the finance department had handed out blue T-shirts with white lettering whose logo depicted worn-out workers collapsed against file cabinets. "I Survived the Fiscal 1983 Close," the shirts read. But there wasn't enough spunk to put out T-shirts in 1984. The unspoken fear in many managerial minds was that these shipments might eventually prove to have been more helpful to Parker Brothers a week later, in the new fiscal year. Would the sales picture be any brighter a year from now? They could only hope that it would be.

Video bust notwithstanding, the nation's toys business was on its way to what would be its best year ever in calendar 1984. U.S. retail sales would grow 20 percent, to a new industry high of $12 billion. But General Mills would not be among the celebrants—that much was clear even at mid-year.

At the close of fiscal 1984, Toy Group sales increased 7.5 percent, to $782.7 million, thanks to record sales and earnings at Kenner. But earnings plummeted 31 percent, to $72 million, largely the result of red ink in video. Instead of the $225 million of the original spring program, Parker Brothers's electronics operations lost $10 million on volume that the company had punched and prodded up to $117 million. Adding insult to injury, the Toy Group was forced to take a $21 million writedown—a "redeployment charge," General Mills called it—on its unsuccessful creation of the operations division, T-GOD.

The optimism that had characterized the pronouncements out of New York and Minneapolis early in the fiscal year had given way to a pensive anxiety, as reflected in the sober prose of the annual report. At last General Mills gave up its bullishness on video. "The chaotic state of the software market has created uncertainty about the future of this business," stated the document released in August of 1984. "Parker Brothers has scaled back its expense base to contain risk while assessing future market opportunities." Newspapers quoted Fifield was quoted as saying he didn't expect video to make a dime until fiscal 1986.

Still, at headquarters in Minneapolis there was a palpable feeling of relief. General Mills finished fiscal 1984 with earnings of $398.7 million on sales of $5.6 billion. Sales were up 1 percent, while earnings were off 4.8 percent, thanks to declines not only in Toys, but in the Fashion and the Restaurant Groups. Nonetheless, thanks to an aggressive stock buyback effort, earnings per share were $4.98, eking out a twenty-second year of uninterrupted growth with an increase of nine cents from 1983. Return on equity was 19 percent, as planned. Dividends per share were $2.04, up 10.9 percent.

Any student of General Mills history could sense change on the horizon. The conglomerate had squeaked through the year by the skin of its teeth. If past performance was any indication, this self-proclaimed "fair-weather company" was nearing the point at which it would take cover from the storm. In the name of its security-loving stockholders, and with the goal of saving face on its own managerial mistakes, the conglomerate would soon do something to reduce its exposure to the volatility of its non-food markets—that is, unless the divisions could turn themselves around, and fast.

General Mills was not alone in its impatience with its non-food operations. Already food-based conglomerates such as Quaker

Oats, Pillsbury, and ConAgra were making moves to abandon some of their diversification efforts and re-consolidate themselves as food processors. Analysts were starting to ask what was taking General Mills so long to get on the bandwagon.

For Stearns, the second half of calendar 1984, the beginning of fiscal 1985, was fragmented and bizarre—a time that would later play in his memory like a blurry movie on fast-forward. Even as he was stepping into his new presidential role there was pressure from all sides to stop the skid of video losses, to turn the company around and find solid ground once again. He knew, as did everyone, that if that solid ground existed it would consist of cardboard and plastic, the stuff of the long-ignored traditional side of the company.

It seemed ironic. Here Stearns was, the video *wunderkind,* now president of a company that effectively *had* no video business. When he was promoted, his job—executive vice president of electronics—went unfilled. For all his taunts about "tortured cardboard" in his younger days, he was taking over the reins of a company that would now produce mostly that. And the real kicker? Not even the traditional side of the business was in the black, thanks mostly to the idiosyncrasies of corporate accounting.

The company's books allocated overhead based on sales volume. Therefore, when video revenues made up for half of the company, that side of the business was soaking up half of the overhead, no matter how much it was truly responsible for. In essence, as long as video remained healthy, the traditional side of the business had been getting a "free ride," as Stearns was wont to put it. After video crashed, most of that floating overhead went back to traditional games and though people on that side of the business resented it, it was the reason that layoffs went beyond mere video programmers and designers. "It's hard to get it through people's heads," Stearns complained to all who would listen, "that, ha-ha,"—the jeer was more bitter than gleeful—"board games are a disaster too." In fact, it was already clear that video might have a better chance of breaking even, when all was said and done, than traditional games.

Any turnaround Stearns might be able to pull off was going to have to be executed with what cash he already had, that much was certain. General Mills was not in a mood to be writing checks for reinvestment. What's more, even if he could get the money, he had no magic bullet waiting to vanquish his video losses, as video had done for hand-held electronic games. What choice did he have? He'd have to make a go of it with traditional toys and games, plus a category that was new in 1983: books.

The book division was off to a boffo start, but it was still merely a $15 million business. And in accordance with the Toy Group's wall-to-wall licensing strategy, it had become heavily dependent on now-maturing Kenner licenses such as *Strawberry Shortcake* and *The Care Bears*. The books were, in fact, little more than illustrated brochures for Kenner's products—and who knew how long the likes of these characters would remain popular? *Strawberry Shortcake* was in its fifth year.

A phonograph-record division that had been started at approximately the same time as the books emerged looked even less reliably profitable—despite the fact that the *Cabbage Patch Kids* record went gold in July of 1984, selling over 500,000 copies. All the in-house research showed that records would probably be up one year and down the next for the foreseeable future, tied to the individual popularity of whatever character or subject Parker Brothers chose. But Parker Brothers had few options to pursue other than books and records. And General Mills would entertain none that would cost it money.

Stearns put the whip to his workforce in the hope of spurring higher sales on existing products and developing new ones. He was particularly keen to share with the traditional side of the business the hustle lessons he'd learned in video. He set out to ride Parker Brothers, and particularly its board-game marketing staff, of its "namby-pamby, ivory-tower image" in the toys industry. He wanted them to quit relying on facts and figures and start acting more like what he thought of as salespeople. In so instructing, he was beginning to sound more like the guys with the cigars than the diploma-packing MBA he had been on arrival, now nearly eight years ago.

"You've got to call on customers," Stearns exhorted. "Be where the action is. You've gotta have dinner with the guys in the leisure suits." Throughout his video days he had learned from painful experience how adept other companies were at sniping from the sidelines, leaving victims wondering where the shooting was coming from. "Arnold Greenberg's got somebody behind every potted palm," Stearns said, referring to Coleco's president. "It's not 1883. This is not the world of cobblestones and carriages anymore. We're in Wyoming with a tomahawk, fighting off the Indians. That's the reality of toys today."

By fall of 1984, when it came time to select products for the coming year's Toy Fair in February, Stearns was heartened by the jerry-built line of products arrayed before him. Parker Brothers expanded its lines of children's books, records, and tapes with new titles, such as the *Rose-Petal* line developed by Kenner and Hallmark. Table pool and baseball were to join *Nerf*'s foam toy line. A line of action figures based on a comic-book series, still on the drawing boards, looked promising. Seeing the potential for growth in the $600 million pre-school market thanks to a yuppie baby boom, an *Ewoks* line—a series of characters related to the *Star Wars* products—was being developed. Hoping to piggyback on that old *MONOPOLY* magic, the company introduced a spinoff game called *Advance to Boardwalk*. There was even an attempt to reprise *Riviton* with less tragic results, through a new construction-toy entry called *The Construction Company*. Through it all, Parker Brothers was still milking the trivia boom with *People Weekly*, and hoping to develop a new strategy-game staple with *Pente*, the backgammon-like game it acquired in 1983, after a year of negotiations.

But trouble continued to shadow Parker Brothers. One of the biggest hopes for fiscal 1985 was dashed when the movie *Dune* received a PG rating. That effectively locked out of the theatres most of the audience to whom Parker Brothers had hoped to sell its licensed toys and games. Instead, the movie hit of the year proved to be *Gremlins,* a license Parker Brothers rejected, labeling the script too violent.

While some of the setbacks were the result of bad luck, candor demanded that others be labeled as examples of managerial mistakes. Still, most were casualties of video in one way or another. In hindsight it was clear that Parker Brothers's obsession with video had hobbled the development of many of the products that were now the company's best hopes for filling the revenue crater left by video.

By its own admission, Parker Brothers had initially paid considerably more than it should have to buy *Pente,* offering a 10 percent royalty at a time when 7 percent was the average in board games. The company also set the guaranteed minimum sales figure far too optimistically. The deal was renegotiated, but that didn't prevent snags from developing with the retail trade. The game's designers had made a practice of doing special deals with some stores and chains. Parker Brothers abruptly refused to continue them. Nor would Parker Brothers allow these retailers to send back unsold merchandise, as they had to the original inventors. Parker Brothers didn't even follow through on its own competitive strategy. The game wasn't taken into the chain stores as planned; the company stayed in the upscale outlets and altered commission rates and established other hard-and-fast rules that alienated the trade. Furthermore, an expensive ad campaign that was geared to upscale customers gave so little emphasis to the names *Pente* and Parker Brothers that the customer wasn't sure what was being sold. But the biggest problem was that of the sales staff: Still accustomed to the faster pace and bigger margins of video, many key sales staffers were slow to support the product.

The line of children's books was plagued with its own set of bloopers. Working on a shoestring development budget through 1982 and 1983, marketers remained ignorant of key factors that would limit their success in the new market. Part of the problem was a sheer lack of talent—there weren't enough good heads working on the project, as all the hard-chargers that had been hired had been herded into video. Then, as the video shakeout began to threaten the overall future of Parker Brothers, several executives active in the books and records project moved on to newer and, presumably, more secure jobs. It wasn't a good atmosphere for creativity.

Like the people who undid the sweetheart deals on *Pente,* the book team similarly antagonized a segment of its retailers—by refusing to let unsold books be returned to the factory. The stance was no surprise to toy-store owners who had always been responsible for moving their own inventory, but it was a departure from publishing tradition that caused many booksellers to boycott the line. The revolt, in and of itself, shouldn't have presented much of a problem to Parker Brothers—the booksellers represented only about 25 percent of the retail network that Parker Brothers was relying upon. But when the booksellers started yelling, so did many irked retailers who were looking for a reason to pop off. They felt they'd been stuck with a glut of over-priced product— a perception that was the result of several more Parker Brothers bloopers.

Back at the beginning of the project, Bruce Jones had failed to win exclusive book rights to *The Care Bears* from M.A.D.— which was now the clearinghouse that handled all of the Toy Group's licensing, even that of Parker Brothers's much-shielded *MONOPOLY*. Instead, Jones was granted a so-called split license with Random House, the New York City publisher. Sharing the rights to the property might have presented no problem—if the publishing house hadn't sat out the first year and undercut Parker Brothers's prices in the second year.

Then Parker Brothers drew the ire of the retail community by virtually pelting it with product. In its continuing quest for revenue volume, Parker Brothers had rammed books through the distribution channels in awesome numbers in the Memorial Day shipping episode of 1984. In fact, the company trucked out more than double the quantity of books that they had any reasonable expectation of selling. Parker Brothers's own sales department had argued against shipping so heavily, predicting revolt among retailers. But management wouldn't budge. There were targets to be hit. "We'll worry about next year, next year," came the message from New York. So, as the Christmas selling season of 1984 approached, many retailers had shelves stacked with far more books than they could sell. They were sorely displeased.

Ironically, retailers were on their way to what would prove to be a very good year with Parker Brothers's books: Sales would exceed projections. But, true to the warnings, cramming the distribution system with product obscured the happy reality of their success. No matter how many books had actually sold, the still-groaning warehouse shelves convinced retailers that the books were a bust. They did not reorder. The result? Parker Brothers inadvertently killed the only potential golden goose it had in addition to video. Book sales fell from $18 million to $8 million. Too bad, too: Profit margins on these books were comparable to those of the company's better-selling board games—better in fact than *MONOPOLY*.

The man who took the heat for some of these troubles was Brent Andrus, the former European toy company executive whom Fifield had brought in to revitalize the traditional side of the company in the fall of 1983. Just over a year later, Stearns fired him and restored Bruce Jones to his former leadership.

Throughout the fall of 1984, Stearns racked up Frequent Flyer mileage on the Eastern Shuttle, winging in and out of New York almost weekly for one meeting or another—most of them designed to contend with the continuing financial mess that began with the decline and fall of the video market. At each of these monthly tracking sessions, Stearns would show Fifield and his New York cohorts ever-larger figures representing Parker Brothers's potential video writeoffs. But each time Fifield disputed Stearns's arithmetic and, in essence, told him to trash his statistics and get his people to work. "Here," Fifield would say, tapping a finger on the increasingly elusive goals he had set for the company, "is what I need."

Unlike the fall of 1983, when the numbers dance that Stearns and Fifield were doing involved sales revenues for video games, this time it was an issue of managed expenses. Nobody questioned that video was in the hole and would stay there; the only issues were exactly how big the hole was and what combination of traditional-game sales and slashed overhead would be used to fill it. Once again, Fifield's earnings projections seemed extremely optimistic to Stearns and his team and, once again, Stearns took his cues as he saw them. Despite knowing that the hole was quite probably tens of millions of dollars deep, he resolved to reveal it a little bit at a time.

Stearns wasn't taking the gradual tack for the same reason he did in 1983, namely because Fifield seemed to want it that way. This time the decision was made largely on Stearns's own initiative. Since learning that Fifield would write no bailout checks, Stearns had also concluded that Fifield nonetheless expected to keep the Toy Group's revenues and earnings respectable, whatever it took. Fifield made no secret of the fact that he had a formula in mind for doing so—a formula that Stearns found unacceptable.

For example, if Stearns wanted to take his sales forecast down by $15 million, Fifield would demand the heads of seventy-five employees—or a chunk of the ad budget, or most counter-productively, a reduction in the number of product introductions. Stearns would be left sputtering. "Jim, we've got a long-term business here," he complained, "and you're impairing the ability of the company to survive at all."

Fifield assured Stearns that the two of them had the same interests at heart; he simply disagreed as to where to draw the line between cutting enough and cutting too much.

Stearns thought Fifield was already on the wrong side of the line. Each layoff had cost Parker Brothers key employees, many of them directly to pink slips, but just as many indirectly—to the uncertainty that caused them to seek and find new jobs. With these people departed the energy and expertise that were sorely needed to revitalize the company. Worse, as Stearns watched, each layoff further demoralized those who remained. Sooner or later Stearns would be turning off the lights on an empty building if he didn't take some action to protect the company.

Amid the wrangling, resentment began to build against Parker Brothers within the Toy Group. As the Group's overall financial picture became uglier, it was the gamesmakers in Beverly who got the blame. Long-simmering sibling rivalry issues that had laid dormant of late returned to the fore. Parker Brothers was doing the Toy Group in, the whispers said.

Some of these observers, watching Stearns's efforts to cushion the full impact of the losses by revealing the figure slowly, pronounced Parker Brothers management a pack of liars. Vic Rado, now on the Toy Group staff in New York after the T-GOD debacle, told people he thought Stearns was either lying or stalling, maybe both. Fundimensions president Art Peisner felt Stearns and company had forgotten they were in the toys business: How else could he explain internal forecasts that minced a predictable $5 million lower each month, never owning up to the full magnitude of the loss?

These critics knew that Jim Fifield was putting considerable pressure on Parker Brothers to keep its forecasts high. But they considered Stearns gutless for not pulling in his horns and writing off some sizable portion of the growing stockpiles of video inventory—that is, until it was discovered that Parker Brothers had no reserve to cover such writedowns. With that revelation, Stearns didn't seem as gutless as he did stupid.

The critics had a point: Parker Brothers could and should have set up reserves for any possible inventory writedowns that might arise. But what they didn't know was that Stearns and Barton had suggested just that sort of precaution some time ago. They had asked to be allowed to sock away some money for a rainy day, but their requests were turned down.

It happened back in 1983, when video was in full bloom. At the time Stearns had described the situation as having four years' worth of silver jingling in his pocket. Did General Mills want to dip in four times? Twice? Or just once? At the end of fiscal 1983, General Mills took it all in a big-fisted grab. Parker Brothers figuratively turned out its pockets and went into fiscal 1984 with no reserves.

Barton, Stearns, and their financial advisors were outraged. Didn't Parker Brothers deserve some sort of cushion after the fantastic year they had just produced? Barton couldn't remember the last time the company had been unable to salt something away. Even then, before any of the troubles in Fashion or Restaurants had been revealed, it seemed clear that Fifield was either ringing the bell for his own political ends, or he was solving somebody else's profitability problems. Either way, it wasn't fair—and in robbing Peter to pay Paul, it didn't seem prudent business practice.

But Parker Brothers wasn't the only division to feel it had been robbed. Nowadays Kenner had the same complaint. Executives in Cincinnati were angry for having to make up Parker Brothers's losses, and for Fifield's increasing tendency to shove Parker Brothers's growing functional deficiencies its way. Why, for example, should Kenner be asked to conduct marketing studies for its east-coast sibling, just because Parker Brothers no longer had a marketing research department of its own? Furthermore, Kenner executives feared that the sort of juggling they were having to do with shipments and inventory to cover Parker Brothers could well leave their own company dangerously exposed somewhere down the line.

Stearns had little sympathy. "If anybody's smoking dope about what's going on, it's Kenner," he said. He found Kenner's 1985 program to be ludicrously optimistic. More than 50 percent of Kenner's projected sales were slated to come from products that hadn't shipped yet. If Kenner were to hit those projections, its two new products—*Hugga Bunch* dolls and the *M.A.S.K.* line of transformable action figures—would have to become the numbers one and two product introductions in the history of the industry, by Stearns's reckoning.

It was fine to have optimistic expectations for public consumption, but "you don't plan on them," Stearns contended. The figures seemed especially optimistic in light of the fact that the other 50 percent of Kenner's projections had to come from the aging line of *Care Bears* products and its arguably moribund *Star Wars* and *Strawberry Shortcake* lines. Stearns didn't begrudge Kenner success; he just didn't want to see the company's "pipe dreams" hurt the already-wounded Parker Brothers. "They've got 900 employees to our 200," Stearns grumbled, speaking of ratios, not actual numbers. "Why's Jim kicking us? The layoffs ought to be happening in Cincinnati."

As Stearns judged it, Fifield was embittered by the failures of his vaunted video strategy, and was taking it out on both Parker Brothers and its young president. Stearns hadn't expected to remain his boss's fair-haired boy; he had, in fact, recommended that Parker Brothers, as a company, receive the lowest possible rating for the year. And, as president, he expected to suffer some of the consequences. But Stearns was shocked when he didn't share in the modest bonuses his subordinates received in fiscal 1985. By denying Stearns even a cent's worth of recognition, Fifield had departed from General Mills tradition—if not policy.

Complaining of punitive treatment against the company and its managers, several Parker Brothers executives began leaking financial documents and Fifield anecdotes to high staff officers in Minneapolis, in the hope that their whistle-blowing might convince Bruce Atwater to take some action. Stearns himself hinted at problems when he crossed paths with the usual conduits to Atwater—people in administration, corporate communications, and similar staff departments in Minneapolis. But mostly he tried to keep mum. If there was one thing he had learned from Ranny

Barton, it was the protocol of executive loyalty. And, like Barton, he would have resigned before he would have harmed his reputation by betraying a boss. Fifield, for all his perceived faults, still wasn't stealing from widows or children. Perhaps the worst of what he had done was to create a climate in which executives dared not speak their mind, for fear of the consequences. And that was no crime; unfortunately, it was all too often business as usual.

Wheels that had been turning for at least six months began to pick up speed after General Mills's annual shareholders meeting in September of 1984.

Concerned about the legacy of its diversification program, plus the fact that consumer food-based conglomerates were increasingly marked as targets for takeovers, General Mills announced a focus shift it had hinted at a year before: From then on, it deemed its major emphasis to be Consumer Foods (particularly ready-to-eat cereals) and Restaurants (led by Red Lobster). Despite the recent trouble in Restaurants, it was believed that each of these divisions promised steady growth and high returns. Collectively, these businesses would position General Mills well for the future, chairman Atwater declared. During the next five years, General Mills further pledged to support these businesses with approximately $1.5 billion in new fixed assets.

Shortly thereafter, in October, the vice chairman in charge of the non-food groups, Don Swanson, was forced into early retirement after thirty-five years of service to General Mills. It was generally understood that he had been asked to step aside because he wasn't deemed to be taking steps to rectify problems in his non-food groups. Removing the Restaurant Group from his responsibilities was the final sign of corporate dissatisfaction with his performance.

Swanson's chair was still warm when it was announced who would sit in it. The man tapped to fill the number-three job in the conglomerate was Jim Fifield. Although he didn't get Swanson's title of vice chairman—his new title would be merely group *executive* vice president instead of group vice president—the move still put Fifield two small hops from the presidency and a board appointment. But to get any further, he would probably have to singlehandedly rescue the non-food groups and save face for General Mills.

It continued to be the Fashion Group, and in particular, its sportswear division, Izod, that attracted the most concern and criticism, both inside and outside the corporation. Almost concurrent with Swanson's retirement, General Mills had announced a 50 percent slide in Izod sales, wiping out all of the company's profit gains and suggesting the probability of an operating loss of several million dollars for fiscal 1985. This shortfall was expected to reduce General Mills's per-share earnings by between forty-five and fifty-five cents. Still, Atwater promised securities analysts in New York that last year's per-share earnings of $4.98 would be exceeded.

The Izod news was substantially worse than the company had led analysts to expect in its dog-and-pony shows just two months earlier, when the word was that the company would break even. Volume now proved to be about half the $400 million in sales that Izod posted three years earlier, at the height of the alligator-shirt craze. Having tried some managerial and marketing changes that failed to pump life into the shirt line, General Mills planned to trim Izod's 2,000-member workforce by several hundred, and to reduce inventories and other expenses by a third.

Interestingly enough, as most other non-food groups were forecasting gloom and doom, the Toy Group was expected to finish the first half of the fiscal year with 25 percent sales growth, despite admittedly disappointing second-quarter results. The widely held assumption was that Fifield got his promotion because his was the only non-food group projecting a profit in the third quarter. It was a projection that most insiders considered completely out of whack. But General Mills's top echelon apparently remained blissfully unaware of how wildly optimistic the figure was until Fifield's successor got a look at Parker Brothers's financials.

Jeff Jacobson, Fifield's poker-faced right-hand man in New York, took over the management of the Toy Group in November. Within weeks of his title change, Jacobson called his first tracking meeting, the last of the calendar year. By then Stearns and his team had a very clear picture of the expected losses in video, and with a new and presumably more open-minded man in control of their destiny, they decided to give him a good long look at what was really going on.

With several key New York staff members flanking him in what had been first Bernie Loomis's, then Jim Fifield's, and now his own heavily mirrored and chromed office, Jacobson perused the gray pages of figures that Stearns and his team had provided. When he hit the bottom line, he looked up, open-mouthed, as Stearns and the others had known he would. Jacobson, like everybody else associated with the Toy Group, had suspected that Parker Brothers had been putting an inordinately good face on things. But never had he expected the truth to be so devastating. Jacobson demanded to know where the red ink was coming from, and furthermore, why New York hadn't been apprised of the impending losses sooner. Stearns shrugged. He and the others had been trying to play this tune for months, he said, unable to get anybody to dance. In past meetings there had been room for bits of optimism, but now that pre-Christmas shipping was long over, two things were painfully clear: There was going to be inventory carryover on video merchandise, and at the same time, the new lines of games and toys weren't going to be as strong as everybody had hoped.

Jacobson said he would have to pass this information up the line as soon as possible—past Fifield and on to Atwater in Minneapolis. Before closing the meeting, the young Toy Group executive set his jaw and made Stearns, Jones, and company promise that they would never again try to keep a good face on an ugly situation, no matter what purpose they might think was being served.

If Jacobson had been shocked by what he learned, the news had to come as twice the bombshell to Atwater and his staff. The General Mills chairman had known that the bloom had been off the video rose for quite some time. But Fifield's earnings promises had apparently remained optimistic enough to convince him that Parker Brothers would scale back and survive the decline and fall of the category in fine style, as Atwater had included that prediction in a particularly upbeat speech he had just given to the investment community.

Now here was yet another potential $50 million earnings shortfall dropped in his lap, another Red Lobster- or Izod-style embarrassment, just when he and the corporation needed it least. In the first six months of fiscal 1985, earnings would skid 29 percent on sales up 1.6 percent, compared with the same period in fiscal 1983. According to all the intelligence that anybody in Beverly could gather, Atwater was feeling a mite perturbed—and more than a little betrayed by his protege, Jim Fifield.

From all outward appearances, Atwater's and Fifield's was a mentoring relationship. Atwater had reason to have known all along that the Toy Group didn't like Fifield as much as he did, however. Just about anybody at Parker Brothers who had access to Atwater's staff in Minneapolis had made disparaging comments about the man and heard their opinions shared; it was hard to believe that the gist hadn't found its may to Atwater's office. There had been vocal speculation, for example, that Ron Jackson's decision to give up his heir-apparency at Parker Brothers to preside over The Talbots was influenced by his desire not to work under Fifield in the Toy Group, and that the same factor might have pushed him out the door to Stride Rite Corporation, a New England shoe manufacturer, when Fifield's promotion gave him oversight of Jackson's Specialty Retailing Group.

But, until these recent announcements, Atwater had seemed to give Fifield the benefit of all doubts. Publicly, Atwater championed him as a brilliant strategist and proven producer. If Atwater now chastised Fifield for the failures of the Toy Group, as many suspected, it was a matter that stayed between them. But the suspicion seemed to gain credence with Atwater's next major announcement: Atwater had appointed a former Federal Reserve official, Mark H. Willes, to the position of chief operations officer (COO), leapfrogging Fifield for the job. It appeared Fifield's star had fallen, just weeks after he'd gotten his dream promotion.

Many who knew Fifield assumed he had to be furious over this fateful turn of events. A man of his ambition and temperament, someone capable of confronting street punks and ripping telephones out of the wall, was not likely to take a *c'est-la-vie* attitude toward the apparent slap. But Fifield kept his own counsel, as General Mills tradition dictated he should. Business went on pretty much as usual from the Beverly perspective, with one exception: Minneapolis suddenly had a seemingly insatiable appetite for facts and figures.

General Mills had always requested reams of paperwork in triplicate, first quarterly, then weekly. But now the requests for statistics and forecasts seemed endless. Each of the last few weeks in 1984 there had been some new and major report requested, and it before Stearns and his team began to suspect some sort of Big Move. "Everything they do says, 'Hi, guys, you're for sale,'" commented a chagrined Jones during one huddle in controller Dennis Miller's office.

Unbeknownst to anyone in Beverly or New York—and revealed only to a few in Minneapolis—Mark Willes's first job as COO had been to do a comparative analysis of each unit within the Toy and Fashion Groups, stacking their levels of performance against those of competitors. It was his project that had inspired the sudden fascination with figures that had Beverly in a tizzy, and Jones's tongue-in-cheek assessment of its import wasn't wrong. A divestiture or two wasn't at all outside the realm of possibility.

If there was one thing General Mills didn't appreciate, besides declining earnings and stagnant share prices, it was corporate embarrassment—and the conglomerate had endured plenty at the hands of these non-food divisions of late. Pressure had increased from shareholders, institutional investors, and of course, from its own food-side managers, to dump these volatile businesses. Through it all, Atwater and his top executives put the blame for their difficulties on the inherent incorrigibility of the industries represented in their non-food groups. But the drums began to speak of mismanagement as a factor—even before the depth of the troubles in the Toy Group had become known outside the company.

Perhaps the most humiliating of a series of public critiques came on December 4, 1984, when General Mills's troubles with the non-food groups became the topic of the *Wall Street Journal*'s influential "Heard on the Street" column. The plain-spoken and devastating article made one barbed point: Those who were focusing on Izod as the one and only problem that General Mills had were sadly mistaken. Several securities analysts quoted in the story said the troubles at Izod were symptomatic of deep, inherent weaknesses in General Mills's management skills and corporate style. Not only was General Mills slow to respond to the faster pace and the changing trends of its trendier businesses, it stifled entrepreneurship with its insistence on research and planning, the analysts alleged. Worst of all, General Mills seemed out of touch with its operating units, the critics added, citing Atwater's quick and public reversal on whether Izod would break even or not. These skeptics announced that they had reduced their short-term earnings forecasts for the company, and some very openly questioned the company's long-term prospects.

While Izod took most of the heat, William F. Maguire, food-industry analyst for the Merrill Lynch investment firm, was less sanguine than many in his assessment of Toys. "With the slow-down in the economy next year and no more *Star Wars* movies to help sales, you have to ask how much more toys can grow." He was also dubious about the immediate growth prospects of the Restaurant Group and the Specialty Retailing Group. "The only one I don't have any question about is the food business."

Whatever happened, the *Journal* article concluded, General Mills could be expected to keep a close eye on its earnings per share. General Mills, it was noted, remained "outspokenly proud" of its twenty-two consecutive years of per-share growth and could be expected to do what was necessary to preserve its record. In fiscal 1984, the editors noted, General Mills earned $11.7 million less than in fiscal 1983. But per-share earnings rose, largely because the company bought back 3.2 million shares of its common stock. General Mills had already gobbled up 1.8 million more of its shares in calendar 1984, apparently in preparation for another bad year. Atwater, in his latest letter to shareholders, had characterized another per-share record only as "likely."

In the midst of the growing turmoil in and around General Mills, Parker Brothers's last family president, Ranny Barton, quietly packed the contents of his file cabinets and took his leave. Stearns had wanted to stage a company-wide fete of some sort to send him off, but Barton warned that he would not come to such a shindig. Not only did he dislike such send-offs, he didn't think Parker Brothers could afford to throw one for him. Instead, as December of 1984 drew to a close, several dozen people gathered at the Lyceum, a landmark restaurant in Salem, to toast days gone by.

Oldtimers such as Ron Jackson and Bill Dohrmann returned to participate in what amounted to a celebrity roast in Barton's honor. The featured entertainment of the evening was a belly dancer, on several of whose moving parts was written the word "enjoy." Clowning with the lace of her skirt wrapped turban-like around his head, the 51-year-old Barton shimmied out of the picture with full retirement benefits, leaving Parker Brothers, a family dynasty no more, to meet an uncertain fate in the hands of outsiders.

But Barton did not leave emptyhanded. As was traditional, Ranny's going-away gift was a signed *MONOPOLY* board. Jones and Stearns had written their messages on the Chance and Community Chest boxes. "It's hard to imagine PB [Parker Brothers] without RPB [Randolph P. Barton]," wrote Jones. "We'll try to keep it a company you can be proud of." Added Stearns: "Thanks boss for your patience and kindness and for taking an interest in me. You have taught me well." Others, nudging Barton for his spirited performance with the belly dancer, wrote "Enjoy, enjoy." But it was the wry cynicism of an accountant named Al Hagen that stood out: "Timing is everything," he wrote in stylized block letters.

9

WINNER TAKES ALL

A small crowd was gathering outside Rich Stearns's office before he could pick up the phone. Jim Fifield was on the line, "with something big," according to the talk around the coffee pot. The light on the phone line blinked impatiently as Stearns strode quickly into his office.

It was a morning early in January of 1985, a matter of days after the long New Years' weekend. Word had been passed before the parking lot filled that there had been big doings in Minneapolis over the holiday. Some sort of emergency board meeting had been held, according to Ranny Barton, who had called to tip Stearns off. Apparently Fifield had quite a phone list sitting on his desk, added the usual sources in New York. No further details were offered in either conversation; Stearns was supposed to just wait for The Call.

When Stearns punched the button on the line, Fifield's voice came on sounding dull and flat. It was as if he were reading from a news release. "Rich, the board of directors met in special session this past weekend at which time the decision was made to divest the Toy Group. Here are the details. . . ."

Stearns sucked in his breath pensively as Fifield droned on. He couldn't say he was surprised. Everything General Mills had done and said in recent months had telegraphed the fact that Minneapolis was looking hard at its options. Stearns had been feeling as if the company's life had been put on hold, just as this phone call had. He knew from butting his head up against it daily that General Mills was reluctant to reinvest in the company or help shore up its losses. But, until this moment, he'd have bet on it—it was all due to General Mills's need for short-term profit relief, not any serious intention to abandon the business.

The rest of the news took Stearns even more aback: The Fashion Group was also on the block, and sales were pending on specific parts of Specialty Retailing. Within months, all that would remain of the non-food diversification program that General Mills had begun nearly twenty years earlier were the Restaurants and, perhaps, part of Specialty Retailing. Figures marched through Stearns's head. It had to add up to something in the area of $1.4 billion in sales, he calculated—a quarter of the company was going up on the block.

"[Y]ou will be working with the investment-banking firm of Dillon, Read & Company, Inc., on a prospectus for the sale . . . [W]e will be entertaining offers from interested parties. . . ." Not much of what Fifield was saying registered with Stearns until he heard his own name. "Rich, we'll need your cooperation in this difficult period ahead." If he were faithful in executing his duties in the months to come and his efforts to represent General Mills's interests resulted in a satisfactory sale, there would be a bonus for him, Fifield promised, "and a full severance package, of course, should that become necessary."

Fifield had reason to worry about his own future now that the last of his reasonable expectations of attaining the chairmanship were about to be sold out from under him. Where would he stand in the General Mills hierarchy when his turf had been whittled down to practically nothing? Certainly there seemed little advancement awaiting him. Still, concerned as he may have been, Fifield managed to close the conversation on an up note. The sale would probably be good for everybody, he said. With that, Fifield excused himself and hung up. He had other companies and other executives to call.

Fifield wasn't the only executive burning up the phone lines that morning. Ranny Barton was hearing the same news almost simultaneously from Jeff Jacobson, Fifield's successor at Toy Group headquarters, who reached Barton at his home. After divulging the fact of the pending divestiture—which didn't surprise Barton any more than it did Stearns—Jacobson asked Barton whether he would consider joining him in attempting a leveraged buyout of

Parker Brothers. Jacobson's was to be the first overture, but it would not be the last. In the days and weeks to come, there would be fifteen more buyout propositions made to the former Parker Brothers executive—even Stearns would run the flag up the pole, though just for a moment. None were accepted. "I'd rather go sailing," Barton later told reporters.

The formal announcement of the planned sell-off was made on January 28, 1985. Like Stearns and Barton, most observers found the wide scope of the divestitures the most remarkable part of the plan. As restructuring plans went, this one was a benchmark. General Mills had cut deeper than most observers would have expected or even thought necessary. In its own history, only the closing of many of the company's flour mills and feed businesses in the 1960s was of comparable magnitude and strategic significance.

General Mills declared that the sell-offs would leave it a more highly focused company with more consistent growth patterns and a higher return on equity. No longer would annual profit targets be "either dramatically over- or under-achieved," as Atwater put it. Once these companies were disposed of, about 90 percent of General Mills's sales and earnings would come from Consumer Foods and Restaurants, up from about 70 percent in fiscal 1984. The "redeployment" would also loosen up about $100 million in cash to help retire corporate debt and build up the company's core business.

"As the result of our restructuring," Atwater told his audiences, "we will no longer have to finance the heavy inventory and receivables of toys and fashion, and we will have more than enough cash and financing ability to fund all of the good ideas that are being generated in Consumer Foods and Restaurants."

General Mills was quick to report that it wasn't in trouble; this was no panic sale. Sure, General Mills would end fiscal 1985 with a net loss of $1.63 per share, or $72.9 million—putting an end to the company's much-vaunted and fiercely protected twenty-two-year string of unbroken earnings increases. But, overall, management in Minneapolis was still predicting volume growth of 5 to 7 percent, pushing the company to the $6 billion mark.

The non-food side of the company had become one big trouble spot, and it was all the more irksome for the high visibility of the toys, fashion, and retailing companies therein. For General Mills, the question wasn't whether the problems in the non-food groups could be solved; it was whether the company wanted to bother solving them. It had decided it didn't.

Some observers speculated that things might have been different if General Mills could have rationalized that the ups and downs of the non-food groups were temporary aberrations—spikey performance records that could be tamed with better management, for example. But analysts and shareholders felt, and Atwater agreed, that the company had poured far more management time and talent into the maw than these companies deserved, and still their performance was, well, not poor—the Toy and Fashion Groups together contributed 25 percent of sales and 22 percent of profits in fiscal 1984—but always unpredictable. These very good companies simply required a level of risk-taking and patience that General Mills was no longer willing to devote—especially not when its basic food business and its restaurants were in need of the same resources.

Through all of his interviews and public statements, Atwater was careful to emphasize that the impending restructuring would benefit the soon-to-be divested companies as much or more than General Mills itself. The divestitures would allow the companies in the Toy and Fashion Groups to shake the yoke of having a food company as a parent and regain their "full value and recognition in the marketplace." What he was putting forth in that assertion was a sort of synergism in reverse, interestingly enough—the parts, once deemed worth less than the sum of the whole, were now seen as being worth *more* than the whole.

From this vantage point, the pieces of the puzzle now fit. Sudden as it had seemed, General Mills's action had been a long time in coming. In fact, it seemed clear to many observers in Beverly that General Mills had begun considering the painting of "for sale" signs before many of them went to work for Parker Brothers.

The stage was set back in 1977, when new president Bruce Atwater, widely believed to be less than a fan of the non-food operations, began trimming back the company's diversification efforts. The idea began to take greater shape when he connected the depressed value of General Mills stock to the volatility of the company's non-food groups. On the other hand, Parker Brothers and the rest of the Toy Group probably won reprieves when the companies became major cash generators during the days of *Merlin* and *Frogger*.

But the divestiture talk was revived when other food conglomerates began to cut loose their non-food divisions. The talk then became a plan when divestiture pressure began coming not only from Atwater's own food-group executives—who were concerned about the value of their stock options—but also from the institutional investors who were among the *Fortune* 500's most vocal, if not prized, shareholders. The embarrassment of press scrutiny, which continued even after General Mills had begun to work out plans to restructure, brought the internal clamoring for divestiture to a fever pitch.

In fact, even as the divestiture press releases were being readied in early January of 1985, *Financial World* was bemoaning General Mills's "nagging problems" with a fourteen-year-old diversification program that had, in its words, "struck a reef." Analysts continued to cluck, as "Heard on the Street" first had, that the company lacked a handle on its many and varied businesses.

When the news finally broke, the divestiture decision was almost universally applauded. Buoyed by appreciative shareholders, the conglomerate's stock immediately jumped five and three-eighths points, to $55.25 per share. Within weeks the share price was up to $65.25, or roughly fourteen times earnings. Atwater had not only retained his higher price-earnings ratio, but improved it. Swift appreciation was also predicted in the conglomerate's lagging return on assets, which were expected to rise from 14 percent (operating) in 1984 to 23 percent by 1987.

Even as they cheered, analysts acknowledged that General Mills's strict financial regimen and its slow-going approach to product development had probably combined to hinder the growth of its non-food businesses. But, by and large, observers resisted the urge to do a post-mortem on General Mills's activities. Instead, they let bygones be bygones. What might have been a public relations disaster became something of a red badge of corporate courage, thanks to a little luck and a lot of goodwill from the investment community. In Beverly, Stearns and his management team marveled as they watched the company's corporate communications staff massage and finesse the story. Someday, they commented bitterly to one another, General Mills would look upon this as its finest hour.

Fed up as many Parker Brothers employees were with General Mills, they took scant pleasure in the cheering and back-slapping surrounding their imminent divestiture. On the day of the announcement, reporters stopped about twenty-five people as they left the headquarters building in Beverly, all of whom shrugged and said they knew nothing about General Mills's plans or, in the alternative, didn't wish to say anything about them. In their battle fatigue, few felt clear enough of mind to judge whether independence—something they had all wished for at one time or another—would be good or bad for the company.

From announcement day forward, General Mills's attitude toward its soon-to-be-divested divisions changed markedly. After years of having Jim Fifield looking over Rich Stearns's or Ranny Barton's shoulders, the managers of Parker Brothers found themselves disquietingly alone with the job of running their company.

There was no General Mills representation in front of the cameras in early February, for example, when Stearns and Barton ceremoniously removed a fiftieth anniversary edition of *MONOPOLY* from the Salem assembly line and presented it to Charles Darrow's widow, Esther. There were no last-minute product-review sessions with the New York City staff prior to the opening of Toy Fair in 1985. Nor were Bruce Atwater or Jim Fifield on hand to cut the cake when the anniversary editions of *MONOPOLY* were presented to the City Museum of New York, in a gala that General Mills itself had organized and funded.

With Barton gone, it was up to Stearns and Stearns alone to see the company through the divestiture and help a new parent plot its future strategy. The tasks ahead of him were no different and no less daunting than those of the past year—to get the company back in the black and inspire the ragtag team of managers that remained to dream new dreams. Still, the very fact of the impending sale couldn't help but make the stakes higher—and with them rose the barriers to Stearns's success. How could he tell an increasingly demoralized workforce to look to the future when he could not describe to them *where* that future might be, much less what?

Managing became mostly cheerleading. Stearns and his vice presidents took turns bucking each other up, helping each other keep smiles on their faces as they walked through the gradually emptying headquarters building in Beverly. It seemed a small thing, yet it was crucial: Any hint of despair on high would only increase the mass cynicism and apathy in the workforce, and hasten the employee exodus already under way.

General Mills had done little to help retain and reassure what remained of Stearns's key employees. Generous as it was reputed to be with severance packages, the conglomerate—displaying either ignorance or callousness—had been very selective about which managers received assurances of severance protection. The letters never arrived in most key offices in Beverly, and Stearns found himself having to go to bat for their occupants—not out of the goodness of his heart, but because he needed desperately to keep them feeling secure and committed to his ailing company. "I can't depend on my vice presidents if they aren't protected," Stearns argued to Fifield. "They won't be fighting tooth and nail to save this company; they'll be out looking for jobs. And who would blame them?" Stearns won a few rounds, but he lost most.

At Parker Brothers's annual sales meeting—which fell a matter of days after the formal announcement of the pending divestiture and before the opening of Toy Fair—Stearns did his best to send the troops into this critical selling period psyched. He told them what Fifield had told him, which was that selling the company could be good for Parker Brothers. He said the company would find its feet again with a new corporate parent. Stearns didn't know how much of his own speech he believed, particularly since he'd come to take a pretty dim view of Parker Brothers having *any* corporate parent. But he knew it was nec-essary to give the peptalk.

A strong sales effort was critical in 1985 not only in light of Parker Brothers's troubles, or the impending sale of the Toy Group, but because it was a year of transition in the toys industry. At Toy Fair there was still joy over the way *Trivial Pursuit* had awakened the long-dormant adult category for games, but the trend was clearly on the wane. Already some major retailers were cutting back their SKUs on adult games for 1985 and predicting a shakeout in the many clones and spinoffs of *Trivial Pursuit,* including Parker Brothers's *People Weekly*. With video games all but dead, Parker Brothers was still leaning hard on its relatively new incursion into books and records, hoping that its plans for aggressive expansion of both categories would pan out.

But Toy Fair had importance far beyond selling merchandise in 1985. This year Parker Brothers executives expected to do as many presentations to prospective buyers of the company, or of the entire Toy Group, as to potential retail buyers of toys and games. The likely bidders included Coleco, Western Publishing, Quaker Oats Company (which owned Fisher-Price Toys), Hasbro Bradley Inc., American Greetings Corporation (the Cleveland greeting card company that licensed its *Care Bears* characters to Kenner), MGM/UA Entertainment Co. (the former Metro-Goldwyn-Mayer), and Mattel Inc.

There would be nothing casual about the shopping; Dillon & Read, General Mills's investment-banking firm, saw to that. Most mornings during Toy Fair a representative of the firm telephoned Stearns while he was still drinking his coffee to announce which company would be coming through the showroom that day and at what time. Usually there was some coaching as well—tell 'em this, but don't tell 'em that. Emphasize this, steer clear of that.

As Stearns morosely regarded the situation, Parker Brothers was a wounded body on an operating table—its Toy Fair showroom a surgical amphitheatre. Neither he nor his cohorts had any way of knowing who among the prospective buyers would restore the patient to health, and who would merely harvest the working parts and jab a scalpel into the rest. If Stearns had to guess, he'd say Mattel would be a likely harvester; Coleco might take a similar approach. All he or any of his managers could do as smile pleasantly at whoever walked into the operating room and hope.

"Surreal" was the word Jones used to describe it as he watched from the sidelines. There would be Stearns, pitching products to retail buyers and playing up to the trade press, then the next guy who stepped up would be asking entirely different questions. "What's your ROS [return on sales]? How high are your receivables?" And the question that never failed to make Stearns wince: "How much money are you going to lose this year?" The fact was, Stearns didn't know. Dillon & Read and General Mills couldn't seem to make up their minds how they wished to state Parker Brothers's financial results.

For a time there had been serious discussion of restating the company's financials over the past five years without video, thereby reflecting it as a discontinued business instead of one that had disintegrated on its own. It was not an attempt to rewrite history; it was merely a bid to improve its portrayal. To better the chances for selling the Toy Group, the financiers were attempting to put the financial condition of the Toy Group and its divisions in the best possible light, while still allowing everybody to look an auditor in the eye. Consequently, every few days there would be a call from New York asking for new data to fit the differing assumptions the investment bankers were playing with. Inevitably, each new number threw off all others. After several rounds of this, Stearns was seldom sure which set of books he was quoting—the real ones, the restated ones, or the re-restated ones—much less how to describe Parker Brothers's "true" financial condition.

Stearns did know this much: General Mills had shown the world how fundamentally ignorant it was of the Toy Group's business by putting it up for sale at Toy Fair. If the idea was to use the annual gathering to spur bidding and create an auction-like atmosphere, it backfired, because Toy Fair is traditionally a time when the market is particularly gun-shy of any perceived instability.

The distributors and retailers that visited the Parker Brothers showroom at Toy Fair each year weren't simply picking out products to sell, Stearns knew, they were picking out business partners. They hung around the showrooms to get a sense of who they would be dealing with in the fall, when pre-Christmas shipping began—who, in effect, their business was going to be depending upon. In 1985, nobody knew where Parker Brothers would be when shipping began, or in what condition. As a result, the Parker Brothers showroom was a relative no-man's land. Orders fell, and with them, the company's image as a viable, purchasable company.

Matters had been made even worse by two years of Memorial Day ramming. Because 1984 revenue and earnings figures had been boosted to artificially high levels, and fiscal 1985 was now coming in very low, the year-to-year sales and earnings comparisons on which acquisition decisions were made were anything but impressive. Parker Brothers was now a $110 million company—less than half its former size. Would-be buyers turned away almost at the mention of the numbers. "You can't sell a company when the sales stink," muttered Stearns to colleagues.

The press coverage wasn't helping drum up buyers, either. Despite its calm and measured tones, everything General Mills said and did screamed that the Toy Group was a white elephant that the conglomerate just couldn't wait to get rid of.

Among the handful of serious shoppers that browsed the Toy Group there were those who came away interested in a Parker Brothers purchase, but nobody seemed to want Kenner or Fundimensions, or, God forbid, the whole Toy Group. Parker Brothers had staples, which made it a safer and more enticing buy than the rest—particularly to a company that didn't possess a board-game division. *MONOPOLY, Risk, Clue, Sorry!*—these were the inducements to non-game companies such as Mattel and Coleco. They didn't need Kenner, with its fading licenses and its hyper-trendy toys. Why add to their own risk portfolio? As for the entire Toy Group, well, General Mills's package price was generally deemed "ludicrous."

The Toy Group had assets of $545.2 million as of the end of fiscal 1984, with a pre-tax profit of about $72 million on sales of $787.7 million. Analysts were estimating the group's purchase value at anywhere from $500 million to $750 million, which industry spokespeople said was sky-high at either end—especially when two-thirds of the package was either in the red or heading there fast. Buying in at the bottom of one business cycle might be considered risky, but as *two* bottomed out? That would be downright foolhardy. At the prices General Mills was throwing around, combined with the heavy reinvestment required to restore the companies to health, the payback on a Toy Group deal would be a long time coming indeed.

That same high price had scotched leveraged buyouts as well. Due to tax considerations, General Mills had made it clear it wasn't interested in making a buyout easy for anybody—particularly not if the proposed purchase involved just Parker Brothers. The conglomerate was quickly coming to the realization that its best hope of getting rid of the Toy Group lay in keeping Parker Brothers and Kenner paired.

After several months of considering and rejecting the few low-ball offers it received, General Mills announced it would sell off Fundimensions (minus the manufacturing facilities it had given up to T-GOD) and take Kenner and Parker Brothers public as a combined entity. For a time General Mills was mum on the spinoff's name—prompting some of the stalwarts in Beverly to sarcastically dub it Acme Toy. But within weeks General Mills announced that the new company—a hybrid of two of the strangest bedfellows the toys industry could conjure—would be known as Kenner Parker Toys Inc.

Toy Group staffers in New York saw a new bounce in Fifield's step with the announcement of the spinoff decision. He looked and sounded very much like a man who had gotten what he wanted. In conversations there and by telephone to the various divisions of the Toy Group, Fifield seemed to claim credit for the switch in divestiture tactics—almost as though he considered the spinoff decision his own master stroke. Taking Kenner and Parker public together made good sense to the parent company because it ensured that it wouldn't be left holding the bag on Kenner. Better yet, it allowed General Mills to get the divisions off the books tax free even as it gave the conglomerate's current stockholders some new shares for their portfolios.

But the benefits to Fifield himself were at least as obvious: A spinoff would put him at the helm of a $750 million company— a $750 million *independent* company—virtually overnight. If he had indeed hatched the spinoff scheme for General Mills, he had simultaneously created his own world-wide empire, based in the city he often said he loved too much to leave—New York. As career options went, bystanders thought it easily overshadowed any that might have had him ascending to a throne in Minneapolis. It was certainly one heck of a lot better than the lame staff job he'd have been stuck with if the companies were sold.

Shortly after the spinoff announcement, Fifield feted the managements of the erstwhile Toy Group, including its divisional companies and international subsidiaries, in a private dining room at New York's perennially posh 21 Club. Over the clank and tinkle of china and silver, Fifield and some of his lieutenants

talked loud and long about how lucrative the spinoff would be,
how everyone connected with it was going to get rich—the unspoken code heard by some listeners being, "at investor expense."
Already Fifield and the others were at work on salary and benefit
packages for themselves that would give new meaning, the cynics
said, to the term "golden parachute."

Fifield had no doubt planned the dinner as a celebration, but
it was a jaundiced audience that surrounded him that night. As
much as they wanted to believe his rosy predictions, many found
Fifield less than inspiring with his apparent fixation on stock
incentives and share prices. Each time he said "We'll all do well,"
what was heard by some was *"I'm* going to do well." It took
Fifield's promise to establish a new managerial bonus and incentive
plan to send some members of the crowd home happy.

But any concerns the various managers of the Toy Group
companies felt were largely kept to themselves. When reporters
came to call, seeking reaction to the spinoff, Stearns said he
welcomed the change in plans—if only because it increased the
likelihood that Parker Brothers would survive and continue fairly
intact. In taking the news to employees, he had milked it for its
motivational value. The spinoff was going to be "like leaving home
or the womb," as he put it. The spinoff meant there wasn't going
to be a parent around anymore to shelter Parker Brothers from
the harsh realities of the marketplace. "We're going to be more
directly in the world of survival of the fittest," Stearns said.
Many of his listeners found the young president's enthusiasm
contagious. After weeks of uncertainty, it felt good to have something to focus on again. They didn't realize the extent to which
Stearns's fervor was an acting job.

The truth was, Stearns had found it hard to summon even
a modicum of optimism about the spinoff decision. For more than
a week he was struck by the ambivalence he was feeling. He ran
the sequence of events through his mind again and again—recalling
how the news of the spinoff had come to him through controller
Denny Miller's office, the Parker Brothers equivalent of a Western
Union office. Like the others who gathered around that day
proclaiming profound relief, if not happiness, Stearns had felt
that a weight had been lifted from his shoulders just knowing
there would be no Mattel or Coleco coming in to shut the company

down. But the high hadn't lasted, and it baffled him why. Then
he thought of the evening at the 21 Club and the reason for his
malaise became clear: The spinoff decision meant he was still going
to be working for Jim Fifield.

The more he thought of it, the angrier Stearns became. As
he saw it, Jim Fifield was the man who had let Parker Brothers
steam so far into treacherous waters. He was the captain who
refused to heed the iceberg warnings. Now here he was, scavenging
among the wreckage and the victims for salvage.

After the March 1985 announcement of the spinoff, Parker
Brothers and the rest of the erstwhile Toy Group was marching
to new orders, revised projections, and different business param-
eters. Every day it was another request for numbers, another
suggested budget cut, or another summons to New York to discuss
more numbers and suggested budget cuts. No longer were the
cutbacks motivated strictly by a need to get the old Toy Group
divisions in the black; now the push was on to further downsize
the operations in preparation for the public offering. The smaller
and healthier the companies seemed, the more investors would
throng to it in expectations of revenue and earnings growth.

Stearns, Jones, and controller Miller had landed the unhappy
responsibility of helping Dillon & Read sell the new Kenner
Parker Toys to the public market. In making the assignment,
Fifield assured them it would be fun. Fun, indeed: Together they
were forced to relive, expenditure by expenditure, the decisions
that had been made during the frenzied video era—justifying
actions that looked even less justifiable in hindsight than they
had at the time. It also fell to them to try to teach these financiers
the idiosyncrasies and vicissitudes of the toys and games industries—a task that was difficult in most circumstances, but all but
impossible when the students were beancounters who paled at the
mere mention of risk.

The real treat was the actual drafting of the prospectus,
however. Days stretched into weeks as the Parker Brothers delegation picked apart the prose, and second-guessed the inherent
conclusions of the report. Hadn't these money-changers heard
anything they had said about the toys industry? Couldn't they
understand anything beyond the walls of their opulent offices? In

the end, the team from Beverly threw up its hands in exasperation. Although they didn't feel the prospectus did much to enhance Parker Brothers's or Kenner's standing with investors, it probably couldn't do any more harm than had already been done, they conceded.

General Mills had made itself scarce during the spinoff preparations. The day-to-day details of Parker Brothers's existence had long been of minimal concern to Bruce Atwater and the rest of the headquarters management, and now they mattered even less. Minneapolis cared far more about the progress and the prospects of the spinoff than the health or wellbeing of its Toy Group survivors. These days, the two seemed to have become mutually exclusive.

Per Fifield's instructions, Stearns was trying to juggle the profits and losses in both halves of Parker Brothers—namely video, and traditional toys and games—so that the investment world would see one company making money instead of two lines of business hemorrhaging as one. "Just get me [a profit of] 10 percent on $100 million," Fifield said, assigning the task. He shrugged as Stearns groaned, as if saying "How hard can that be?" Easy as it sounded, Stearns knew it was going to be exceedingly difficult to reach that goal and still have a company left over. Already entire departments, such as marketing research, were gone. Others were down to one or two people. "The surgeon's gonna kill the patient if we don't do this gradually, in several operations," warned Stearns.

But each time Stearns thought it was possible to cut and combine no more, he received another slash memo from Fifield. Soon Stearns found himself agreeing to prepare a plan to sell Parker Brothers's own headquarters building—a draconian move that Fifield seemed to suggest almost nonchalantly.

That decision, more than any other, had brought it home to Stearns how far Parker Brothers had fallen. Just one year earlier there had been talk of expanding the overcrowded facilities for a second time. Now here came Fifield, advising that the whole thing be shuttered. Granted, there was no crowding problem anymore, but the plan still stood to affect hundreds of people. Where would the remainder of the headquarters workforce go?

Fifield didn't lack for answers. Some of the company's administration could take up residence in a refurbished section of the old plant at 190 Bridge Street in Salem, he said. If there was need for more room the company could rent commercial space somewhere nearby. When Stearns balked, Fifield turned surly underneath his smile. Either rent, he told Stearns, or "we'll move the whole thing to Cincinnati and see how you can do with three product managers."

The billeting plan was unwieldy at best, and unworkable at worst. But it was all part of Fifield's continuing efforts to send Kenner Parker into the market with the smallest nucleus possible to leverage the stock price and generate earnings. Even after alternate facilities were established, Parker Brothers stood to save $10 million. As the news releases were being typed on the decision to sell the Beverly building, another one hundred production employees got pink slips. And there were sixty-seven headquarters workers furloughed on the day when Stearns made the formal announcement.

If there had been any doubt among observers of the extent to which Fifield was calling the shots, these latest rounds of layoffs removed them. As recently as the previous week, Stearns had denied any planned layoffs; Fifield hadn't told him of any. Now Stearns was asked again: Would there be more layoffs? "I never say never," Stearns said cooly. "I don't have a crystal ball. But I don't anticipate anything more." Regaining his corporate demeanor, he added what was now painfully obvious: "Morale is definitely at a low ebb. But Parker Brothers is a strong and resilient company. We'll get over this."

Employees took a more cynical view. Many laid off that day had been with the company twenty-five years or more. "If there's no more layoffs now, it will happen in July or September," sighed one woman. "The place is closing. The thing to do now is to start looking for work someplace else." Another woman, an eleven-year veteran still on the payroll, said: "They told us we'll be just like the little Parker Brothers of before [after the spinoff], but we don't really feel that way." Nonetheless, she showed a glimmer of hope. "We really want to make it. We're pretty sentimental."

Feelings of hope and resignation were similarly mixed throughout divisions of the former Toy Group, though uncertainty binded them together in a way that corporate allegiance never could. As what remained of the Toy Group underwent reorganization in preparation for combined operations, there developed something akin to paranoia among the thinned managerial ranks in New York, Beverly, and Cincinnati. Like trench veterans in fear of being fragged, they kept low profiles with their own troops and watched their backs among higher-ups. Rumors were rampant. "Funny stuff" was going on, some of the whispers said—people were "disappearing" left and right.

There was, of course, a kernel of truth in the gossip: Plenty of once-familiar names and faces continued to present their letters of resignation and quietly take their leave. But, as the rumor-mongers preferred to characterize it, these people had demateriaized—leaving room to speculate whether the absent one "got in Fifield's way" or simply wigged out on the way home from work. No matter how much effort was put into quashing the talk, it persisted and spread.

Stress took a heavy toll on Rich Stearns, as it did on many others. But there was only one president of Parker Brothers, and Stearns felt a heavy burden of responsibility for the company. He fervently believed in the company and everything it had stood for over the years. There was a century of tradition to be maintained here, and he didn't intend to let it die without a fight.

Still, like his employees, Stearns had grown less confident with each passing day of his ability to lead the company into a future anywhere near as glorious as its past. Fifield's lean-and-mean strategy would no doubt get the company through its public offering, but what then? Stearns couldn't see how business could go on with the company in such debilitated condition. And worse, he didn't see what he could do to improve it.

These days it was damned hard to be a hero. Anything Stearns did to please Fifield inevitably gored Parker Brothers. Anything he did to protect Parker Brothers made him seem either dumb or gutless in Fifield's eyes, and threatened the success of the spinoff as well. It was a bewildering state of affairs for a man who had been the company's superstar almost since the day he arrived. No longer could Stearns hide the strain behind a smile and well-chosen metaphor or two. He was plagued with stomach problems and outbreaks of hives on his hands. His blond hair became mixed with white, and his baby-faced cheeks grew thin. Compatriots, talking among themselves, said he looked like a dead man.

There was no way to trace exactly where or when it started, nor could be determined just why, but during the weeks following the spinoff announcement, the rumor mill stopped spreading fear and started organizing against Jim Fifield. Maybe it was the management bonus and incentive plan that Fifield still hadn't produced that rankled the ranks; money was one of the few reasons for a manager to stay associated with the Toy Group these days. Maybe it was merely payback time on a series of perceived managerial wrongs committed by Fifield over the years. Whatever the motivation, the anecdotes on the 21 Club party wended their way to General Mills headquarters on the lips of a number of disgruntled attendees. It didn't seem fair that General Mills's misfortune should become Fifield's fortune, they said. Several let it be known that they would leave the company before the spinoff if Fifield remained in charge.

If Atwater heard the messages that were being sent to him, he did not acknowledge them. If he agreed with the widely held assumption that Fifield's concealment of the video losses had burned bridges with his boss, Atwater did not mention it in the increasingly few conversations he had with people in Beverly or Cincinnati. He simply made arrangements to visit Ron Jackson at Stride Rite in Cambridge, Massachusetts, where the former Parker Brothers marketer had started work as chief operating officer just a matter of weeks before. Atwater had a business proposition for him.

In May 1985, at a board of directors meeting in Minneapolis, Jim Fifield was scheduled to make a presentation on the details of the spinoff of the Toy Group. Stearns, who wasn't invited to the session, told cohorts he was certain that Fifield was going to make a case for closing down Parker Brothers once and for all. There had been a new spate of data collection in recent weeks, and all the figures the man had requested had pointed to much deeper reductions, and quite possibly, to liquidation. Stearns would have bet money on it: Fifield had decided to carry out his threat to fold Parker Brothers into Kenner in Cincinnati.

But it was a far more dramatic story that made it back to Beverly that day: Fifield had been fired.

As the scuttlebutt from the headquarters staff portrayed it, Atwater had asked to see Fifield privately before the meeting began. Then, upon entering Atwater's inner sanctum, Fifield was summarily dismissed.

The coup, as depicted, was so bloodless as to seem elegant. Ron Jackson was ushered into the board chambers from a separate room and appointed chief executive officer of the newly emerging Kenner Parker Toys Inc. Jackson and Atwater had purportedly worked out the timing and the terms of his return in secret, over the several weeks since Atwater's visit.

Atwater confirmed the substance of the rumor by telephone. It was another of those news-releasey "conversations" that Stearns had come to know so well. "Rich," began Atwater, "there's been a decision made to make a change in the Toy Group. Effective immediately, Ron Jackson will be president. Jim Fifield and I have talked, and Jim has decided to pursue other opportunities."

Subsequent news stories offered little to dispute that version of the events. In a *Wall Street Journal* article, the 43-year-old Fifield said heading the group didn't fit his "career objective" of managing a broad-based consumer products company. "To make this truly a success would take a five-year commitment from me. I've been wrestling with what I'd like my career to be, and I decided it wasn't here." When queried about the timing of his move, he said he wanted to have taken his leave before the soon-to-be-spun Kenner Parker started meeting with bankers in June about financing. Fifield did, however, reveal some misgivings over certain recent decisions emanating from Minneapolis. Regarding the spinoff, he said he was "personally disappointed in what they were doing," though he "understood it strategically."

In the same article, Jackson, 41, said he never would have left General Mills for Stride Rite if it hadn't been for the opportunity to run a company. Now he would return, he said, for the same opportunity "at a company where I know the people real well and they know me."

The stragglers in Beverly thought their prayers had been answered. Several managers could barely contain their excitement over Fifield's impending departure in telephone calls to friends and colleagues. "Ding dong the witch is dead!" some sang out, the annual spring telecasts of *The Wizard of Oz* still fresh in their minds. Indeed, after two years of spinning out of control, the house had come tumbling down to earth, and to everyone's relief, those were Fifield's shoes sticking out from underneath. If anybody could get the company back to Kansas it had to be Ron Jackson. Old marketing rivalries notwithstanding, Jackson was a capable manager, a proven friend of Parker Brothers's, and despite his well-known reserve, a good-hearted, right-thinking man. Stearns welcomed him as a partner—somebody he could roll up sleeves with.

Ranny Barton approved, too, having originally suggested Jackson as his own successor. From his new office in downtown Beverly, he quickly fired off a note to Bruce Atwater indicating his concurrence with how General Mills was handling the divestiture. He said he heartily approved of the spinoff decision and, particularly, Atwater's appointment of Jackson to run it.

When Jackson arrived in Beverly, he wasted little time unpacking and settling in. He liquidated the New York corporate staff, terminating most of Fifield's cronies—including Jacobson, his successor in running the Toy Group. Jackson also began trimming back the number of vice presidents and executive vice presidents in the Toy Group divisions. There were simply more than the new company would need. He also sent a president packing—Art Peisner of Fundimensions.

Like a handful of others, Bruce Jones had thought he escaped the ax until a humid morning in early July, when he returned to the Beverly headquarters from a short vacation. Most days Jones was one of the first few people in the office, so when he arrived before eight o'clock and saw both Rich Stearns's car and that of the employee relations man who handed out the severance packages, he knew his number was up. He went in, got a cup of coffee, and bided his time. Within minutes, Stearns was there, shutting the office door behind him. There was nothing creative about either the message or its delivery. "It's not working," Stearns said matter-of-factly. "I'm going to have to ask you to leave."

Two weeks later, Jones was having lunch with a former coworker, a longtime employee of the company's legal department. They traded bets on who Stearns would fire next and when. But

by the time Jones got home, the young executive was on the
phone with the message that the ax had already fallen again,
wielded not by Stearns but by Jackson. "Rich is gone," she said.

Stearns was shocked by his dismissal. Even as Jackson was
telling him who to fire, Stearns had enjoyed the misguided security
of feeling his future was assured. So Stearns was expecting a
routine meeting when Jackson called him in one afternoon and
bade him sit down. Instead, Jackson told him what Stearns had
told so many others: that it "wasn't going to work" to have him
stay. He was being let go, though the news release would call it
a resignation. Stearns, seldom at a loss for words, was too numbed
to do more than acknowledge what had been said. Jackson offered
no further explanation, just the usual assurances of severance and
outplacement counseling. So that's what it comes down to after
almost nine years, thought Stearns—five minutes of regrets and
good wishes?

Stearns thought back on all the times he had disagreed with
Jackson back in pre-*Merlin* days, and how markedly their personal
and managerial styles differed. But he chalked up his dismissal
to circumstances. He was damaged goods, somebody who had the
managerial misfortune of being in the wrong place at the wrong
time—just another no-longer-necessary tool to be replaced. Others
suspected that Stearns was dismissed because Jackson felt the
young president wasn't shouldering the strain well anymore.
Stearns, however, persisted in believing that Jackson—like any
incoming president—was appointing a new cabinet to give the
outside world a feeling of a fresh start at Parker Brothers. The
investment community liked to see that sort of thing, warranted
or not, he said.

Rich Stearns "resigned" at the age of 34, on July 19th. Jim
Fifield disappeared from management roster of General Mills's
annual report in September. By then, what was once a workforce
of 1,300 at Parker Brothers was down to 800. The Toy Group's
assets had fallen from $545.2 million to about $385 million since
May alone. But the last, and one of the more disruptive issues of
the spinoff had been settled by Ron Jackson: No buildings would
be sold. Owing to his own lifestyle druthers—which didn't call
for a townhouse in New York City—Jackson announced that the
new Kenner Parker Toys would be based in Parker Brothers

headquarters in Beverly. That welcome announcement was accompanied, however, by the eleventh-hour layoffs of yet twelve more people, all management-level executives. One employee, when asked by reporters how he'd greeted this, the latest in a long series of sometimes contradictory announcements tacked to the bulletin board, said he had scarcely blinked at the news. "They can't surprise us with too much lately."

By August the Parker Brothers parking lot was full again as the top managements of all fifteen of the General Mills Toy Group companies worldwide began reporting to their new digs in Beverly. More than fifty white-collar workers, many of them accountants and lawyers, moved in from Fifield's old digs in New York City.

With the opening bell of the New York Stock Exchange on November 1, 1985, Parker Brothers was clanged out of independent existence. So was Kenner. Kenner Parker Toys Inc., took its place on the stock ticker. General Mills stockholders became owners, as well, of three shares of Kenner Parker and two shares of Crystal Brands—the new name of the other General Mills spinoff, the Fashion Group.

With its combined revenue of $638.31 million and its 5,850 employees, Kenner Parker immediately became the nation's fourth largest toymaker; only Hasbro, Mattel, and Coleco were larger. Amid champagne and souvenir tickertape, the board of directors of the new corporation rather apprehensively toasted the health and wealth of their combined operations. Kenner Parker began trading at about $17 per share—two to three dollars below its book value.

If the luncheon group seemed awkward or uneasy amid the trappings of the celebration, it was for the same reason that the market was lukewarm in its acceptance of the offering: Kenner Parker had been unprofitable in the most recent quarter, posting a loss of $3.9 million on sales of $122.1 million. The next financial statement, due in a matter of weeks, wouldn't be much better—a loss of $10.5 million on sales of $171 million. The company's executives acknowledged they saw little reason to expect Kenner Parker to post a profit for two years. Still, the assessment of those executives, and that of reporters and analysts alike, was that the new Kenner Parker was going to be better off on its own—assuming it survived.

General Mills Chairman H. Brewster "Bruce" Atwater adjusted the microphone and, with little introduction, began to address his employees from the lectern of the city's Harvard Business School Club. "Under close scrutiny it appeared that, with exceptions, our diversification program tended to spread the company resources over too wide an area. To some extent, losses or limited earnings in some activities were eroding much higher returns in others."

Looking up, Atwater lifted a yellowed and tattered piece of paper into the air. "Perhaps some of those statements have a familiar ring in 1985," he said, continuing extemporaneously. The words had been first spoken in 1966, he revealed, by former chairman Edwin Rawlings. The General behind General Mills's diversification strategy was explaining the difficult decisions that led to his jettisoning of the company's namesake flour milling and agricultural products businesses around 1960. Just as Rawlings concluded then, Atwater said he hoped his decision to divest the Toy and Fashion Groups would clear the decks for new prosperity.

The year 1985 was "momentous and difficult," continued Atwater. General Mills had, in one way or another, disposed of twenty-six individual companies within the past two years. Seventeen of these companies had been part of General Mills's diversified operations for more than a decade; nine had been with the company more than five years. But, brightening, Atwater pointed out the restructuring had vastly improved his company's value on the stock market. In fact, share prices had doubled.

Returning to the main issue, Atwater shrugged and added his own assessment of the diversification era now past, and the era of food- and restaurant-based consolidation now beginning: "This is the nature of how you get into new things. If you don't want to make a mistake, you aren't ever going to try anything new." With that, he announced the acquisition of a budding restaurant chain.

Behind the scenes, Atwater seemed anything but nonchalant about the massive restructuring that had taken place on his watch. A sort of soul-searching seemed under way behind his always pensive demeanor, according to those who observed or spoke with him. Much as he believed in the rightness of his restructuring plan, he seemed troubled by the allegations of mismanagement that had cropped in the past year. He seemed to be reaching for some deeper understanding of where the conglomerate's non-food operations had gone astray.

One of those who participated in whatever personal post-mortem Atwater may have been conducting was Ranny Barton. Atwater had telephoned Barton immediately upon receiving Barton's written congratulations over the spinoff decision, apparently to thank Barton for an unexpected vote of confidence.

The call was as much a surprise to Barton as the letter must have been to Atwater; Barton could count on one hand the number of times he had taken a personal call from the General Mills chairman. But Atwater had more than gratitude on his mind.

"Ranny, what do you think went wrong?" he asked.

Another man in Barton's position might have unloaded both barrels, having watched his family empire dissipated and heard the two-year bloodletting referred to as merely a "mistake." But Barton still considered himself "a General Mills fan," so he spent a few seconds of silence sorting out what Atwater was really asking. How could he look back over seventeen-plus years and come up with one succinct answer? There were probably lots of things Barton could point to, if he had time to really consider it. But Montreux was what popped immediately to mind. Staring down at his desk, receiver in hand, Barton could see himself sitting on that balcony with Jim Fifield.

"Well, Bruce, I guess I'd have to go back to Montreux in 1983." That was where Parker Brothers and General Mills seemed to have parted company, strategically speaking. It was certainly where he had parted philosophical company with Jim Fifield.

Atwater apologized; he didn't know what Barton was talking about.

Barton explained the nature of the meeting. Then he detailed the differences of opinion that had shaped up at that time between Parker Brothers and Fifield over the future of video, alluding to his long-standing opinion that Parker Brothers's retrenchment needs had been wrongly subordinated to other goals from that day forward. As Barton talked, he half-expected Atwater to stop him and say he now recalled, and that he had been apprised of the video standoff. Atwater did not. He seemed to be hearing all of this for the first time, and to be deeply disappointed by it.

Ten years earlier, when things were good in the Toy Group, "I could get to the top with a problem," continued Barton. Business life was a two-way street, with Parker Brothers accepting guidance from one direction and respectfully begging to differ on strategy from the other. But half of that avenue had been blocked off, and whatever other mistakes had been made along the way, this—to Barton—was the one ultimately responsible for the fateful events that followed.

Summing up, Barton said he thought General Mills had let Parker Brothers get "too far away." Too far away to truly see and understand Parker Brothers as an unique organization. Too far away to recognize and respond to the ups and downs of its business cycle. And, too far away to recognize that, for all their apparent similarities in goals and style, General Mills and Parker Brothers were playing different games with different sets of rules.

Atwater made noises of understanding, perhaps even concurrence. He thanked Barton, and the two said their goodbyes.

EPILOGUE:

NEW GAMES

MONOPOLY's logo was seemingly everywhere from November of 1985 through most of 1986. Department store windows were decked out with displays of the game and its playing pieces, large ads filled the newspapers, and television news programs featured stories on its lore. As part of the fiftieth anniversary celebration, the rights to the game's many trademarked images—many of them lovingly protected from licensing until this time—were granted to eleven different manufacturers, who used them to sell everything from housewares to stationary to apparel. Even McDonald's fast-food restaurants launched a promotion based on the game, reportedly hiking Kenner Parker's sales of *MONOPOLY* by 30 percent.

Amid all of the publicity, it was scarcely mentioned, if at all, that Parker Brothers—the company that gave birth to this multi-decade craze and took it to thirty-two nations worldwide—had ceased to exist as an independent entity. As long as *MONOPOLY* lived on, who cared?

Still, in the absence of any public recognition of the spinoff, the many Parker Brothers veterans who passed the displays or tuned in the broadcasts regarded the celebration as a personal tribute—a symbolic validation of where they had been and what they had done. For most, reading an ad or passing a *MONOPOLY* display was as close as they were likely to get to the toys or games business for the foreseeable future. Some found that likelihood bittersweet; others considered it a huge relief.

Most of the members of Parker Brothers's last team of executives landed on their feet.

Ranny Barton manages family investments from a cottage-like office in downtown Beverly, jamming his dealings into a hectic schedule of civic, cultural, and non-profit administrative work. His octogenarian father, Robert Barton, works out of an adjoining office when he's not out sailing or wintering in Florida.

The younger Barton stayed in fairly close touch with the new Kenner Parker after the spinoff, occupying something of an elder statesman's role. At the company's invitation, he previewed new products and, with his wife, attended several management fetes.

Rich Stearns moved his family to Philadelphia, where he spent one year as the vice president of marketing for the Franklin Mint. Stearns then spent approximately six months trying to start a mail-order toy company that would focus on positive alternatives to the "violent, sexist, and conformist" toys and licensed characters that he believes dominate the toys market. The effort put him back at Toy Fairs in New York and abroad, rubbing shoulders with all of his former cronies. The enterprise failed for lack of financing, however, and in the spring of 1987, Stearns became president of Lenox Collections, the direct response division of Lenox Inc., one of the nation's oldest dinnerware companies. In his latest job application, Stearns used the names of several former General Mills and Toy Group executives and, as far as Stearns knows, they gave him favorable references.

Bruce Jones spent a six-month stint as vice president of marketing for a Boston-area building-materials retailer. After a prolonged period of renewed job-hunting, he became senior vice president of marketing and programming for American Cablesystems, a cable-television company just down the road from Kenner Parker headquarters in Beverly. Ironically, American Cablesystems was being swallowed in a merger at publication time, and Jones was uncertain of his future.

After leaving Parker Brothers, Bill Dohrmann worked in real estate brokering and development in Boston. Then, in mid-1986, he went back to what he considered his first love—the toys industry. He is one of the few Parker Brothers survivors to go back to the business, and one of just a handful who went back as an employee of a former competitor. Dohrmann is a senior vice president, marketing games and pre-school toys, for Coleco in Hartford, Connecticut.

Bernie Loomis went from M.A.D. to Glad—Great Licensing and Design, a Hasbro-sponsored think tank—in early 1984. That group was subsequently dissolved. In mid-1986 he formed Bernard Loomis Inc., a toys design, development, and consulting firm. At publication time he was involved in joint ventures with several major toys companies.

Many former managers or directors of line departments at Parker Brothers, such as marketing, marketing research, engineering, and design, have landed temporary or permanent positions as consultants in their respective areas of expertise. Despite their MBAs and technical degrees, they have eschewed corporate careers for self-employment, but only as a second choice. "If things could somehow get back to how they were, I think we'd all be lining up for jobs at Parker Brothers," said one former mid-level Parker Brothers executive, echoing the thoughts of several others. "That place spoiled a lot of us for everything else."

Many former Toy Group staffers either returned to General Mills headquarters in Minneapolis after the spinoff, or took jobs in unrelated industries.

In the same month as the spinoff, Jim Fifield became president of CBS/Fox Video, a joint venture of CBS Inc., and Twentieth Century-Fox. The company is one of the largest sellers of pre-recorded videocassettes in the U.S. *Forbes* said Fifield was chosen because CBS/Fox, dominant as it was in its market, was losing market share and needed "somebody with steady nerves in the downside of a product's life cycle." Fifield, who did not respond to repeated requests for interviews over a period of months, is said by friends and former colleagues to have "learned a great deal" from his experience with the Toy Group. They also believe he may feel constrained by any severance agreement he might have with General Mills from discussing his tenure there.

Jeff Jacobson, the lieutenant who took over the Toy Group vice presidency when Fifield was promoted, went to work at Coleco.

Mark Willes, the Federal Reserve official that leapfrogged Fifield on his way to a job as chief operating officer, became president of General Mills in 1986.

Former non-food vice chairman Don Swanson is retired and living in Florida.

Former General Mills Chairman Jim McFarland is deceased.

Craig S. Nalen, the point man on General Mills's incursion into toys, spent more than a decade managing small companies and starting new ones, having discovered how much he enjoyed managing emerging companies when assembling the Toy Group. He is now a federal appointee, heading OPIC, the Overseas Product Investment Corporation, based in Washington, D.C.

General Edwin W. Rawlings maintains a retirement home in Hawaii. In 1987, at the age of 83, he published his memoirs, entitling them *Born to Fly.*

In a December 1985 article in *Business Week,* General Mills Chairman Bruce Atwater said he was happy to be back in businesses that grow a ploddingly predictable 1 to 3 percent per year— namely, packaged foods and restaurants. "I feel more comfortable about where we're going than I have for a long time," he said. Still, the restructuring continues. Besides Olive Garden, the eight-restaurant chain Atwater bought near the time of the spinoff, General Mills has purchased a maker of ice cream snacks and, for just a year's duration, a group of Minneapolis-St. Paul Chinese restaurants. In January of 1988 it was announced that General Mills was exploring the sale of the last divisions of its Specialty Retailing Group, especially the women's apparel chain, The Talbots.

Despite nearly two decades of enthusiastic approval, analysts and investors have grown progressively more critical of General Mills, its diversification strategy, and its management skill. Atwater's performance as a CEO—once almost universally lauded— is now judged more harshly in some quarters.

Some of the people reported happiest after the spinoff were those higher-echelon Parker Brothers employees who continued working in Beverly for the new Kenner Parker—among them former video marketer Bill Bracy, controller Dennis Miller,

R & D man Phil Orbanes, and of course, the former marketer who became Kenner Parker's president and CEO, Ron Jackson.

Under Jackson, the newly combined company regained its independence. He ditched the old crop year and went back to the calendar year. He replaced the old growth-and-earnings ethic with an atmosphere that encouraged creativity as it tolerated the cyclical ups and downs of the marketplace. Jackson also reclaimed a more conservative reputation for the company, positioning Kenner Parker as the maker of traditional board games and other staples. At the corporate headquarters in Beverly, a measure of the collegial style that had characterized Parker Brothers returned as well.

Among the things that didn't change post-spinoff was the rivalry between Kenner and Parker Brothers. The two companies remained as different in style, suspicious in nature, and chauvinistic in outlook as ever (Parker Brothers still wouldn't contract out to a plant reporting to Kenner). But Jackson kept the two at arm's length from one another. He drew a clear and indelible line down the center of the company: Kenner did toys, Parker Brothers did games, and ne'er did the twain meet but on the balance sheet.

Thus reorganized, the newly combined entity went back to square one and rolled the dice anew on *Play-Doh* and *Strawberry Shortcake* from the Kenner side, and *MONOPOLY, Clue,* and the *Nerf* line from Parker Brothers. Even *Instant Insanity,* the runaway hit of the merger year of 1968, went back in the Parker Brothers line.

Kenner Parker languished in the red for several quarters. But pre-tax profits doubled as a percentage of sales by mid-1987, and Kenner Parker became the third-largest publicly traded toys and games company in the world.

It was perhaps too happy an ending. In the summer of 1987, after twenty-one months of independence, Kenner Parker became the target of a hostile takeover bid by New World Pictures, Inc., a Los Angeles-based production company that specialized in B-movies *(Godzilla 1985, Nice Girls Don't Explode, Soul Man),* television shows ("Crime Story," "Santa Barbara"), and *Marvel* comic books.

New World saw synergy in using Kenner Parker licensed characters and properties in its ventures. Its CEO, Harry Evans Sloan, called the proposed merger "the best fit I've ever seen between two companies." But most analysts saw the match-up as ridiculous. "Can a group of conservative Massachusetts toy company executives get along with a bunch of entrepreneurs from L.A.? That's the question," said one.

Believing itself better off independent, Kenner Parker went to court to try to stop the $47-per-share, $460 million takeover bid. It was stall tactic, really—an attempt to buy time for management to consider a leveraged buyout or find a more satisfactory corporate parent.

In late August of 1978, Kenner Parker found its white knight in the form of Tonka Corporation, a Minnesota-based maker of toy trucks and other playthings. Despite being but half Kenner Parker's size, Tonka made the acquisition at a purchase price of $51 per share. The financing on the deal alone was expected to wipe out all of Tonka's earnings for the year. When the final papers were signed, Tonka officials said they expected "substantial continuity" following the merger. Kenner Parker would remain headquartered in Beverly, and its management team would "probably" continue.

But Tonka soon changed its position. With a solid push from the new parent corporation, Kenner Parker's corporate staff bailed out in golden parachutes worth more than $1 million apiece. Jackson himself was reported to have received $5 million.

Once again morale in Beverly plunged. Parker Brothers alums who had praised Jackson for returning Kenner Parker to health now blamed him for letting the company become too cash-rich, and therefore vulnerable to hostile takeover.

Once again an organization was in upheaval. Kenner laid off hundreds of people, and the growing speculation was that Tonka might sell off some chunk of the Kenner Parker purchase to pay down its debt.

And, once again, the survival of a grand old games-making tradition was in doubt. In the early weeks of 1988, nobody connected with the transitional organization seemed certain what would become of the company that used to be Parker Brothers.

A NOTE ON RESEARCH

*T*he primary research for this book consists of more than 100 hours of interviews with people who either lived this story or closely observed it.

In preliminary discussions, it was a concern of many interviewees that they not be quoted passing judgment on people or events from today's perspective. Many recognized that they would be judged—rightly or wrongly—to have an ax to grind of one type or another. To avoid both the fact and the appearance of publishing self-serving judgments with 20/20 hindsight, I decided to construct the research in a way that would allow the book to unfold as the real-life story did, leaving the commentary to the characters, and the final analysis to the reader.

To achieve the necessary richness of detail, interviews were long (up to four hours each, in initial stages of the research). They generaly proceeded chronologically, from the beginning to the end of the interviewee's involvement with the people, companies, and events of this story. Pains were taken to compare and contrast the accounts given by the various interviewees. Predictably, there were instances in which one interviewee would recall incidents that others did not, or tell the same story with a different perspective. When "new" information came to light, it was cross-checked with other interviewees in follow-up sessions. When accounts remained at variance, third, fourth, and even fifth parties were consulted, inconsistencies were laid bare, and the resulting point-by-point comparisons were used to clear up the confusion and reach a concensus on the disputed fact or occurrence. In most circumstances, the resulting concensus served to refresh the interviewee's memory. Any disputes that remained are described in the notes section.

In addition, to gain as full an appreciation as possible for the physical appearance, style, manner, and personal history of the book's main characters, interviews with key sources included filling out a two-page character-sketch questionnaire on themselves, and on other characters. The questionnaire I used can be found in a book called *Writing Fiction, Nonfiction, and How to Publish,* by Pat Kubis and Bob Howland, Reston Publishing Company, Inc., 1985, p. 73–74.

Not everyone named in the book participated in its research; on the other hand, not even one-quarter of those who participated in the research will find themselves named in the book. For example, a variety of investment analysts, industry consultants, and executives in related businesses were interviewed to gain a more generalized understanding of General Mills and Parker Brothers and their respective positions in the marketplace. Their insights are incorporated without attribution, as are those of lower-echelon and shorter-term employees of both organizations who filled in gaps in chronology or perspective.

It is important to the reader's understanding and evaluation of the material, however, that four key characters who did not participate in the research be identified here: General Mills Chairman and CEO H. Brewster "Bruce" Atwater, Jr.; former General Mills vice chairman Donald F. Swanson; former General Mills Toy Group executive vice president James G. Fifield, and Kenner Parker Toys President and Chief Executive Officer Ronald J. Jackson. All four declined repeated requests for interviews. Atwater and Jackson, through intermediaries, cited continuing shareholder relationships between General Mills and Kenner Parker; Swanson and Fifield said, in essence, that they had put their General Mills years behind them.

In all cases in which a source was not available, special research attention was devoted to the necessary task of becoming acquainted with the uninterviewed person's activities and personality. With rare exception, incidents in which uninterviewed sources are portrayed are based not on one person's recollection, but on the descriptions and impressions of those who witnessed them in action or were reliably informed of their actions. Where such direct corroboration was not possible—for example, a two-person conversation for which the author had access to only one direct source—efforts were made to substantiate the tone and detail of the account through others whose similar experiences with the characters, or their subsequent awareness of related events, left them competent to judge the recollection of the interviewee. Some published materials were also useful. For example, the memoirs of a former member of the General Mills board of directors, Gerald S. Kennedy, were invaluable in depicting certain characters and recreating their inner-sanctum discussions.

Physical descriptions of General Mills headquarters in Minneapolis, Parker Brothers facilities in Salem and Beverly, Massachusetts, and the setting of the annual Toy Fair in New York City are largely the result of the author's personal visits to these sites, aided by recollections of interviewees and published descriptions. Maps were consulted to gain information on certain geographical locations and features. Descriptions of temperature, humidity, precipitation and cloud cover were derived from federal climatological records and the recollections of interviewees.

Other sorts of documentary material were used to corroborate facts, check context, or contribute color—including published books, trade publications and reports, academic case histories, reference works, and a host of popular magazines. Please consult the notes section of each chapter for sources on specific quotations and for generalized information on published sources. Certain personal notes and memorabilia also served to enrich the research process, but as they are the personal property of sources, these items are not cited.

Still, because many corporate records are maintained on the premises of General Mills, Kenner, Parker Brothers, and the new Kenner Parker Toys Inc., none of which lent corporate support to this project, the author has been heavily dependent upon the recollections of the interviewees even for dates, times, numbers, and other data. To ensure the highest level of accuracy possible, every unpublished fact, every description of person or place, and every account of a chain of events has been checked and cross-checked with others whose knowledge puts them in a position to confirm, correct, or augment the information. Key research participants patiently endured dozens of follow-up interviews and fact-checking queries from the author. By the end of the research, virtually every incident or impression in the book had been discussed many times, from as many angles and perspectives as was feasible. As a final precaution, significant portions of the manuscript were read to key sources for corrections and comments.

It will be obvious to the reader that scenes, dialogue, and to large extent, minutiae such as gestures, speech patterns, and body language, have been recreated by the author. In the case of quoted dialogue, no speaker should be assumed to be the only source—indeed, even among the sources—of the dialogue. The words do not purport to be exact, but pains have been taken to make them representative of the tone and content of the statement, as well as of the conversational style of the speaker.

For example, if specific slang or terminology is used, it is because the author has been reliably informed that these words were part of the speaker's lexicon. The same is true of certain assertions of attitude, gesture, and posture. In many cases interviewees have been able to describe how someone looked and moved in a given circumstance. In other instances, the author has inserted likely descriptions derived from a variety of interviewees who observed the subject over a period of time. These insertions are not gratuitous, nor were they chosen lightly. Rather, they are included with the hope that these word-props and bits of scenery will create or revive mind's-eye pictures of the characters for the reader.

NOTES

Prologue

1–4

Information on presentation of *MONOPOLY* games to City Museum of New York: press packet detailing the *MONOPOLY*-related events in Salem and New York City.

2

Peak revenues and earnings contributions of the Toy Group to General Mills: "General Mills Steps Back to the Future," Business/Twin Cities, *St. Paul Pioneer Press and Dispatch,* September 23, 1985.

2

Parker Brothers suffers a $10 million loss on its video-game business: "General Mills Posts Losses for Lines Being Spun Off," *Wall Street Journal,* October 30, 1985.

3

Wall Street's approval of the divestiture announcement: "It's Back to the Kitchen for General Mills," *Business Week,* February 11, 1985.

3

Parker Brothers, the Tiffany of the games business: "Where Monopoly Is Not A Dirty Word," *Business Week,* March 26, 1967, p. 180.

4–5

Background information on the effects of mergers: "The Hidden Costs of Failed Mergers," by Walter Adams and James W. Brock, *The New York Times,* June 21, 1987.

5

Porter on diversification: "From Competitive Advantage to Corporate Strategy," by Michael E. Porter, *Harvard Business Review,* May–June, 1987, p. 43.

Chapter One

General sources for historical information on Parker Brothers and General Mills include their company histories: *Ninety Years of Fun, 1883–1973: The History of Parker Brothers,* 1973, by Parker Brothers; and *Business Without Boundary: The Story of General Mills,* by James Gray, University of Minnesota Press, 1954. An earlier source on the organization that became General Mills is *Medal of Gold: A Story of Industrial Achievement,* by William Crowell Edgar, 1925, The Bellman Co., Minneapolis, Minnesota.

8

Headlines of February 14–15, 1968: *The New York Times* and the *Boston Globe.*

9

Information on Toy Fair: "History of the American International Toy Fair," a news release from the Toy Manufacturers Association, February 1987.

9

General Mills's willingness to change and diversify: "From Cheerios to Marvin Gardens: The Widening World of General Mills," *Corporate Report,* March 1976. "Big G Stands for General," by Robert Terry, *Dun's Review,* January 1968, p. 44.

9

Comparative information on profit margins in games and foods: "General Mills: Growth Minded," *Financial World,* March 4, 1970, p. 13. "General Mills: Toymaker," *Financial World,* November 4, 1970, p. 20.

9–10

Information on General Mills's reputation for scientific management skill: *Forbes,* September 1, 1932, as quoted in General Mills Annual Report to Shareholders, Fiftieth Anniversary Summary, 1978.

10

Robert Barton's reluctance to bring Parker Brothers into mainstream toys: "Where Monopoly Is Not a Dirty Word," *Business Week,* March 26, 1967, p. 180.

11

Salem history: "Games New Yorkers Play," a catalog of an exhibition of games, Museum of the City of New York, *Horizon,* January–February, 1985. *Illustrated History of Salem and Environs,* from the historical collections of the Essex Institute, Salem, Massachusetts. *Salem, Massachusetts,* by William Bentley, Massachusetts Historical Society Collections, 1799, vol. 6, p. 212–288. *Salem, Massachusetts,* Essex Institute, Historical Collections, vol. 1–67, 1954. *Merchant Venturers of Old Salem,* by Robert Ephraim Peabody, Houghton Mifflin, Boston and New York, 1912. *Chronicles of Old Salem,* Frances Diane Robotti, Essex Institute, 1948. *Salem and the War of 1812,* W. D. Chapple, Essex Institute, Salem, Massachusetts. *Old Naumkeag: An Historical Sketch of the City of Salem, and the Towns of Marblehead, Peabody, Beverly, Danvers, Wenham, Manchester, Topsfield, and Middleton,* by Charles H. Webber and Winfield Scott Nevins, 1877.

11–13

Evolution of games in America, formation of Parker Brothers: "Games People Played," *Yankee,* February, 1978. "The Game Game, Or What You Can Learn From an Oobi," *Saturday Review,* December 9, 1972, p. 63. *Warman's Antique American Games 1840–1940,* first edition, by Lee Dennis, 1986, Warman Publishing, Elkins Park, Pennsylvania. "Toys and the American Toy Industry," a February 1981 news release from the Toy Manufacturers of America, Inc., based on material from *Toys in America,* by Inez and Marshall McClintock, Public Affairs Press, Washington, D.C., 1961. "Games New Yorkers Play," a catalog of an exhibition of games, Museum of the City of New York, *Horizon,* January–February, 1985.

11

Puritan attitudes about games: *Warman's Antique American Games 1840–1940,* first edition, by Lee Dennis, Warman Publishing, Elkins Park, Pa., 1986.

13

Parker Brothers and play-testing: "Games People Played," *Collectibles Illustrated,* May/June 1982. "Where Monopoly Is Not A Dirty Word,"

Business Week, March 26, 1967, p. 180. *The Salem Evening News,* Centennial edition, Oct. 16, 1980.

13
Parker Brothers's pledge: *Ninety Years of Fun, 1883–1973: The History of Parker Brothers,* by Parker Brothers, 1973.

14–15
Robert Barton, his policies and his Depression-era times: "Where Monopoly Is Not a Dirty Word," *Business Week,* March 26, 1967, p. 180.

15 16
MONOPOLY and Charles Darrow lore: *MONOPOLY Rules and History: The Story Behind the History-Making Game and Rules for Play,* Parker Brothers. *A Toy is Born,* Marvin Kaye, Stein & Day, New York, 1973. "U.S. Journal: Berkeley, Cal., Monopoly and History," *The New Yorker,* February 13, 1978, p. 90. "Darrow's Myth—Once Again," by David Warsh, in a column entitled "Economic Principals," *Boston Globe.* "Where Monopoly Is Not a Dirty Word," *Business Week,* March 26, 1967, p. 180. "The Game Game, Or, What You Can Learn From an Oobi," *Saturday Review,* December 9, 1972, p. 63. "The Story of *MONOPOLY,*" a news release prepared for the game's fiftieth anniversary press packet.

14
Darrow quote beginning "Taking the precepts of *MONOPOLY* . . .": *A Toy Is Born,* Marvin Kaye, Stein & Day, New York, 1973.

16
Barton quote beginning "Lightning never seems to . . .": "Where Monopoly Is Not a Dirty Word," *Business Week,* March 26, 1967, p. 180.

16–17
General Mills's penchant for (and pride in) periodic restructurings: "From Cheerios to Marvin Gardens: The Widening World of General Mills," *Corporate Report,* March 1976. "More Than Just Wheaties: General Mills' Diversification Brings in Peak Profits," *Barron's,* August 6, 1979, p. 41. "Far-Reaching Overhaul Enriches General Mills," *Barron's,* August 8, 1966, p. 26. "Paradox at General Mills," *Forbes,* November 1, 1968, p. 32.

16

General Mills's "adaptability. . . .": General Mills Annual Report to Shareholders 1978, which contains a fiftieth anniversary summary.

17–18

Cadwallader Washburn's mill becomes the Washburn Crosby Company, and the Washburn Crosby Company becomes General Mills: *Land of the Giants,* by Don W. Larson, 1979, Dorn Books, Minneapolis, Minnesota. Larson's work is also excerpted in "The Midwest Grain Trade and How It Grew," *Corporate Report,* November 1979.

17

Washburn quote beginning "heartless, soulless . . .": *Business Without Boundary: The Story of General Mills,* by James Gray, University of Minnesota Press, 1954.

18–19

The Washburn Crosby Company becomes General Mills, buys WCCO Radio, creates Betty Crocker: *Land of the Giants,* by Don W. Larson, Dorn Books, Minneapolis, Minnesota, 1979. *General Mills Annual Report to Shareholders,* 1978.

18

Bell quote beginning "Our biggest assets . . .": *Business Without Boundary: The Story of General Mills,* by James Gray, University of Minnesota Press, 1954.

19

Wheaties jingle: *Business Without Boundary: The Story of General Mills,* by James Gray, University of Minnesota Press, 1954.

19–20

General Mills dividend record: *Business Without Boundary: The Story of General Mills,* by James Gray, University of Minnesota Press, 1954.

20–22

The Rawlings era divestitures and restructuring, Duncan Hines, Louis B. "Bo" Polk and his new-ventures role: "Where Youth Sets the Style," *Business Week,* May 17, 1969, p. 118. *General Mills Inc.: Yoplait Custard Style Yogurt (A),* Harvard Business School case study #9-586-087, 1986.

21
General Mills seeks "management capability": General Mills Annual Report to Shareholders 1978.

23
Definition of "synergy". According to *Barron's Dictionary of Business Terms,* Jack Friedman, editor, Barron's Educational Series, 1987: "Action of a combined enterprise to produce results greater than the sum of the separate enterprises. For example, a merger of two oil companies, one with a superior distribution network and the other with more reserves, would have synergy and would be expected to result in higher earnings per share than before."

24
General Mills facilities in Golden Valley, the culture of the organization: "From Cheerios to Marvin Gardens: The Widening World of General Mills," *Corporate Report,* March 1976. "How We Perceive The Corporate Animal," *Corporate Report,* December 1977, p. 36.

26
Kenner and its background: "Betcha Didn't Know," a pamphlet published in 1986 by the Toy Manufacturers Association of America, New York, N.Y. "Where Toys Come From," by David Owen, *The Atlantic Monthly,* October 1986, p. 65.

27
A player who sits back (when playing *MONOPOLY*) deserves to lose: *Modern Board Games,* edited by David Pritchard, Games & Puzzles Publications, 1975.

27–28
Robert Barton's self-assessment as a manager, *MONOPOLY*'s asset value: "Where Monopoly Is Not a Dirty Word," *Business Week,* March 26, 1967, p. 180.

28
Barton quote beginning "We want to make . . .": "Where Monopoly Is Not a Dirty Word," *Business Week,* March 26, 1967, p. 180.

31
Other consumer companies that followed General Mills into the toys industry: "Toys and the American Toy Industry," a February 1986 news release from the Toy Manufacturers of America, Inc.

32

Nalen quote beginning "The most precious thing . . .": "General Mills Uses Venture Team to Develop Toy Market, Other Fields," *Advertising Age*, December 25, 1967.

32

Barton quote beginning "This is the kind of business . . .": "Where Monopoly Is Not a Dirty Word," *Business Week*, March 26, 1967, p. 180.

Chapter Two

33-34

Information on Toy Fair: "History of the American International Toy Fair," a news release from the Toy Manufacturers of America, Inc., February 1987. *Toy Industry Fact Book*, Toy Manufacturers of America, 1986 edition.

34

Revenues of Craft, Game, and Toy division: *Minutes and Moments*, the memoirs of a former member of the General Mills board of directors, by Gerald S. Kennedy, 1971, p. 263.

35

General Mills as modern marketing machine: "How We Perceive The Corporate Animal," *Corporate Report*, December 1977, p. 36. "Where Youth Sets the Style," *Business Week*, May 17, 1969, p. 118.

35

Sixteen-hour days at General Mills: *Business Without Boundary: The Story of General Mills*, by James Gray, University of Minnesota Press, 1954.

36

Bell on individual mistakes: *Business Without Boundary: The Story of General Mills*, by James Gray, University of Minnesota Press, 1954.

38

Bell quote beginning "Our aim is to give . . .": *Forbes*, September 1, 1932, as quoted in General Mills Annual Report to Shareholders, Fiftieth Anniversary Summary, 1978.

39

Badger, Browning & Parker was later named Humphrey Browning and MacDougall. The name changed again in 1986 following a merger. It is now known as HBM/Creamer Advertising.

40

Parker Brothers regarding itself as a publishing entity: *Ninety Years of Fun, 1883-1973: The History of Parker Brothers,* by Parker Brothers, 1973.

42

General Mills as "a power to be reckoned with . . .": "General Mills Moves Afield," *Financial World,* May 25, 1971, p. 14.

43

Kennedy quote beginning "feverish haste to . . .": *Minutes and Moments,* the memoirs of a former member of the General Mills board of directors, by Gerald S. Kennedy, 1971, p. 248.

44

General Mills compared to Ford Foundation: "Where Youth Sets the Style," *Business Week,* May 17, 1969, p. 118.

44

Kennedy quote beginning "The letter to the stockholders . . .": *Minutes and Moments,* the memoirs of a former member of the General Mills board of directors, by Gerald S. Kennedy, 1971, p. 251.

45

James P. McFarland, Polk's departure: "Where Youth Sets the Style," *Business Week,* May 17, 1969, p. 118. "From Cheerios to Marvin Gardens: The Widening World of General Mills," *Corporate Report,* March 1976.

45

McFarland quote "This is no one-man fiefdom, . . .": "From Cheerios to Marvin Gardens: The Widening World of General Mills," Corporate Report.

45

McFarland quotes beginning "We're just broadening our base . . .": "Where Youth Sets the Style," *Business Week,* May 17, 1969, p. 118.

46–47

The cyclical nature of the toys industry, shortness of product cycles, and rarity of staple products: "Some Toys Never Grow Old," *Boston Globe,* February 13, 1987, p. 33. *Toy Industry Fact Book,* Toy Manufacturers of America, 1986 edition. "Where Toys Come From," by David Owen, *The Atlantic Monthly,* October 1986, p. 65. "The Game Game, Or, What You Can Learn From an Oobi," *Saturday Review,* December 9, 1972, p. 63. "Staying Power," *Forbes,* March 26, 1984, p. 186.

48–49

Product development, General Mills-style: *General Mills Inc.: Yoplait Custard Style Yogurt (A),* Harvard Business School case study #9-586-087, 1986. "The General Mills Brand of Managers," *Fortune,* January 12, 1981, p. 98. "From Cheerios to Marvin Gardens: The Widening World of General Mills," *Corporate Report,* March 1976.

49

Bell on product development "instinct": *Business Without Boundary: The Story of General Mills,* by James Gray, University of Minnesota Press, 1954.

49–53

Product development, Parker Brothers-style, with accounts of *Oobi, Tiny Tim's Game of Beautiful Things,* and *Nerf: The Salem Evening News,* Centennial edition, Oct. 16, 1980. *Ninety Years of Fun, 1883–1973: The History of Parker Brothers,* by Parker Brothers, 1973. "The Game Game, Or What You Can Learn From an Oobi," *Saturday Review,* December 9, 1972, p. 63. "Parker Brothers Plays the Game," *Chain Store Age,* General Merchandise Trends, February 1985.

49

Barton quote "We connive and we cheat": "The Game Game, Or What You Can Learn From an Oobi," *Saturday Review,* December 9, 1972, p. 63.

51

Dohrmann on *Oobi:* "The Game Game, Or What You Can Learn from an Oobi," *Saturday Review,* December 9, 1972, p. 63.

54–55

Atlantic City and *MONOPOLY: Ninety Years of Fun, 1883–1973: The History of Parker Brothers,* by Parker Brothers, 1973. *MONOPOLY Rules and History: The Story Behind the History-Making Game and Rules for Play,* Parker Brothers. "The Story of MONOPOLY," a news release prepared for the game's fiftieth anniversary press packet.

54

Parker quote beginning "Would you like to . . .": *Ninety Years of Fun, 1883–1973: The History of Parker Brothers,* by Parker Brothers, 1973.

55

Quote beginning "Baltic and Mediterranean Avenues have . . .": "The Story of MONOPOLY," a news release prepared for the game's fiftieth anniversary press packet.

Chapter Three

60–62

Construction of new Parker Brothers headquarters and controversy: "Parker Brothers Will Build $2M Office in Beverly," *The Salem Evening News,* Salem, Mass., May 9, 1974, and May 18, 1974. *Playthings,* January 1978, p. 19. *Playthings,* February 1978, p. 46.

63

Anti-Monopoly: "U.S. Journal: Berkeley, Cal., Monopoly and History," *The New Yorker,* February 13, 1978, p. 90. "Who Ya Gonna Call for Anti-Monopoly II? Trustbusters!" *St. Paul Pioneer Press and Dispatch,* November 1, 1985, p. 10D. "Darrow's Myth—Once Again," David Warsh, Economic Principals column, *Boston Globe.* "The Name of the Game," by Donna Sammons, *Inc.,* September 1983, p. 28.

63

Over the years, the toys, games, and crafts companies that made up the Creative Products Group would have various names; for clarity's sake the author will simply refer to the group as the Toy Group from this point forward.

66–69

General Mills's brand-management system: *General Mills Inc.: Yoplait Custard Style Yogurt (A),* Harvard Business School case study #9-586-087, 1986. "The General Mills Brand of Managers," *Fortune,* January 12, 1981, p. 98.

73

Parker Brothers's product line included twenty games per year: "The Game Game, Or, What You Can Learn From an Oobi," *Saturday Review,* December 9, 1972, p. 63. Also, for the sake of comparison, a 1936 catalog produced by the Toy Manufacturers of America, Inc., showed 22 items from Parker Brothers.

75–84

Development of hand-held electronics, including inventors Bob and Holly Doyle, and products *Code Name: Sector, P.E.G.S.* and *Merlin:* "Electronic Shock in Toyland," by Diane McWhorter, *Boston,* October, 1978, p. 104. "Electronics Light Up Parker Brothers Sales," and "Push a Button, Beep Beethoven," *Beverly Times,* December 7, 1978. "The Traditional Toys Lead the Sales Parade," *Business Week,* December 15, 1980.

77–78

Comp IV: A reader might wonder how Parker Brothers knew what Milton Bradley was doing. Well, hearing the name *Comp IV* was an early tipoff. It sounded like an electronic game, a theory borne out by later leaks and intelligence. Parker Brothers and Milton Bradley had been revealing the names of their products to one another each year since the two put out goblin games with similar names—Milton Bradley's was Which Witch?; Parker Brothers's was Witch Pitch. The name-sharing process would eventually serve its purpose in 1981, preventing the two from marketing games that each had named *Light Fight.* Parker Brothers changed the name of its entry to *Reflex.* For details on how *Comp IV* is played, see *Electronic News,* March 7, 1977, p. 82.

79

Hand-held electronics and their appeal to older children and adults: "Who'll Survive the Toy Shakeout?" *Financial World,* October 15, 1980, p. 106. *Advertising Age,* June 13, 1977, p. 2.

79

Origin of *Tic-Tac-Toe: The Study of Games,* E. Avedon and B. Sutton-Smith, John Wiley & Sons, 1971.

80

How microprocessors transformed game-playing: *Advertising Age,* June 13, 1977, p. 2. *Electronic News,* March 7, 1977, p. 82.

82–83

Engineers add notes to *3-T:* "Electronic Shock in Toyland," by Diane McWhorter, *Boston,* October 1978, p. 104.

83

Quotes beginning "Hoodoo, voodoo . . .": *The New Roget's Thesaurus,* revised edition, G.P. Putnam's Sons, 1961, 1978.

83–84

While most sources don't disagree with the accounts that have Stearns taking the lead on naming *Merlin,* some credit designer Arthur Venditti, a known fan of magic and magicians, with coming up with the name at the same time or earlier than Stearns.

84

Quote beginning "Where's *Merlin,* where did he go? . . .": *Advertising Age,* June 13, 1977, p. 2.

86–88

Riviton, introduction and recall: *Parker Brothers,* Harvard Business School case study #9-480-047, revised March, 1982. *Parker Brothers (A),* Harvard Business School case study #9-580-085, revised July 1985. *Parker Brothers (B),* Harvard Business School case study #9-580-086, revised September, 1982. *Parker Brothers (A) and (B) Teaching Note,* Harvard Business School, 5-585-034. "The Death of *Riviton,*" *Corporate Report,* April 1979, p. 36. *Wall Street Journal,* November 27, 1978, p. 2.

87

Effect of $8.9 million writedown on Toy Group and General Mills overall financial results: "More than Just Wheaties: General Mills' Diversification Brings in Peak Profits," *Barron's,* August 6, 1979, p. 41.

88–90

Proliferation and impending collapse of hand-held electronic games, predictions of likely survivors, Rubik's Cube, Atari's early lead in video: "Who'll Survive the Toy Shakeout?" *Financial World,* October 15, 1980, p. 106. "The Traditional Toys Lead the Sales Parade," *Business Week,* December 15, 1980.

89

Ideal Toy Company and its waning enthusiasm for hand-held electronic games: *Electronic News,* March 7, 1977, p. 82. "Who'll Survive the Toy Shakeout?" *Financial World,* October 15, 1980, p. 106.

90-91

The 1977 video bandwagon, Coleco's troubles: "Who'll Survive the Toy Shakeout?" *Financial World, October 15, 1980, p. 106.*

Chapter Four

92

Toy Group contributions to General Mills revenues and earnings: See General Mills Annual Reports to Shareholders for appropriate years.

92-93

Barton quote beginning "Certainly the company, had it remained . . .": *The Salem Evening News,* centennial edition, October 16, 1980.

93

General Mills and its planning exercises: "The General Mills Brand of Managers," *Fortune,* January 12, 1981, p. 98.

94-112

Personal history of Bernard L. Loomis, development of *Star Wars* and *Strawberry Shortcake* licenses, his establishment of M.A.D.: "Where Toys Come From," by David Owen, *The Atlantic Monthly,* October 1986, p. 65. "Hasbro Gets Its Guns," *Industry Week,* April 30, 1984, p. 17. "A Grown-Up's Winning Touch in Toys (Usually)," *The New York Times,* February 14, 1985, p. D1.

98-103

Toys, licenses, and Saturday television; licensing as a toys industry strategy, the development of extendible licenses; controversy over licensed toys and their television promotion: *Toy Industry Fact Book,* Toy Manufacturers of America, 1986 edition. *Chain Store Age,* General Merchandise Trends, February 1985, p. 113. "The Christmas Zing in Zapless Toys," by Steven Flax, *Fortune,* December 26, 1983. "Could Your Product Be a TV Star?" *Industry Week,* October 31, 1983, p. 67.

99

Mattel's growth-inspired difficulties: "Putting Barbie Back Together Again," *Fortune,* September 8, 1980, p. 84.

100

Loomis describes research as "toyetic": "A Grown-Up's Winning Touch in Toys (Usually)," *The New York Times,* February 14, 1985, p. D1.

103

According to the Toy Manufacturers of America, Inc., close to 50 percent of the toy industry's sales were of licensed products by the mid-1980s, and there were about twenty toy-based series on television ("Gobots," Wuzzles," "Snork," "M.A.S.K.," etc.), all of them financed directly by toy companies or their licensing partners.

105

The action figure ROM: General Mills Annual Report to Shareholders, 1979.

108

Sources say this sort of lockout did prevent General Mills from boosting revenues after 1984, when Toy Group revenues began to suffer.

112–113

Biography of James G. Fifield and his career path: *Standard & Poor's Register: Directors and Executives,* volume 2 of 3, Standard & Poor's Corporation, 1987. General Mills Annual Report, 1976.

113

Mrs. Bumby's Potato Chips, Potato Buds: "The General Mills Brand of Manager," *Fortune,* January 12, 1981, p. 98.

113

Atwater quote beginning "If you have an idea . . .": "The General Mills Brand of Managers," *Fortune,* January 12, 1981, p. 98.

114–115

Bernie Loomis's predictions regarding the Toy Group: Several sources confirm Loomis's role as soothsayer. Loomis himself says he probably made plenty of pithy comments of this nature as he prepared to leave Toy Group management, but doesn't think anyone should have taken them as predictions—certainly not on anything so concrete as a divestiture. "If I were that clairvoyant," he quipped later, "why would I have gone to M.A.D. [and stayed with the Toy Group]?"

Chapter Five

118

Merlin becomes in the industry's bestselling plaything: General Mills Annual Report to Shareholders, 1981.

119–120

Growth and proliferation of home video market (facts and figures in Stearns's presentation to Toy Group management substantiated): "The Riches Behind Video Games," *Business Week,* November 9, 1981, p. 98. "Milton Bradley: Playing Catch-Up in the Video-Game Market," *Business Week,* May 24, 1982, p. 110. *The Winners' Book of Video Games,* by Craig Kubey, Warner Books, 1982. "Video Games Are Suddenly a $2 Billion Industry," *Business Week,* May 24, 1982, p. 78. "The Video-Game Shakeout," Newsweek, December 20, 1982, p. 75.

125

Fifield quote beginning "Somebody will come along . . .": Apparently he enjoyed using the metaphor. Fifield is quoted making a similar comment in "The Christmas Zing in Zapless Toys," by Steven Flax, *Fortune,* December 26, 1983.

128

Atwater lauded in *Business Month:* General Mills: All-American Marketer," *Dun's Business Month,* December 1981.

128

General Mills's increasing revenues and earnings compared to marine platoon: "The Other GM," *Financial World,* June 15, 1981, p. 28.

129–130

General Mills refocuses management, clamps down on divisions in an effort to boost earnings, and thereby, share prices: "The Other GM," *Financial World,* June 15, 1981, p. 28. "How to Manage Entrepreneurs," *Business Week,* September 7, 1981, p. 66. General Mills Annual Report to Shareholders, 1980.

130

Swanson quote beginning "We can deal with problems . . .": "How to Manage Entrepreneurs," *Business Week,* September 7, 1981, p. 66.

130

Atwater quote beginning "You've got to do things differently . . .":
"How to Manage Entrepreneurs," *Business Week,* September 7, 1981,
p. 66.

131

Barton quote "They seem realistic,": "How to Manage Entrepreneurs,"
Business Week, September 7, 1981, p. 66.

134

Frogger, how it's played: *The Winners' Book of Video Games,* by Craig
Kubey, Warner Books, 1982.

134

The "video athlete": *The Winners' Book of Video Games,* by Craig Kubey,
Warner Books, 1982.

136

Toys companies and their participation (or lack thereof) in video market,
continued proliferation of video, Hasbro a has-been: "Milton Bradley:
Playing Catch-Up in the Video-Game Market," *Business Week,* May 24,
1982, p. 110. "Hasbro: Merging with Milton Bradley to Get Nearer the
No. 1 Spot," *Business Week,* May 21, 1984, p. 90.

136–137

Business Week on video games growth: "Video Games Are Suddenly a
$2 Billion Industry," *Business Week,* May 24, 1982, p. 78.

139

Stearns quote beginning "We almost missed the boat . . .": "Parker
Fires "Videogame Salvo," *Advertising Age,* June 27, 1983, p. 6.

Chapter Six

143–144

Video as popular craze, source of physical ailment, and psychological
symptom: *The Winners' Book of Video Games,* by Craig Kubey, Warner
Books, 1982. *Mind at Play: The Psychology of Video Games,* Geoffrey R.
Loftus and Elizabeth F. Loftus, Basic Books, 1983. *Journal of the
American Medical Association,* September 1982.

143

Survey shows half of video game players are over twenty-six: *Electronic Games,* May 1982.

143

Video's appeal to adults (a trend that began with hand-held electronics): "Who'll Survive the Toy Shakeout?" *Financial World,* October 15, 1980, p. 106. "Video Makes Toy Stores Believe in Santa," *Business Week,* December 20, 1982, p. 25.

144

Koop says video games cause behavior aberrations: *Mind at Play: The Psychology of Video Games,* Geoffrey R. Loftus and Elizabeth F. Loftus, Basic Books, 1983.

145

Atari spends $20 million on the E.T. license: "Atari's Struggle to Stay Ahead," *Business Week,* December 20, 1982, p. 25.

145–146

No time for market research—given the speed of the video market. The average arcade game peaks and falls within weeks of its intro: *The Winners' Book of Video Games,* by Craig Kubey, Warner Books, 1982.

146

Skyskipper purchase: "General Mills: Toys Just Aren't Us," *Business Week,* September 16, 1985, p. 106.

150

Milton Bradley's supremacy in board game market: "Electronic Shock in Toyland," by Diane McWhorter, *Boston,* October 1978, p. 104.

151

Fifield derides "bored games": "Not Kidding Around: Video-Zapped Toy Makers Turn to Old Reliables," *Barron's,* February 20, 1984, p. 32.

152

Retail disinterest in traditional board games: "Trivia Breathes Life Into Board Games," "Is There Life After Trivial Pursuit?" *Chain Store Age,* General Merchandise Trends, February 1985.

152–153

Popularity of fantasy games, *Dungeons & Dragons,* and *Pente:* "Is There Life After Trivial Pursuit?" *Chain Store Age,* General Merchandise Trends, February, 1985, p. 113.

153

New attempts to promote board games, "People Together" campaign: "Parker Brothers Puts Its Chips on New Boards," *Advertising Age,* August 22, 1983, p. 44.

154–156

Development of children's books, use of *Care Bears* license in books: "Parker Brothers Puts Its Chips on New Boards," *Advertising Age,* August 22, 1983, p. 44. "Parker Brothers Ventures into Children's Book Publishing," *Publishers Weekly,* February 18, 1983, p. 112. "Parker Brothers Plays the Game," *Chain Store Age,* General Merchandise Trends, February, 1985, p. 113. "General Mills: Toys Just Aren't Us," *Business Week,* September 16, 1985, p. 106. "The New Kid in Children's Books," *Business Week,* February 28, 1983, p. 98.

156

Keller quote beginning "The old way was to . . .": "Fleeting," *New Yorker,* February 27, 1984, p. 38.

156

Jones quotes beginning "We're now really the keepers . . .": "Fleeting," *New Yorker,* February 27, 1984, p. 38.

156

Christmas slow, but video business remains hot as Parker Brothers goes into planning for its 1984 spring program: "Video Makes Toy Stores Believe in Santa," *Business Week,* December 20, 1982, p. 25.

157–158

Video market attempts to switch from cartridges and consoles to software and computers, the development of two separate markets: "Video Games Are Suddenly a $2 Billion Industry," *Business Week,* May 24, 1982, p. 110. "Atari's Struggle to Stay Ahead," *Business Week,* September 13, 1982, p. 56.

157–158

Barton quote beginning "The video game business will never . . .":
"Video Games Are Suddenly a $2 Billion Industry," *Business Week,*
May 24, 1982, p. 78.

158

Ditomassi quote beginning "You've got a bloodbath coming . . .":
"Milton Bradley: Playing Catch-Up in the Video-Game Market," *Business Week,* May 24, 1982, p. 110.

158

Kassar quote beginning "For the video game . . ."; "Video Games Are
Suddenly a $2 Billion Industry," *Business Week,* May 24, 1982, p. 78.

161

Atari announcement of sales downturn, retail demand high as inventory
glut grows, Imagic cancels public offering. Yet Parker Brothers is
expected to be among the strong competitors likely to survive any
shakeout that might result: "Fierce Competition in Video Games Behind
Dive in Warner Stock Price," *Wall Street Journal,* Friday, December
10, 1982. "The Video-Game Shakeout," *Newsweek,* December 20, 1982,
p. 75. "The Real Trouble in Video Games," *Business Week,* December
27, 1982, p. 31.

161

Stearns quote "Atari's feeling the bite of all us little gnats,": "Fierce
Competition in Video Games Behind Dive in Warner Stock Price,"
Wall Street Journal, Friday, December 10, 1982.

163

Fifield predicts home electronics sales will increase: "New Products to
Pace Food Rebound," *Advertising Age,* February 28, 1983, p. 71.

168–169

Parker Brothers files anti-competitive lawsuit against Atari, ultimately
drops it: "Deny Parker Brothers Injunction on Atari Distribution Pacts,"
Electronic News, April 4, 1983, p. 84. "Parker Brothers Would Drop
Atari Suit," *Electronic News,* May 2, 1983, p. 82.

169

Anti-Monopoly ruling: "Who Ya Gonna Call for Anti-Monopoly II?
Trustbusters!" *St. Paul Pioneer Press and Dispatch,* November 1, 1985,

p. 10D, "Darrow's Myth—Once Again," David Warsh, Economic Principals column, *Boston Globe.* "The Name of the Game," by Donna Sammons, *INC.,* September 1983, p. 28. "Monopoly Name Doesn't Pass Go," by Richard L. Gordon, *Advertising Age,* February 28, 1983, p. 3. "No Monopoly on Monopoly," *Business Week,* February 27, 1983, p. 72. "Trademarks and the Anti-Monopoly Case," by Carl E. Person, *Advertising Age,* p. 37.

169–170
Skyro flying ring: General Mills Annual Report to Shareholders, 1980.

Chapter Seven

171–172
Parker Brothers's fiscal 1983 performance and industry ranking in video: "Parker Brothers Puts Its Chips on New Boards," *Advertising Age,* August 22, 1983, p. 44. "No Biz Like Toy Biz," *Industry Week,* March 5, 1984, p. 21.

172
Toy Group performance in fiscal 1983: "Parker Brothers Puts Its Chips on New Boards," *Advertising Age,* August 22, 1983, p. 44. "General Mills Continues to Weed Units," *Advertising Age,* October 3, 1983. General Mills Annual Report To Shareholders, 1983.

172
Atwater called "great strategic thinker,": "A Great Strategic Thinker," *Financial World,* March 1983.

173
Video game strategy as compared to Toy Group video strategy: *The Winners' Book of Video Games,* by Craig Kubey, Warner Books, 1982.

173
Barton predicts tripling of sales: *Advertising Age,* January 10, 1983, p. 8.

173
Atari's video market share plunges, according to A. G. Becker study: "Cartridge Share Plummets: Can Atari Recover?" *Advertising Age,* February 7, 1983, p. 3.

174

Expected home computer proliferation by Christmas of 1983: "Video Games Are Suddenly a $2 Billion Industry," *Business Week,* May 24, 1982, p. 78.

174

General Mills calls itself home-entertainment software supplier: General Mills Annual Report to Shareholders, 1982.

174

Texas Instruments announces a $119 million loss in its home computer business: *Wall Street Journal,* July 25, 1983, p. 3.

174–175

Toys being run like food, additions to toy product line resemble introduction of flanker *Fruit 'n Bran Wheaties* to Wheaties: "New Products to Pace Food Rebound," *Advertising Age,* February 28, 1983, p. 71. "General Mills Looking to Grow From Within," *Advertising Age,* October 1, 1984, p. 28.

175

Age of certain General Mills food and cereal products, and the company's strategy for keeping them popular: *General Mills Inc.: Yoplait Custard Style Yogurt (A),* Harvard Business School case study #9-586-087, 1986. *General Mills Inc.: Yoplait Custard Style Yogurt (B),* Harvard Business School case study #9-586-088, 1986. "The General Mills Brand of Managers," *Fortune,* January 12, 1981, p. 98.

175

Food-group executive quote: "There is no such thing as a product life cycle": "The General Mills Brand of Managers," *Fortune,* January 12, 1981, p. 98.

175

Hasbro and its reintroduced *GI Joe:* "Where Toys Come From," by David Owen, *The Atlantic Monthly,* October 1986, p. 65. *Business Week,* May 21, 1984, p. 90.

176

The stop-production memo for *MONOPOLY* in 1936: "The Story of *MONOPOLY,*" a news release prepared for the game's fiftieth anniversary press packet. *Ninety Years of Fun, 1883–1973: The History of Parker Brothers,* 1973, by Parker Brothers.

176

McFarland quote "Without failure . . . growth cannot occur": "From Cheerios to Marvin Gardens: The Widening World of General Mills," *Corporate Report,* March 1976.

178

SKUs are stockkeeping units—referring to a quantity of merchandise held in inventory.

180

Parker Brothers's new ad campaign: "Parker Fires Videogame Salvo," *Advertising Age,* June 27, 1983, p. 6.

180

Stearns quote beginning "We plan to take . . .": "Parker Fires Videogame Salvo," *Advertising Age,* June 27, 1983, p. 6.

180–182

Q*bert, the game, the marketing strategy, Doris Divelle: "Licensing Bounty Awaits Arcade Game Winners," *Advertising Age,* April 11, 1983, p. 36. "Parker Bros. Puts Its Chips on New Boards," *Advertising Age,* August 22, 1983, p. 44.

180

Popeye was the licence that Barton had hoped to win when he bought the known also-ran, *Skyskipper.*

180

As Hasbro had no video business of its own, Parker Brothers had acquired the video rights to *GI Joe.*

182

Late 1982 slowdown in arcade video market: "Atari's Struggle to Stay Ahead," *Business Week,* September 13, 1982, p. 56.

182

Movies and trademark characters to be licensed for video games: "Parker Brothers Puts Its Chips on New Boards," *Advertising Age,* August 22, 1983, p. 44. "Parker Fires Videogame Salvo," *Advertising Age,* June 27,

1983, p. 6. "GF Pours it on for Kool-Aid Videogame," *Advertising Age,* June 20, 1983, p. 71.

183

Decline in video play value: "Cartridge Share Plummets; Can Atari Recover?" *Advertising Age,* February 7, 1983, p. 3.

183

Segmentation analysis: As defined by Rosenberg's *Dictionary of Business and Management,* segmentation analysis is the "division of a market into subgroups with similar motivations."

184

Industry-wide, orders down for video through September of 1983: "The Christmas Zing in Zapless Toys," by Steven Flax, *Fortune,* December 26, 1983.

184–185

General Mills (Parker Brothers) likely to survive video shakeout: "The Video-Game Shakeout," Newsweek, December 20, 1982, p. 75.

188

General Mills and its twenty-year record of earnings increases: "General Mills: All-American Marketer," *Dun's Business Month,* December, 1981.

188

Basis for "pulling a Coleco": "More Than Just Wheaties: General Mills' Diversification Brings in Peak Profits," *Barron's,* August 6, 1979, p. 41.

190

Atwater announces closing of companies: "General Mills Continues to Weed Units," *Advertising Age,* October 3, 1983.

190

Sales of snack food companies in 1982: "General Mills Continues to Weed Units," *Advertising Age,* October 3, 1983.

190

The management of one company, Goodmark, a $70 million processor of meats, told *Business Week* that its former parent hadn't understood its business. Second to go was Tom's Foods in mid-1983. Its sales of $200 million had earned $24 million in profits before taxes, which

General Mills acknowledged was "good performance." But it too had distribution patterns that were unfamiliar, and therefore uncomfortable, to a supermarket-supplying company like General Mills.

190
Atwater calls food and restaurants "primary growth vehicles": "General Mills Continues to Weed Units," *Advertising Age,* October 3, 1983.

193
Lionel's production in Mexico, 13,000 tools: *Boston Globe,* Monday, January 12, 1987, p. 2.

193–194
The cost to dismantle T-GOD: General Mills Annual Report to Shareholders, 1979.

194
McFarland says General Mills products "traveled the avenue to the home": *Business Without Boundary: The Story of General Mills,* by James Gray, University of Minnesota, 1954.

196
Fifield divides Parker Brothers in half: "Parker Brothers Puts Its Chips on New Boards," *Advertising Age,* August 22, 1983, p. 44.

196–197
Texas Instruments withdraws from home computer market: "TI Exits Home Computer Market," *Electronic News,* October 31, 1983, p. 1. "Why TI May Well Return to Home Computers," *Business Week,* November 14, 1983, p. 48.

197
Parker Brothers layoff attributed to "miscalculation": "New Era for Parker Bros.," Beverly Times, April 25, 1984, p. 1.

Chapter Eight

200
Video crashes at Christmas of 1983, traditional toys (including board games and dolls such as *Cabbage Patch Kids*) surge according to Commerce Department: "No Biz Like Toy Biz," *Industry Week,* March 5, 1984,

p. 21. "The Christmas Zing in Zapless Toys," by Steven Flax, *Fortune,* December 26, 1983. "Not Kidding Around: Video-Zapped Toy Makers Turn to Old Reliables," *Barron's,* February 20, 1984, p. 32.

200–202

Trivial Pursuit and the market it created, Parker Brothers's *People Weekly:* "No Biz Like Toy Biz," *Industry Week,* March 5, 1984, p. 21. "Betcha Didn't Know!", a pamphlet published in 1986 by the Toy Manufacturers of America, Inc., New York, N.Y. "Trivia Breathes Life Into Board Games," "Board Games: New License Vehicle," and "Is There Life After Trivial Pursuit?" *Chain Store Age,* General Merchandise Trends, February 1985, p. 113. "Not Kidding Around: Video-Zapped Toy Makers Turn to Old Reliables," *Barron's,* February 20, 1984, p. 32.

201–202

According to "Betcha Didn't Know!" a pamphlet published in 1986 by the Toy Manufacturers of America, Inc., New York, N.Y., over 24 million units of *Trivial Pursuit* would be sold in 1984. That multiplied Selchow's pre-*Trivial Pursuit* sales revenues by a factor of ten.

203

Hassenfeld quote beginning "This year has absolutely destroyed . . .": "The Christmas Zing in Zapless Toys," by Steven Flax, *Fortune,* December 26, 1983.

203–204

Shakeout begins, speculators bail out of video in droves, touching off a new era of consolidation: "Where Toys Come From," by David Owen, *The Atlantic Monthly,* October 1986, p. 65. *Business Week,* May 21, 1984, p. 90. "Who's Who in Toys," *Chain Store Age,* October 1984, p. 69. *Toy Industry Fact Book,* Toy Manufacturers of America, 1986 edition.

204–205

The inventory glut and resulting price-cutting on video cartridges and software, losses at Atari, Mattel, and Activision: "The Christmas Zing in Zapless Toys," by Steven Flax, *Fortune,* December 26, 1983. *Forbes,* January 14, 1985, p. 169. "Who's Who in Toys," *Chain Store Age,* October 1984, p. 69.

205

Parker Brothers has three of the top five arcade-based titles in cartridges and software, and 15 percent of the market: "No Biz Like Toy Biz," *Industry Week,* March 5, 1984, p. 21.

206

General Mills named most admired food company for 1983: *Fortune,* January 9, 1984, p. 58.

206

General Mills's mixture of product lines bolsters one another: "General Mills: All-American Marketer," *Dun's Business Month,* December, 1981.

207

Donald F. Swanson speaks to analysts about the non-food groups and their performance: *The Wall Street Transcript,* April 9, 1984, p. 73,415.

208

Izod and Red Lobster not doing well: "General Mills Continues to Weed Units," *Advertising Age,* October 3, 1983. "When Business Got So Good It Got Dangerous," by Bill Saporito, *Fortune,* April 2, 1984. "Nagging Problems for the Other GM," *Financial World,* January 9–22, 1985, p. 84. "Shoo, Alligator," *Selling and Marketing Management,* February 6, 1984, p. 40.

209

Izod marketing executive quote beginning "In a changing market . . .": "Shoo, Alligator," *Selling and Marketing Management,* February 6, 1984, p. 40.

209

Quote beginning "What's wrong?": "General Mills: Toys Just Aren't Us," *Business Week,* September 16, 1985, p. 106.

209–213

Barton resigns, Stearns promoted; a second layoff: "New Era for Parker Brothers," *Beverly Times,* April 25, 1984, p. 1.

211

Stearns calls presidency "a sacred responsibility": "New Era for Parker Brothers," *Beverly Times,* April 25, 1984, p. 1.

212

Barton introduces Stearns as new president to press: "New Era for Parker Brothers," *Beverly Times,* April 25, 1984, p. 1.

213

General Mills increases return on shareholder equity goal to 19 percent: General Mills Annual Report to Shareholders, 1983.

213-214

Memorial Day inventory-loading episode of 1984: "General Mills: Toys Just Aren't Us," *Business Week,* September 16, 1985, p. 106.

214-215

Toys industry, General Mills, and General Mills Toy Group results for calendar 1984 and fiscal 1984: "When Business Got So Good It Got Dangerous," by Bill Saporito, *Fortune,* April 2, 1984. General Mills Annual Reports to Shareholders, 1984 and 1985.

215

Fifield doesn't expect video to make a dime until fiscal 1986: "New Products to Pace Food Rebound," *Advertising Age,* February 28, 1983, p. 71.

215

$21 million "redeployment charge" on T-GOD: General Mills Annual Report to Shareholders, 1983.

215-216

Why General Mills could now be expected to bail out of a bad situation, other food companies divesting non-food lines: "General Mills Puts Toy, Fashion Lines Up For Sale, Plans to Emphasize Food," *Wall Street Journal,* January 29, 1985. "General Mills Outlines Plan of Divestiture," *Wall Street Journal,* March 27, 1985.

217

The books division, its performance and prospects: "Parker Brothers Plays the Game," *Chain Store Age,* General Merchandise Trends, February, 1985, p. 113. "General Mills: Toys Just Aren't Us," *Business Week,* September 16, 1985, p. 106.

217

Sales of phonograph records, despite a gold album, aren't doing well: "General Mills: Toys Just Aren't Us," *Business Week,* September 16, 1985, p. 106. News release.

218

Parker Brothers's new products: The author has obtained copies of news releases on these products.

218

Dune debacle: "Licensed Games: More than a Name," *Chain Store Age,* General Merchandise Trends, February, 1985, p. 113.

225

General Mills shifts its focus to just food and restaurants: "General Mills Continues to Weed Units," *Advertising Age,* October 3, 1983.

225

Donald F. Swanson forced into retirement: "General Mills Puts Toy, Fashion Lines Up For Sale, Plans to Emphasize Food," *Wall Street Journal,* January 29, 1985.

225–226

Continuing Izod trouble reduces General Mills's earnings, but Toys still project a revenues increase: "General Mills Expects Lower Share Earnings, Citing Losses at Izod," *Wall Street Journal,* November 15, 1984.

227

General Mills's results first half of fiscal 1985: "General Mills Puts Toy, Fashion Lines Up For Sale, Plans to Emphasize Food," *Wall Street Journal,* January 29, 1985.

228–229

Mark Willes's appointment, his analysis of the non-food groups: "General Mills Still Needs Its *Wheaties,*" *Business Week,* December 23, 1985, p. 77.

229

General Mills criticized for its handling of the non-food groups: "General Mills' Izod Woes Are Said to Reflect Broader Problems of Company's Management," in "Heard on the Street," *Wall Street Journal,* December 4, 1984.

230

General Mills buys back shares to preserve earnings record: *Wall Street Journal,* February 24, 1984, p. 19.

Chapter Nine

232–233

General Mills announces plans to divest the Toy and Fashion Groups, an unexpectedly large reshuffling: "General Mills Puts Toy, Fashion Lines Up For Sale, Plans to Emphasize Food," *Wall Street Journal,* January 29, 1985. "General Mills Outlines Plan of Divestiture," *Wall Street Journal,* March 27, 1985.

233

The non-food groups for sale totaled thirty-two percent of assets.

233–234

Barton considers and rejects leveraged buyout propositions: "General Mills Won't Get Top Dollar for Planned Sales of Units," *Wall Street Journal,* February 7, 1985. "Parker Brothers Ex-Head Won't Seek Unit of General Mills," *Wall Street Journal,* February 25, 1985.

234

Atwater says profit targets will not be over- or under-achieved: "General Mills Steps Back to the Future," Business/Twin Cities, September 23, 1985, *St. Paul Pioneer Press and Dispatch.*

234

Atwater quote beginning "As the result of our restructuring": "General Mills Steps Back to the Future," Business/Twin Cities, September 23, 1985, *St. Paul Pioneer Press and Dispatch.*

234

Projected fiscal 1985 finish for General Mills: "General Mills Won't Get Top Dollar for Planned Sales of Units," *Wall Street Journal,* February 7, 1985.

235

Toys and Fashion together contributed 25 percent of sales and 22 percent of profits to General Mills: "General Mills Puts Toy, Fashion Lines Up For Sale, Plans to Emphasize Food," *Wall Street Journal,*

January 29, 1985. "It's Back to the Kitchen for General Mills," *Business Week,* February 11, 1985.

235

Divested units will regain value in the marketplace, reverse synergism: "General Mills Steps Back to the Future," Business/Twin Cities, September 23, 1985, *St. Paul Pioneer Press and Dispatch.* "The Hidden Costs of Failed Mergers," by Walter Adams and James W. Brock, *New York Times,* June 21, 1987.

235

Atwater says divestiture will be good for the sold companies: "General Mills Outlines Plan of Divestiture," *Wall Street Journal,* March 27, 1985.

236

Financial World comments on General Mills's diversification: "Nagging Problems for the Other GM," *Financial World,* January 9–22, 1985, p. 84.

236

Reaction to General Mills divestiture plan, including rise in stock price due to anticipated boost in lagging return on assets: "It's Back to the Kitchen for General Mills," *Business Week,* February 11, 1985.

237

MONOPOLY fiftieth anniversary events in Salem and New York City: "Games New Yorkers Play," a catalog of an exhibition of games, Museum of the City of New York, *Horizon,* January-February, 1985. The author also has obtained copies of news releases pertaining to the observances in Salem and New York City.

238

Employee reaction to divestiture: "Parent Firm Eyes Parker Brothers Sale," *Beverly Times,* January 29, 1985, p. 1.

238–239

The year 1985 is a transitional year for toys and games, post *Trivial Pursuit* and video: "Who's Who in the Changing Toy Game," *Chain Store Age,* October 1984, p. 69. "Is There Life After Trivial Pursuit?" and "Parker Brothers Plays the Game," *Chain Store Age,* October 1984, p. 69.

239–241

The companies likely to bid on the Toy Group or its component parts, expected sale price, reason why Parker Brothers (now $110 million in revenues) is the most attractive division within the group, investment community reaction: "Mattel Weighs Bid for Parker Brothers," *The New York Times,* February 14, 1985, p. D5. "General Mills Inc. Won't Get Top Dollar for Toy, Apparel Lines, Executives Say," *Wall Street Journal,* February 7, 1985, p. 14.

239

Dillon, Read & Company handles divestiture for General Mills: "General Mills Outlines Plan of Divestiture," *Wall Street Journal,* March 27, 1985.

241

General Mills price for Toy Group considered ludicrous: "General Mills Won't Get Top Dollar for Planned Sales of Units," *Wall Street Journal,* February 7, 1985.

241–242

General Mills elects to spin off the Toy Group and the Fashion Group, a more tax-effective strategy: "General Mills Outlines Plan of Divestiture," *Wall Street Journal,* March 27, 1985. "General Mills Inc. Discloses Details of Planned Spinoffs," *Wall Street Journal,* September 24, 1985, p. 14.

242

Spinoff temporarily dubbed "Acme Toy": *New England Business,* April 1985, p. 49.

243

Stearns reaction to spinoff: "An Uncertain Future for Parker Brothers After Planned Spinoff," *New England Business,* p. 49.

245–246

Consideration of sale of Parker Brothers headquarters building in Beverly, a third layoff: "Parker Brothers Will Close Office," *Beverly Times,* May 10, 1985, p. 1.

246

Stearns on layoffs: "Parker Brothers Will Close Office," *Beverly Times,* May 10, 1985, p. 1.

246

Employees on layoffs: "Parker Brothers Will Close Office," *Beverly Times,* May 10, 1985, p. 1.

249

Fifield on being fired and Jackson on taking over company: *Wall Street Journal,* May 22, 1985.

250–251

Jackson cleans house: "Jackson Makes the Right Moves," *Beverly Times,* August 12, 1985, p. 1.

251

Total impact on Parker Brothers workforce from layoffs: "Parker Brothers Names Moore," *Beverly Times,* August 10, 1985, p. 1.

251

Decline in Toy Group assets from May to November 1985: "General Mills Inc. Details of Planned Spinoffs," *Wall Street Journal,* September 24, 1985, p. 14.

251

Decision not to sell Beverly headquarters: "Parker Brothers Will Reorganize, Stay," *Beverly Times,* July 23, 1985, p. 1.

252

Employee on contradictory announcements: "Parker Brothers Will Reorganize, Stay," *Beverly Times,* July 23, 1985, p. 1.

252

The spinoff, its stock distribution, its less than rosy prospects, and Kenner Parker's first quarterly results: "General Mills Inc. Details of Planned Spinoffs," *Wall Street Journal,* September 24, 1985, p. 14. "General Mills Posts Losses for Lines Being Spun Off," *Wall Street Journal,* October 30, 1985. "Can the General Mills Babies Make It on Their Own?" *Business Week,* November 18, 1985. "Beverly Toy Company Expects to Get Down to Business in '86," by Charles Stein, *Boston Globe.* "Kenner Parker Reports a Loss," *Boston Globe.*

253

Atwater quote beginning "Under close scrutiny . . .": "General Mills Steps Back to the Future," Business/Twin Cities, *St. Paul Pioneer Press and Dispatch,* September 23, 1985.

253–254

Bruce Atwater offers a post-mortem on the non-food diversification "mistake": "General Mills Steps Back to the Future," Business/Twin Cities, *St. Paul Pioneer Press and Dispatch,* September 23, 1985.

Epilogue

258

Jim Fifield goes to CBS/Fox Video: "Coming Attractions," *Forbes,* June 2, 1986, p. 228.

259

Bruce Atwater happier in food and restaurants: "General Mills Still Needs Its *Wheaties,*" *Business Week,* December 23, 1985, p. 77.

259–260

Changes wrought in the new Kenner Parker Toys Inc.: "Beverly Toy Company Expects to Get Down to Business in '86," by Charles Stein, *Boston Globe.* "Kenner Parker Reports a Loss," *Boston Globe.*

260–261

New World Pictures Inc. attempts hostile takeover of Kenner Parker: "New World Offers $475 Million for Toy Company," *Los Angeles Times,* July 18, 1987, p. IV–1. "New World Pictures Inc. Offers $429 Million for Beverly-Based Toymaker," *Boston Globe,* July 18, 1987, p. 33. "New World Bids $41 a Share for Kenner, Sending Toy Firm's Stock Up to $45.875," *Wall Street Journal,* July 20, 1987, p. 4. "Too Good to Stay Free," *Boston Globe,* August 20, 1987, p. 33.

INDEX